I0817065

HÒT'A!
ENOUGH!

Georges Erasmus's Fifty-Year Battle for Indigenous Rights

WAYNE K. SPEAR
and GEORGES ERASMUS

Foreword by the Honourable Dr. Jody Wilson-Raybould, P.C., O.B.C., K.C.

Publisher: Meghan Macdonald | Acquiring editor: Kathryn Lane | Editor: Susan Fitzgerald
Cover designer: Karen Alexiou
Cover image: Wayne K. Spear

Library and Archives Canada Cataloguing in Publication

Title: Hòt'a! Enough! : Georges Erasmus's fifty-year battle for Indigenous rights / Wayne K. Spear and Georges Erasmus ; foreword by the Honourable Dr. Jody Wilson-Raybould, P.C., O.B.C., K.C.
Names: Spear, Wayne K., 1965- author. | Erasmus, Georges, author. | Wilson-Raybould, Jody, 1971- writer of foreword
Description: Includes bibliographical references and index.
Identifiers: Canadiana (print) 20240412222 | Canadiana (ebook) 20240413067 | ISBN 9781459752900 (softcover) | ISBN 9781459752917 (PDF) | ISBN 9781459752924 (EPUB)
Subjects: LCSH: Erasmus, Georges. | LCSH: Indigenous peoples—Canada—Government relations. | CSH: Indigenous leaders—Canada—Biography. | LCGFT: Biographies.
Classification: LCC E92 .S6567 2024 | DDC 971.064092—dc23

Canada Council for the Arts Conseil des arts du Canada

We acknowledge the support of the Canada Council for the Arts and the Ontario Arts Council for our publishing program. We also acknowledge the financial support of the Government of Ontario, through the Ontario Book Publishing Tax Credit and Ontario Creates, and the Government of Canada.

Printed and bound in Canada.

Dundurn Press
1382 Queen Street East
Toronto, Ontario, Canada M4L 1C9
dundurn.com, @dundurnpress

I would like to dedicate this book to my family, especially my sons, Kristen and Che, for their many years of love and support.

CONTENTS

FOREWORD

I confess that when Georges asked me to write the foreword to *Hòt'a! Enough!,* I was a little uncertain about whether I should say yes. I was not sure I would be able to find the right words. How can one adequately write about an individual who has done so much to shape the lives of Indigenous Peoples, and of Canada itself, when the impacts of their work are still unfolding every day?

Georges is part of a generation of Indigenous leaders that will be recognized as fundamentally transforming Canada. They are the generation of leaders that, when the opportunity came, courageously and with determination stepped into the light. For so much of this country's history, the struggle for Indigenous rights had to be in the shadows, as state oppression and violence made it so. But the resistance and resilience of so many Indigenous Peoples, for so long, created an opportunity to drive change into the public sphere — into the consciousness of Canada — and when that opportunity came, Georges was one of those who seized on it.

I do not know Georges very well — we have only met and talked a few times — but I do know his generation well. My father, Hemas Kla-Lee-Lee-Kla (Bill Wilson), is one of them, and at times he and Georges sat around the same tables. In my experience, theirs was and is not a generation of leaders that is intent on getting praise and recognition. They were, and are, intent on making impactful and real change.

As such, it was no surprise to read in *Hòt'a! Enough!* that Georges is a very private person and perhaps not the most amenable to being the subject of, and writing, a book about his life. But it is also no surprise that such an inclination to focus on effecting change, and not just talking about it, has resulted in such a unique and insightful book — one that should be read and studied by young and old alike for years to come.

The form of the book, a biography written methodically by Wayne K. Spear interspersed with commentary and reflections by Georges, is almost a metaphor for Georges's life as a leader. He observed what he saw in Canada, reflected on it, and then told you what it really meant, as well as the way things should be. And then he went out and made it that way.

Georges stands at the epicentre of seismic events for Indigenous Peoples in Canada that will shape us for decades to come — from the adoption of Section 35 of the Constitution Act, 1982, to the Royal Commission on Aboriginal Peoples, to seeking justice and healing for the Survivors of residential schools, to the fundamental work of upholding the inherent right of self-government. On all of these issues and many others he has led, whether as president of the Indian Brotherhood of the NWT, National Chief of the Assembly of First Nations, co-chair of the Royal Commission on Aboriginal Peoples, co-chair for Indigenous Survival International Canada, or as president of the Dene Nation.

By chronicling Georges's life, *Hòt'a! Enough!* provides us with insight and understanding of these topics in a way that a biography of no other person could. Revealed before us is not only an understanding of what happened but also of the thinking and motivations that were driving them, and the wisdom that comes from looking back on one's life.

When reading the book, I not only felt like I was in a deep conversation with Georges and learning new things but also that I was in an encounter with a life lived with consistency and clarity. And that I was being called and challenged to bring more consistency and clarity to the way I live my own life, and, indeed, to the work of upholding Indigenous rights. This makes sense, as Georges has long played a role as a conscience for Canada.

Famously, in the chaos of the Meech Lake Accord, Georges stood before Canada's power-bearing elites and gave an "off the cuff" oration that called out the hypocrisy and complacency that has so long kept down Indigenous Peoples in Canada:

> I believe we can do something different. We want to do something different. We are sick and tired of coming to events like this and being your conscience, absolutely sick and tired of it. We'd love nothing more than to be able to go around and dance and feel good about ourselves. But by God, we have too many real things to be concerned about.

Well, the Georges who gave that speech is the Georges of *Hòt'a! Enough!*. It is not in any way surprising that he ends the book with a clarion call to action, to carry forward the work, to persevere:

> Because it takes so long to achieve the proper recognition of Aboriginal Rights or Treaty Rights, it might mean sometimes that the generations that fought for certain rights being recognized are not necessarily alive when the recognition happens. In other cases, the struggle for recognition might be over only for the struggle for implementation to begin. For the young people taking up the struggle of your forefathers and mothers, don't despair. It will take time to get what you want, but history is on your side. Move forward with a confident stride, and like the generations before, you will prevail — if you stay the course.

Being Indigenous in Canada is hard and will remain hard. But there certainly have been times when it has been more difficult. One of the reasons we are where we are today is because of the leadership of Georges and others of his generation. By stepping into the light, Georges and others were able to redirect some of that light and shine it on Canada's wrongs and harms and reveal pathways of reconciliation, redress, and rebuilding.

We are, all of us, responsible for carrying forward that work today, honouring the legacy of those that paved the way. Read *Hòt'a! Enough!*. It will help you fulfill that responsibility.

— The Honourable Dr. Jody Wilson-Raybould, P.C., O.B.C., K.C.

INTRODUCTION

I met Georges in August 1999, when I was a newly hired communications officer at the Aboriginal Healing Foundation, and he was the president and chair of the board. By then he was a mountain of a man in Native politics, fifty-one years of age and in the early days of salt-and-pepper hair. Here I should explain why I wanted to write this book and why I think a reader may benefit from reading it. First, Georges's life has been inherently interesting. He has played a public role during many of the most consequential events of the past fifty years of Canadian history, from the Berger Inquiry and the constitution talks to Oka and Indian residential schools. Second, there is wealth in Georges's story for the reader who wants to understand the character of Native perspectives. Third, in many respects this is a book about Canada, and I should hope at least some readers will believe there is value in better understanding the country in which they live. As for Georges, he is widely regarded among his peers as a model of good, effective, and far-sighted leadership. I consider his decades-long career a model worthy of study, and I hope young people (and especially young Indigenous people) will take up this book for the lessons it contains.

For fifteen years, from 1999 to 2014, I was Georges's speech writer. Toward the end of that work, I pitched this book. He was noncommittal at first and a few years later, when the AHF shut down, he told me there was no time in his life for a memoir. I moved on, having concluded that the book was a non-starter. Then, just after dinner on October 10, 2017, Georges sent me a text:

> Wayne are you still open to doing a book with me? If so can you send the outline again. I may be prepared to do one. Georges

Work began on November 20 at Georges's apartment in the Tip Top Lofts, adjacent to Toronto's Billy Bishop Airport. Over the next few years we met in Toronto and in Yellowknife, conducting interviews and reviewing drafts. Georges drew up a list of the people he wanted to include in the book. We spoke to most of them, but unfortunately a few died over the years it took to complete this project.

A writer doesn't know what a book is about until it's written. In my view this memoir, despite its title, is as much an "our" battle story as it is a "my" battle one. Everything Georges did required a collective effort. In pulling together, Indigenous people displayed their passion and intelligence and strength. Like any biographer, I also wanted to delve into the private world of Georges, and I knew that was going to be a challenge. I'd worked with him for more than five years before we had a conversation that trespassed on his personal affairs. He's easily the most private person I've ever known. Over time I discovered a few tricks that would open him up, like asking about Yellowknife. I learned that Georges loves the land, that he loves gardening, and that he much prefers feeding animals to hunting them. These and other details gave me an early insight into the private man and suggested a nurturing character.

Yes, Georges is passionate and gnashes at injustice, but he's also gentle and thoughtful and sweet. Not once in the many years I observed him did he raise his voice. Working with First Nations, Métis, and Inuit, he was calm, cool, thoughtful, deliberative, and patient, and he listened far more than he spoke. Most remarkable to me was his humility. My work has brought me into the orbit of a good many politicians, and Georges is the only one among them I would characterize as without ego. He had to be talked into every leadership position he ever had, by people who could see his unique capabilities. I have to admit that I dug Georges the Angry Native Radical, but if you focus on that you miss Georges the Calm Consensus Builder.

One of the questions I set out to answer was "What made Georges a great leader?" I think it's the span of his talents. He knew when aggression was required, and he could deliver, but he also knew the time for patience and restraint. He has a keen and logical mind, but he also feels deeply. My work with Georges makes it clear that he has a powerful ability to catch every misplaced detail, and yet somehow he can keep his eye on the big picture. He never tried to impose his thinking on others, but he could see the way forward and he would express his ideas with such clarity and command that others would want him to lead. Georges could bridge the big and small, the soft and tough, the simple and complex, the head and the heart.

Other people of course have their theories. According to Jerome Berthelette, Georges's leadership benefitted from his "unflappable nature and his ethics. There's no question about his moral and ethical framework." Herb Norwegian says, "It was, first of all, family. The big thing is his mom. I thought that's where a lot of that came from. His leadership was based on common sense, on making the right decisions at the right time." Janet Pitsiulaaq Brewster says that "aside from the obvious, his wicked smartness and his experience, he was humble and absolutely willing to look at everybody as human beings and as potential representatives for absolute human goodness." "I certainly respect him and see his knowledge," says Richard Lafferty. "He's able to disseminate information in a very calming and clear fashion. There's no ambiguity when he's finished explaining what he wants to say." Dan Gaspé recalls Georges as a voice of calm in a stormy time: "I was really impressed with his ability to cut to the real issues and communicate them clearly." Marilyn John says that Georges was "very well respected, especially by the Elders and by Aboriginal people right across the country." Georges himself seems to agree with the assessment of Patrick Scott, that "it must be because he is so tuned into Elders."

I'm not suggesting Georges is without limitations. I've noted how private a person he is, and for some that could read as distant, mysterious, intimidating, even cold. Georges has a warm heart, but you would never guess that at first glance. He couldn't be more different in private than he has been in public. This dissonance — the Native radical who loves nothing more than going home to his nine cats — has always been a source of amusement to me. But there's no law that says you can't be a fighter and a lover too. I wanted to show that Georges's life has been about the battle, but not only about the battle.

I knew that readers of this book would want to see the personal side of Georges, but how was I going to access it? An idea came to me. As the chapters started to take shape, I asked Georges to write his personal reflections on what he was reading. Why did he make the decisions he made? What was going on in his life at the time? What was he feeling? I proposed that we include these reflections in the book, setting them in a distinct font so it was clear to the reader that these were Georges's own words. It's an unusual way to write a biography, but in this case it made sense.

Looking back, it's hard not to feel that the world of Native politics is diminished. The Dene Nation has never been more powerful and effectual than in the days when Georges was leader. "During that time," Freddie Greenland told me, "we had really strong leadership. Everybody was together and knew what they were talking about. It's just too bad that, as we went along, everything fell apart." Under National Chief Erasmus, the Assembly of First Nations did some of its most consequential work. Today it is plagued by scandal and internal conflict. ("Georges's leadership style was appreciated," an AFN employee told me. "It's more like a bureaucracy now.") The Royal Commission on Aboriginal Peoples (RCAP) was the last instance of the royal commission, and we are unlikely ever to see a project of that scope and ambition again. The Aboriginal Healing Foundation was an arm's-length, government-funded, national agency created and run by Indigenous people for Indigenous people. No government today would turn to an agency of this sort. There's a disconnect between Indigenous communities and the Ottawa-based Indigenous politicians that didn't exist a generation ago, and it's led to a drifting of the national organizations into irrelevance. That's my personal opinion, but many people I interviewed had reached the same conclusion. Echoing many others, Garnet Angeconeb told me, "I have to say that the leadership back then was really different from the leadership today. We had issues that needed to be addressed and put forward to the Canadian conscience. I never saw dialogue at a level that I did back then." The point isn't to judge, it's to inspire. If this book has one purpose, it's to tell the young people that they are limited only by their imaginations.

A note on terminology

Throughout this book, I've used various terms for the people indigenous to what is now called Canada. For the most part, I've used the words that were common at the time. Up to the 1970s the words "Indian" and "Native" were commonplace, and beginning in the 1980s the term "Aboriginal" (sometimes capitalized, sometimes not) crept in. Then, in the early 2000s, "Indigenous" came to be the dominant term. So, for instance, if I am writing about the constitutional talks of the early 1980s, I will tend to use "Aboriginal." Such are the rules, and I've reserved the right to break them whenever doing so avoids a repetitive or clumsy phrase.

— Wayne K. Spear

1

YOUNG GEORGES

Yellowknife is a land of glacial-scoured igneous metamorphic rock, lakes, grasslands, fens and peat bogs, and forests of Jack pine, spruce, and paper birch. It is home to ducks and geese, as well as to boreal chickadees, ptarmigans, magpies, ravens, redpolls, woodpeckers, white-winged crossbills, snow buntings, squirrels, hares, house sparrows, and jays. Occasionally you'll see a coyote, wolf, wolverine, or black bear, and often red foxes. Ten thousand years ago the Laurentide Ice Sheet retreated to form Glacial Lake McConnell and, later, the ancestral Great Slave Lake. Now, lichen-covered basalt outcrops and coarse-grained gabbro recall an ancient past, when lava rich in magnesium and iron spilled from the fault lines that intersect Yellowknife's foundations. Yellowknife is austere and beautiful.

The city receives more sunlight annually, on average, than any other in Canada. Situated at the shore of Great Slave Lake, the second-largest lake entirely within Canadian borders, Yellowknife is 150 kilometres south of the tree line. The name derives from the knives fashioned by the Tetsǫ̨t'ıné — copper, or metal, people — from ore harvested at the shores of the Coppermine River. In the Great Slave Lake region, Dene speakers of Slavey, Dogrib, and Chipewyan hunted, fished, and trapped for thousands of years prior to the arrival of settlers.

Yellowknife, Old Town, early days.

Yellowknife became a town where the gold was paved with streets, and soon arrived many seekers of prosperity. In the mid-1930s, the establishment of the Con Mine brought immigrants from Germany, Italy, Sweden, and elsewhere. Anticipating development of the area, Canada designated Indian Affairs a branch of the Department of Mines and Resources and, from 1939 to 1953, Yellowknife was governed by a largely appointed administrative council controlled by the distant Ottawa government. Between 1941 and 1951, the population nearly doubled, going from 1,410, to 2,724. The Old Town, situated on The Rock and Latham Island, reached the limits of its growth. In 1945, when the war ended and the second boom began, the "New Town" was established to the southwest. The decision was mocked by some locals, who assumed that Yellowknife would be abandoned when the mine was exhausted and thus derisively referred to the New Town expansion as "Blunderville." The reality was that the terrain of Old Town was not well suited to residential expansion, the mining companies were not keen on drawing large numbers of non-miners to the island, and the volume of business had surpassed what the existing settlement could manage.

On August 8, 1948, Georges Henry Erasmus was born in Fort Rae, known officially since the 2005 Tłįchǫ agreement as Behchokǫ̀. Georges describes it as "a wonderful settlement in the heartland of the Tłįchǫ." One hundred kilometres northwest of Yellowknife, near the end of the Great Slave's north arm, Behchokǫ̀ takes its name, "Big Knife Community," from the Tłįchǫ language. Georges was born to mother Florence, née Smith, and father Fred, both from Behchokǫ̀. He would be the first of thirteen children: Georges, Violet, Roy, Bill, Ron, Margaret, Guy, Marilyn, Joanne, Jeannette, Sean, and Shannon. (Bertha would be lost to what was then known as crib death.)

In the 1950s, Yellowknife was very much a mining town. In 1953 it would become a municipality, with its own council and town hall, and in 1967 it would be designated a territorial capital. In the meantime, Yellowknife was a cosmopolitan village of Dene and settler, dotted with wooden houses, hotels, shops, and cafés. The Yellowknives Dene communities, N'Dilo and Dettah, were then as now situated at the tip of Latham Island six and a half kilometres southeast across the north arm of Great Slave Lake, respectively. A small but growing town, Yellowknife in Georges's early youth had a local municipal council, a modern airport, a hospital, a federal school, a Catholic separate school system, and a non-Indigenous population keen to develop a resource-based economy in what some of them saw as the last outpost of empire.

The Tłįchǫ and Yellowknives Dene communities had close ties. The Dene would flow back and forth. Not long after Georges was born, Fred took work at the Yellowknife Con Mine. Although born in Behchokǫ̀, Georges would spend his first few years in N'Dilo, where Fred moved the family when his eldest son was a few months old. "It's kind of hard now to think that N'Dilo was not part of Yellowknife," says Georges, who recalls the family as "kind of isolated." Travel into town from N'Dilo required a canoe ride or a short walk over "the rock," a six-story hill that dominates Latham Island. The family travelled by dog team in winter and by boat in summer.

Dad was a bit of a jokester sometimes. He demonstrated it one April 1, while we were still living at N'Dilo. He went to all the homes around us, loudly knocking on doors and telling hunters to get up and quickly bring their rifles because caribou were right there in front of us on the lake. Imagining fresh caribou in all the ways it could be cooked, everyone came out with their gun, partially dressed, looking for the caribou. When everyone was up and outside, Dad yelled, "April Fool's!" and burst out laughing. Everyone ended up laughing, but I would not be surprised if some thought about returning the favour someday.

Jimmy Turner was an Englishman and a commercial fisherman who built the Erasmus family's skiff. He married Georges's aunt Catherine, Fred's sister. Fred put the skiff to good work, visiting the net once or sometimes twice a day to bring home the haul. Some fish would be used fresh, some would be sold, and some would be made by Florence into dryfish. The Erasmus kids had a variety of freshwater fish as a regular part of their diet, along with caribou and moose and ducks. In Georges's younger years, there was a lot of fishing in the family:

An activity in the fall was catching a large amount of lake fish and processing them by putting ten fish on a long stick and hanging them by the tail on a stage high enough off the ground that animals couldn't reach them. Dad would catch hundreds of fish, mostly whitefish. They would be sun or air dried and then frozen. We called this stick-fish. It was fed to the dogs during the winter and was also a source of protein for us.

One winter Dad decided to put a fishnet in the water around Christmas, or a little later. He and another fellow started making a large hole in the ice that was much bigger than would be the case if the net were being set earlier when the ice was thinner. After going down about three feet, they jumped into the hole and took turns chiselling a deeper hole, while leaving a shelf on one side to stand on. They went down at least two more feet before hitting water. They then had to dig another hole just as deep further out for the other end of the net. They used a jigger to find the spot for the other hole for the net. Normally if the ice is not too deep, the jigger can be seen as it moves forward under the

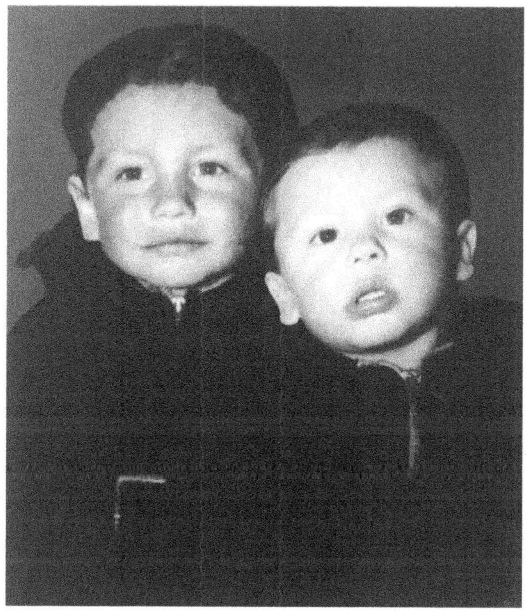

Georges and younger brother Roy, about 1952, ages four and two.

ice, but because the ice was so deep and the snow cover on the lake was so plentiful, it was not possible to see the jigger. After much effort, Dad and the other guy were able to put the net in the water. Dad went back to setting his net earlier so that it was easier to set the net. Once the net was set it had to be visited every day. We had a whole variety of freshwater fish that we would have as a regular part of our diet along with caribou and moose and ducks.

Georges recalls tending to the nets on Great Slave Lake. "Beautiful sunshine, and Dad has me in the back of his little canoe. We're going out to see what kind of fish he's caught during the night."

One spring morning when I was about five, my dad did me a wonderful favour, inviting me to join him in his canoe. We visited his net on the other shore across the bay. I was instructed to be careful and not to upset the canoe. Then we were off. Dad had a tub in front of him to hold the fish he caught. It was a beautiful sunny day with no wind, the water was still like glass. As we paddled into the sun, the only sounds were birds in the trees and Dad's swift breaking of the water as he paddled across the lake. In no time we were across, and he was visiting the net. As he took fish out of the net, he was telling me what kind we were getting and the proper way to take the fish out of the net. I remember looking back across the lake and seeing our little home from an angle I had not seen before. We were just above the lakeshore on a little ledge with easy access to the lake.

The Erasmus children grew up with strong parents well-versed in Dene traditions. Florence was one of the first teachers at the kindergarten school. Prior to her marriage, she did a variety of jobs at the Fort Rae (Behchokǫ̀) hospital operated by the Catholic Church. She was a gifted seamstress who made moccasins and mukluks and parkas and traditional gloves. Florence was patient with the children and committed to helping them fulfill their innate potential. Like Georges, she wanted to go to school. "She's the one person I know who cried because she *didn't* go to residential school," Georges says. Although she would never receive a formal education, Florence taught herself to read and write.

Mom would take the moose and caribou hides and make clothing for us — mitts, moccasins, coats, jackets, and parkas. She would add beautiful beading or embroidery. She also made everyday moccasins, without the fine beadwork, which we would use to play outside. These moccasins would need regular repair, sometimes more than once a year. Later in life Mom started sewing articles of clothing for sale, but in the early years it was enough just to supply us all with what we needed for the winter season in the north.

One of the fall activities was to pick berries as a family. I used to love going on these little day trips to one of the lakes north and east of us, to get away from any berries that might have been affected by the arsenic fallout from the two gold mines. We were all taught at an early age not to eat the berries locally, as they would be contaminated by the arsenic in the air from the mines. I remember one fall going up the Yellowknife River, doing the portage at the rapids and going across Prosperous Lake to a south-facing hill, picking loads of cranberries. It was one of those winters where we had all the berries we needed for jam or whatever. Blackcurrant and cranberry were my favourites to have in a jam.

In the late fall, when the ice begins to form, you'll notice small black clumps of aquatic vegetation rising to the surface of lakes and ponds. This is the muskrats gathering material to make their winter living space, essentially a covered hole in the ice where they will have protection and air to breathe. These "pushups," as they're known, will soon be covered by winter snow. While the muskrats swim the trappers walk the ice, opening the pushups and placing their traps. A day or two later they will return for the harvest. Trapping is typically done in winter because the fur of animals is then at its prime. One year, shortly after leaving N'Dilo, Fred was gone so long on a weekend hunt that Florence became concerned. Eventually he returned with a large haul of muskrats. The meat would be shared widely among the extended family, and the skins would be fleshed, all fat and traces of meat removed. Then the pelts would be cured or dried in preparation for sale. Hunting and harvesting supplemented the family income and ensured the household necessities.

We had wonderful dogs, and Dad was proud of them. The dogs stayed not far from the house amongst the trees. They were so important for everything: hunting, fishing, trapping, transportation, and hauling wood. Dad would go hunting with the team in winter and return after a few days with a sled full of fresh caribou meat that he hunted sometimes alone and at other times with other hunters. I loved to play with our dogs and rode my dad's lead dog, Rover, like a horse. He was very strong and gentle, and he was bigger than most of our other dogs.

I remember going up the hill and keeping an eye on the return winter trail in the snow on the lake for my dad to return from the hunt. One of the winter chores that I sometimes helped my dad with was to go with him to get firewood with the dogs. We would go across the lake, heading east, and travel inland until we found the woodlot that dad wanted to harvest. I would ride in the toboggan carryall going for wood but run behind on the return. I was taught to be useful and to do what I could with household chores. I was glad to be of help.

One year my dad decided he would enter the 150-mile Dog Derby race — fifty miles a day over three days — that used to be organized at the end of March of every year and continues to this day. He did all right, was even ahead sometimes, but he had one dog that had lots of extra fur around his paws that kept clumping up in the melting snow. He had to stop regularly to clean its paws. He ended up putting the dog in his sled as a passenger. He never did cut off the extra fur that our dog had on his paws. He thought it was an important insulator.

As Georges recalls, Fred worked a variety of jobs. "I was in the old St. Patrick's Elementary School, and there's my dad, climbing up and putting tar on the roof." Fred's work was mostly seasonal, spring to early winter. Like many Dene, he was looking to create a life where he could take the necessary part-time jobs in mining and so on so he could continue to hunt, trap, and fish. "My dad was trying to do what many Dene have tried hard to do," says Georges. "In more recent times, mining companies have been trying to figure out how to operate in a way that accommodates Indigenous workers, three weeks on and three weeks off, or whatever it is, because Indigenous people are yearning to continue their culture and way of life." Unfortunately, in Fred's day accommodation of this sort was well in the future. He eventually took full-time work in the federal government's DPW (Public Works) garage, leaving him no time for going out on the land. That's when Fred sold his dogs.

Georges and his eleven siblings were taught by Fred and Florence to be responsible, to help the elderly, and to contribute to the community. Georges's sister Joanne, born in 1965, remembers her dad sitting the children down to teach them in traditional ways. "I got used to being part of a family and part of a community," Georges says, "where you're taught to do what you can."

Some of my earliest memories are of me living at the end of Latham Island, at N'Dilo, surrounded by trees, bush, and beautiful rocks that were little hills both south and north of us. We had a few immediate neighbours: elderly Granny Lafferty right beside us and three other log homes where my mother's brother, Uncle Teddy, and his family lived. Uncle Teddy's eldest son, Jean Paul (later to be known as John Smith), was one of my playmates. We played all over the local rocks when we were small, first with my cousin John and later with my brother Roy. We got to know every seam or crack in the rocks and all the great places amongst the trees and bushes where we could hide.

Granny Lafferty was not Georges's actual grandmother, but she was a relative. She and Georges would gather kindling in the thick brush around N'Dilo, mostly dried willow. Granny Lafferty had a trick that made an impression on the young Georges: "She'd organize our wood for carrying just using rope. She would tie the wood into two bundles and make armholes so we could hoist the wood onto our backs." Granny Lafferty was very clever and was open to letting Georges spend time with her. Georges loved her company.

Uncle Teddy's log house caught fire and was damaged beyond repair. He and his family left N'Dilo for town. Folks assumed that the fire was started by an abandoned cigarette. The fire was put out using forest-firefighting equipment, including mobile pumps with bladders that could be put on one's back. Sometime after the house fire was put out and the firefighting crew had left, Granny Lafferty and Georges found the beginning of a forest fire at the base of a small hill a few thousand feet away from the burnt house. They immediately began to fight the fire using damp rags and anything else they could find. Someone sent word that the fire was back. Eventually the crew returned to finish the job. When they left the second time, they provided backpack pumps to fight any additional fires. This would be Georges's first but not last round as a firefighter. He would think about this day years later, when he would spend his summers fighting fires with the forestry department.

When Georges was about four, he and some friends collected cigarette butts discarded by Florence and others. They had tried to make cigarettes from dried leaves but found the result disgusting. Now they were after the real deal. Once again, Georges found the experience truly disgusting. Early in his life, he abandoned the idea of smoking.

A very early memory was being given matches to always carry on me as survival gear and being taught how to make fires with dry wood from willows, dried birch bark, and dead trees. We were instructed that matches were not toys and should never be played with or used irresponsibly. We were taught how to use knives and axes and allowed to have pocket knives. At an early age I was taught to shoot a gun and to know different types of firearms. Again, it was strongly reinforced that guns were not toys and always had to be used responsibly.

There was a time when Georges was keen on hunting. Ptarmigans with slingshot in winter. Later, hunting with a bow and arrow and, later still, with a gun. A .22 calibre for ptarmigans, a shotgun for ducks in summer and fall. When Georges was married with children, hunting supplemented a tight family budget. One successful outing would fill the freezer. But Georges now says he's gone to the other extreme.

Dad taught us how to shoot fairly early. Before Ski-Doos, we walked across ice on the lake. You could hear ptarmigans feeding in the trees. We used an over & under .22, a 410 single-shot. More than enough to hunt ducks, but you had to have a good shot because you only got one. I was a pretty good shot, though, so I didn't mind. I went to the shooting range and out in the woods, and I took the time to be proficient at killing rather than merely wounding animals.

I don't think I could kill. Today, I'm feeding the ptarmigans and ducks. It happened gradually but really took hold twenty to twenty-five years ago. I was on a winter hunt with Herb Norwegian and my dad. We drove out on the ice road to the mines. Went into hunting grounds. As soon as we drove up, there was a herd of caribou on the lake. We hunted and butchered them there, camped for a night or two, and came back. That was the last time I did a hunt.

Georges spent a lot of time as a child with his paternal grandmother, Mary Erasmus. She lived a few minutes away at N'Dilo. One spring day when Georges was around five, Mary decided to start a garden. They cleared a small area of plants and saplings, removing roots and debris. Granny Erasmus cut up some potatoes, showing Georges the eyes they would use to propagate cuttings. He was fascinated by this new information and skill. Together they covered the rows of potatoes with dirt. Over the summer Georges would water the potato patch, learning what weeds or unwanted growth to pick. To this day, he loves to plant potatoes, "no doubt because of the early start in growing things in the garden with my granny." In later years, Mary moved into a house with a wood stove and a big porch. Georges stacked wood while his grandmother made fry bread. She taught Georges to use trees as firewood stacking-ends.

Georges would walk with his grandmother across the bridge to a restaurant called the Busy Bee, where they'd order bacon and eggs. Or they'd go to Weaver & Devore, a general store established in 1936. In the days before television, the children were rarely in the house. Georges and his younger siblings, Roy and Bill, played prospector on the rocks behind their house, or a game somewhat akin to baseball called "Skin." Here's how brother Bill Erasmus describes it:

> If you made a home run, it was called a skin. A skin was like a life. If you had a skin, and then you went out, you're still alive because that skin would give you one life. Your whole team had to go out before the other team batted. If the last batter made a home run, a skin, then everybody went up to bat again. To make an out, a person could catch a fly or one bounce. They could put you out by touching you with the ball as you ran to the base. Or they could literally throw it at you. If they hit you with the ball, when between bases, you were out. People would leave and, in-between innings, other people would join. The game would go on for hours. I'm surprised it didn't carry on. I guess TV put an end to that.

The older Erasmus children made many of their toys. Georges made slingshots and spears for hunting and play. In those days youngsters got good at fashioning toys from wood, nails, and other scrap materials. Georges recalls an elaborate, multi-level riverboat cobbled together by an acquaintance from nails and wire. "I thought I was pretty good at carving, but I couldn't hold a candle to this young fellow. He was an artist." Georges and Roy played for hours with swords that their father made of willow.

From a young age, the movies provided another means of entertainment. The most popular were Westerns and adventure films, featuring castles and sword fights and daredevilry. A viewing of *Moby Dick* inspired Georges and Roy to make spears, which they spent hours throwing at snowbanks. But nothing could beat arrows, which Georges eventually bought rather than made.

During the springtime thaw they would go out on the "rotting" candle ice, honeycombed by melting water and dirt. As the candle ice disintegrates and the floating shards bump one into another, the ice makes a distinct clinking sound. The structure of candle ice is vertical. No matter how thick the ice is, the person who falls through it will have nothing firm to grab. Fred warned his children not to go out on the melting ice. Knowing that they would, he told them to take a pole to stop them from falling through.

Young Georges waged war with handmade slingshots, spears, bows and arrows, and fireweed. The kids would establish a fort atop a rock, and another team would be tasked with conquering the fort from below. In winter, they would build snow tunnels and igloos. Georges played baseball and, like many in Yellowknife, curling. Even as a young child, he was an avid reader, saving up his money to buy comics. In those days, the comic books had Joe Weider ads with cut-out mail-in forms for "absolutely free muscle building information on how to build a handsome body." That sounded pretty good to Georges.

Off went his order to Montreal and back came an envelope. He dutifully followed the exercise instructions and got results too. Soon, Georges was ordering instructional materials for karate and kung fu. The only thing missing was a sparring partner, so he enlisted a friend to (as Bill puts it) "experiment" on. "He'd tell Archie to put him in a headlock from behind. Georges had read the instructions and knew a way to get out of it. But he didn't tell Archie that. Archie would do what Georges told him, and Georges would stomp on his foot and throw back his head, almost breaking Archie's nose."

A large family in a small house meant no room for martial arts. In the wintertime, Archie and Georges would dress in heavy winter clothes and do their karate "experiments" outside, on the ice. "Growing up, we spent the whole winter outside," Georges remembers. "And when we had twenty-four hours of daylight, we spent the whole day outside."

Georges's parents decided to keep him out of school, at least for a while. In 1955, when Georges was seven, the family moved fully into the Yellowknife community so that he could go to school. In January of 1956 Georges began to attend classes.

Apparently, Dad's sisters in Yellowknife were hounding my parents to move into the town proper so I could start school following my sixth birthday. I was not aware of any of this until sometime later. We moved one December just

Florence and Fred Erasmus, mid-1950s.

before Christmas, dogs and all. We rented a log house that was mostly empty from the Liske family, as the family lived at Trout Rock, in the north arm of Great Slave Lake. The school bus stopped near the house. At this point in my life, I spoke Tłįchǫ and French. The biggest challenge for me was to quickly learn English, as it was the only language used in the school. The other option for my parents was to stay where we lived at N'Dilo, on Latham Island, and send me to residential school for ten months of the year. Dad had gone to residential school in Fort Resolution and disliked it so much that he swore his children would not go to any residential school.

My first day at St. Pat's Elementary School was quite an adventure. Because we had been living at the end of the island and away from most people, I didn't know very many children on the bus or in the school. Living closer to people meant more interaction with other children. I learned to play cards and gamble for pennies and other coins. Blackjack and different poker games were the order of the day. I found, once I learned the games, that I was pretty good at gambling. But I learned that you could lose as well as win. I still enjoy a good game sometimes.

I could speak Tłįchǫ to the few Dene children that were in school or French to one teacher in another grade. I had to get a handle on English ASAP, and I did. Mom and Dad stopped talking to me in Tłįchǫ and mostly spoke English so I could pick up the language quickly. I did a lot of homework, not because it was asked of me but because I wanted to master the English language. One of the exercises that my mom helped me with was to know my readers inside out. I read them so much I could tell you what was written on any page by heart. I stood facing the wall and answered my mom when she asked, "Okay, what is on page three?" Another way I worked at learning the English language was to do the shopping for the family at a small store-cum-café called the Rex Café. Everything was behind the counter so shoppers would have to ask for what items they wanted to buy.

I could not believe when I did not pass into grade two at the end of June. Here I am, eight years old, and I'm going back into grade one. No doubt the teacher thought she was doing me a wonderful favour. I was pissed right off. I'm still pissed!

Georges and family in Fort Rae, 1956.

In short time Georges learned English, but at a cost. “Now, I have trouble thinking in Tłı̨chǫ. I have to really work hard at it. It’s a tiny voice, as opposed to a very loud voice in English.” In time Georges returned to school, but once again he would suffer a setback.

It’s the fall of 1959. School had just started and I’m feeling listless. My mother brings me to the doctor, and they say it’s nothing, he’s just lazy. A week later she’s back with me again because I’m in really bad shape. I’m sitting there in the waiting room, and there’s a doctor going through. He takes one look at me and says, “Take that child to the hospital right now!” I start hallucinating. I’m coming in and out of consciousness, and they can’t figure out what’s going on. My parents are, like most Dene, Roman Catholic. I was baptized the same day I was born, for crying out loud. They captured me, right then and there. So now I’m being given last rites, before they medevac me off to Edmonton. On the way to Edmonton, I have an out-of-body experience. All of a sudden, I pop out of my body and right out of the plane. I can see through the skin of the wall of the plane like it’s nothing. The plane is hurtling along, and I’m right there with it. And, holy, I really wanted to explore, but I didn’t want to die. Somewhere my consciousness was very clear: “You can explore, but if you go too far, or you stay too long, that’s gonna be it for you.”

Georges drifted for a while in this state, eventually, in his words, popping back into his body. He woke as the plane landed at the industrial airport, not far from Charles Camsell Indian Hospital, where he would soon be diagnosed with tuberculous meningitis. Already behind at school, he would spend eighteen months in hospital, returning to Yellowknife in the spring of 1961. As bad as this was, it could have been worse. Georges had the good fortune to receive a new treatment ("miracle drugs," as Georges puts it) that drastically improved the speed of his recovery. "Prior to this time, people would spend five, ten, or more years in hospital. I probably could have been sent home in December, but to them even the idea of an eighteen-month recovery was radical."

A number of things happened while I was in Edmonton at the Charles Camsell Indian Hospital. One was that my dad decided to sell our dogs. Once he found employment with the federal public works department, he had less and less time to use his dogs. So, when an occasion arose to help a friend that was still very much using dogs, he ended up letting our wonderful dogs go to another family. I only found out after the fact, and I was grateful I did not actually see this transpire. It would have been heartbreaking. The only dogs we had after this were pets, usually just one at the time. One summer, Dad had a job in the High Arctic. He returned with a big husky puppy that he named Arctic. We loved him, but we were not used to exercising dogs, outside of traditionally harnessing a team to a sled. So poor Arctic did not get the exercise he needed. That's something I look back on and still feel bad about. This was obviously part of the transition in lifestyle that we Dene were going through. We were starting to live a different way of life, spending more time in settlements or organized communities that led to new habits. There were many other adjustments for Dene who were used to a traditional way of making a living. One was taking a regular, nine-to-five, everyday job. This meant giving up the control that the Dene had of their activities — what, when, and where to do at any given time.

Georges returned to Yellowknife in the Spring of 1961. He quickly lost the extra weight he'd put on lying in a hospital bed, unable to run and play.

While their son was in hospital, Florence and Fred bought a house not far from the one they'd been renting. Georges helped with the ongoing renovations, removing nails from the lumber they'd acquired at construction sites. Georges watched and learned as walls and floors were framed, covered, and insulated. This knowledge would help enormously in later years, when Georges would become a builder himself.

In the spring of 1961, Georges was on the cusp of his teenage years. Already he'd had a number of jobs, or perhaps in some cases "jobs." As a child he'd recycled nails and sold newspapers and collected empty beer bottles for redemption at Grimshaw Trucking or Byers Transport. The money would be split between Georges and the children he'd recruited for the task. The empty bottle trade was a gold mine, according to the family. For a time, Georges worked in a grocery store after school hours, stocking shelves, packing groceries for shoppers, cleaning up after closing, preparing the store for opening the next day, and helping with various odd jobs. At around seventeen, he took up forest firefighting. In later years he would recruit just about anyone to help him with carpentry, a skill he'd picked up from his father, just as his father had learned from his father. Georges was always doing something to keep busy.

Georges's late entry into the school system, now compounded by an eighteen-month absence, meant that brother Roy (born February 12, 1951) was his classmate. Despite the setbacks and frustrations, Georges would eventually finish high school. But for the next few years he'd be in and out of the school system, taking various jobs like digging ditches and laying down water pipe and cooking for the highway construction crew.

I had just turned sixteen. Someone came to the house looking for someone to work in a work camp. The highway to Pine Point and Fort Resolution had been built some years before. Now an extension to Fort Smith was being added. The man talked to my dad, asking if I might be interested in this job. It meant not returning to high school, but rather spending several months working in the kitchen with the camp cook. Dad said, "Ask Georges, he can decide what he wants to do." I jumped at the chance. Next thing I knew I was on a bus to Hay River with another Dene who was going to join the road crew on the same job.

I always looked for ways to relieve my parents of having to supply me with spending money while I still lived at home. In high school I had summer jobs — at the town public works digging ditches, laying water and sewer lines, or with private contractors like the one that built the Bush Pilot's Monument. For a few summers I worked at the forestry department fighting forest fires. I loved all my jobs and look back on them fondly, particularly my forest-firefighting experience. In those days, there were no regular, trained, year-round firefighters. Anyone wanting to fight forest fires would gather early in the morning at the forestry yard, where the head of the local forestry department would pick how many were needed for each new fire that was to be fought, including who was to be foreman of the crew. I was amazed to be chosen as a foreman very early on over a large crew on a serious fire. Nearly everyone had more experience than me, which I acknowledged from the start. I was open to advice from the older and more experienced men. I was one of those people that wanted to put the fire out as soon as possible with as little damage to the northern terrain. We made use of the long days of twenty-four-hour sunlight, and we put in very long hours. Before too long, perhaps within a few days, we had the perimeter secure. This meant that we could now work shorter days, doing patrols to make sure the fire had been put out and that it had not spread. Then it was back to town and on to another fire.

In 1967, Georges took a summer job helping to build the Bush Pilot's Monument on the Old Stope Hill. He was hired as a general labourer, working with a crew on the monument's wooden stairs and on other tasks related to building the monument. The stonemason had no assistant, so any time he needed help, Georges would oblige.

It was just an extension of the labour I had working on the stairs. The fellow they brought in to do this masonry work had been doing it a long time, and he was really good. He told me how to do what he was doing. I really, really enjoyed the work. In addition, I helped with the rocks and stone and did some carpentry. But I was saving up my money to leave.

In 1967, Yellowknife became the capital of the Northwest Territories. It was the Centennial of Canada and the Summer of Love. Georges says he was "entertaining the idea of heading to Montreal to see Expo 67 or going to San Francisco to see the hippies at Haight-Ashbury, who were all over the news. Never got beyond Edmonton that summer."

As it happened, a friend named Earl Dean was going to university in Edmonton. Georges decided to tag along. The university had purchased expropriated land with beautiful three-story houses in anticipation of a future expansion. It would be years before they needed this land for development, so the university had decided in the meanwhile to allocate the properties for student housing.

An ad had gone out seeking furniture donations for students. Georges and his friend moved into one of these student houses and got involved in picking up and delivering this donated furniture. For a while it was fun. At the end of July, they decided to get another job. Georges's friend wouldn't start university for another month, and Georges still hadn't decided whether he was going to Montreal or San Francisco. So they took a job canning motor oils and antifreeze and other petroleum products, until life picked up again. Georges learned that motor oil "is all the same, just in different cans" but the larger mystery of his life plan eluded him. He didn't go to Montreal or to San Francisco, and within a couple months his friend was immersed in his studies and Georges was on his own. Living on a university campus had got Georges excited. "I was involved in all kinds of things. And the learning, the books, all the things going on … holy jumping, I was on fire to go to university."

By the time Georges had made the decision to go to university, Christmas was approaching and money had run out. There was another wrinkle. For years Georges had been popping in and out of high school and still had two years to complete. How could he finish, and quickly? In November, he went to the Indian Affairs office in Edmonton for support. "Look," he said, "I want to go to university next fall, and here's how I can do it." Georges's proposal was to complete two years of high school in Edmonton over two semesters, enabling him to enter university the following autumn. A long shot, but it was an idea. All Georges had was the bit of cash he'd earned and his ideas.

"I'd love to help," the Indian Affairs person replied, "but there's nothing I can do." Because Ottawa was providing high school education funds to the government of the Northwest Territories, Georges was advised to go home. At the end of 1967, Georges was back in Yellowknife to complete grade 11, which he did in 1968. "I have to hand it to the nuns," he says. "Thank God they never closed the door on me. They did everything possible, doubling up my classes and, most amazing of all, dropping Religion class." Georges put in long, hard days of lessons, working through lunch and every spare period. A grade of 85 percent or better by Easter meant that you didn't have to write the final exam. Georges scored a grade of at least 85 percent in all but one subject.

This rapid conclusion of the high school business made Georges impatient. Now that he had done what was needed, he wanted to get on with his life. With a few months to fill, he occupied himself by kicking around Yellowknife and working on the high school yearbook. His life then took another unanticipated turn.

I'd never really had girlfriends until Cynthia "Cindy" Chambers, in my final year of high school. She was on the pill, but in 1969 she got pregnant. She was due in September. After much discussion with teachers, friends, and family, we decided to get married in May of 1969. This meant I needed to provide for my young new family, so getting a good job became priority number one. I approached Plains-Western again to see if I could now get a full-time job. They said of course, you're a good worker, come on back. I returned to Plains-Western immediately after school was out, in June 1969.

At Plains-Western, Georges learned to climb poles and to be a junior member of the electrical crew. He looked forward to going to work each morning. This was his first job that required driving, and he loved driving the company trucks to the work site. Georges and the crew strung wire to new sites in Yellowknife as the town expanded. He discovered he enjoyed heights and had no issues climbing as high as was necessary. One summer day, an accident near the airport took out the power lines and Georges was up the pole for nearly twelve hours, on his spurs. He had a great boss and a foreman who graciously passed on his skills. During the summer of 1968, when he first worked at Plains-Western, Georges had befriended another Dene. They got to know one another and a few times they partied into the night.

In the early 1960s Georges had worked on the foundations of Yellowknife's water and sewer systems, and now he was installing the city's first traffic lights, at the main intersection of 50th Street and Franklin Avenue. Yellowknife's population was taking off again, from 3,741 a year before its designation as the territorial capital to over 6,122 in 1971. The city's growth gave Georges plenty of work opportunities. It didn't matter to him whether he was digging ditches, or climbing poles, or laying pipe, or fighting fires. He loved whatever he was doing. "You could see something for your effort by the end of the day, unlike politics and stuff around Ottawa."

In the fall of 1969, Georges's son Kristen was born. He became a father even as his parents were still having children. Kristen had an uncle and aunt close to his own age and grew up with them as if they were siblings. Georges was very excited and overjoyed with his new son.

He was a constant joy to me. I had no idea that I would be so happy to become a father. As he discovered the world, I saw the world in a new way. Coming from a big family, I was used to people around me and having extended family living with us sometimes. Over the next number of years, I had at least one of my uncles living with us from time to time. Sometimes for a few weeks, sometimes all winter. My uncles would help in different ways with our young family, cooking, babysitting, even going caribou hunting with me on occasion. If we went on a fall hunt, we would fill our large freezer so that we would have meat for the winter.

Cindy suggested to Georges that they have another child. "She didn't want our son to be an only child. Coming from a big family, I totally agreed with having another child." Che was born just over two and half years after Kristen.

In 1969 "politics and stuff" was at the doorstep of the twenty-year-old Georges Erasmus, even if he didn't yet know it. On April 20, 1968, Pierre

Trudeau was sworn in as prime minister of Canada. When Georges was climbing poles, Trudeau released the "Statement of the Government of Canada on Indian Policy" — better known as "The White Paper." The White Paper was a document that laid out the Trudeau government's legislative intentions related to First Nations people. It proposed to abolish the Indian Act and the Treaties, and to assimilate First Nations. These ideas provoked Indigenous people across Canada. One of them was a young Plains-Western Gas and Electric Company employee about to embark on a five-decade career, fighting for the interests and rights of Indigenous people.

At the end of the 1960s, Georges took interest in the politics of the Dene, noticing that the band and the local Dene community were not well organized.

I wasn't giving up on university, but I decided to put it off for a while. Instead, I would volunteer some of my evenings and weekends to helping organize the local Dene community in Yellowknife. I was so disgusted with how our people seemed to be marginalized that I wanted to help the beginning of the re-emergence of the strong Dene people I had been hearing from all my life. I was brought up with the Dene world view, which included our belief that we had not surrendered our land or our right of self-government. But I was not seeing Dene control anywhere.

Georges offered his services to some local leaders. One was Antoine Liske, who seemed to Georges a natural leader people wanted to follow. Georges would go to local homes and generate discussions. What should be done about how decisions were being made all around us without our say? His first gig was as a volunteer secretary to the community leaders. Here, Georges and his fellow Dene began the long process of taking control of their lives.

As elsewhere, Yellowknife was being shaped by 1960s counterculture and radical politics. Even as many of the local Dene hunters had taken up jobs in the mines, young Canadians were coming north to experience what they considered a more authentic existence, in harmony with the land and away from the alienating arrangements of capitalism. Best of all,

Yellowknife in the 1960s was a place where anyone with a bit of gumption could get ahead. The jobs were plentiful and the real estate abundant. But from Georges's perspective, the Dene weren't getting ahead; they were falling further behind.

Yellowknife was flourishing. It had two mines and was now considered the capital. Civil servants were pouring in from Ottawa. So I decided that I was going to help organize the local community. Nobody said to me "we're going to make you secretary," but unofficially I had been doing the job as part of community development at the Company of Young Canadians (CYC), even though I'd started that work before my time with the CYC.

Erasmus family Christmas, early 1970s.

Although he was now working full-time and had a young family, Georges volunteered his weekends and nights to help the Yellowknife Band Council get more organized and engaged. Former journalist and Chief of Tulita (known as Fort Norman until January 1, 1996) Paul Andrew recalls that "as far as we were concerned, the Band Councils were our governing system. The Government of the Northwest Territories' mandate was to work with municipal governments. That's what the White Paper was all about, creating municipal governments and getting rid of our Band Councils. The Elders fought against this because they wanted to establish and maintain and even strengthen the Chief and Council."

The local band comprised Yellowknife, where most of the people lived, and the village outskirts where the Chief and council resided. Georges recalls that "we kind of had the equivalent of a local sub-chief for what was going on in Yellowknife, and so that's who I started working with." No one objected to the arrangement. The Indian Brotherhood of NWT (IBNWT) operated out of a tiny office atop the Tog Shop, a Yellowknife clothing store. "Like everybody else," recalls Antoine Mountain, "I just walked into the Indian Brotherhood office. Harold Glick had a clothing store on the first floor and we were up on the second." Under Georges's tenure, the band held frequent meetings and in general became more active.

The origins of the IBNWT go back to a Fort Smith meeting of the sixteen Dene chiefs who together constituted the Advisory Regional Council, a body set up by the Indian Affairs Branch to exchange information between Ottawa and the Dene. At this meeting, the Chiefs were informed that, as part of the White Paper policy, the Indian Affairs Branch would shut down in the NWT and responsibility for Status Indians would be given to the newly formed government of the NWT. (In fact, Indian Affairs did withdraw from the NWT for a few years, but later returned as a consequence of Dene pressures.) The Dene Chiefs of the Advisory Regional Council concluded that the time had come to take direct action. On October 3, 1969, the Indian Brotherhood of the NWT was born.[1]

With a family, a full-time job, and a volunteer gig, Georges lacked the time to pursue university. But it remained his intention to do so. As he saw it, higher education was something he'd put aside "for a little while" until things quieted down. What Georges couldn't know was that there would be no lulls in his long career. The "little while" he imagined would be a matter of months that became years, and then decades. Over and again he would be called upon, and over and again he would step up. His work with the Band Council was noticed by an outfit called the Company of Young Canadians, or CYC.

They came to me a number of times and said, "You're right in the heart of what's going on here. How about you come and work for us?" I wasn't aware that the Company of Young Canadians had field staff, called "volunteers," doing the same kind of organizing or community development. One day I was approached by Peter Puxley, the local staff person managing the Company of Young Canadians' volunteers. He offered me a job, as a volunteer, to continue doing what I was already doing in community organizing. I asked what he was paying, and he told me the most he could offer was $250 a month. I told him that I was already making twice that and finding it hard to live on. So no, thanks.

The offer went nowhere, until the CYC returned in the spring of 1970 with a solution: they would make both Georges and Cindy volunteers, bringing the household income close to what Georges was earning at Plains-Western. Even this amount, however, would be a struggle. While at Plains-Western, Georges had been taking jobs on the side, doing residential electrical work and occasionally helping a friend with cleaning at the Yellowknife hotel, bar, and café. But the work of community organizing was now pulling at Georges and beckoning him to a new direction.

Founded in 1966 by Prime Minister Lester B. Pearson, the CYC Great Slave Lake Project was a youth program modelled roughly after the American Peace Corps. Georges's CYC colleague Rick Fader says that "Pearson liked the idea of giving young people the chance to do odds and ends for the community. I don't think he expected us to be social animators." To the dismay of the Pearson government, the initiative received accusations of abetting political radicalism and took on the nickname "Company of Young Communists." As the CYC director in Yellowknife, Peter Puxley, would write many years later, the Company of Young Canadians "was an unusual example of the government enabling activities and movements that would often become a thorn in its side."

For Georges, whose reputation as a Native radical and rights crusader was still years into the future, the CYC was simply an extension of the work he'd already been doing. At the CYC, he could do even more. The cut in pay was compensated by the fact that Georges could now commit himself full-time to community work, which he saw as an element in his education. Always an avid reader, Georges now dove into political literature, particularly the writing of Paulo Freire, Frantz Fanon, Karl Marx, and Eldridge Cleaver. "Colonization and decolonization were subjects I could not get enough material to read. I spent a lot of time reading about revolutions across the Third and Fourth World," he says, "an interest I had for many years and that really took off after spending five months in Edmonton on the UOA campus in the fall of 1967." At the time Georges joined, the CYC had volunteers in a number of communities around the Great Slave Lake. Over time the work of CYC volunteers had an impact on the political evolution of the Dene communities.

Within a year and a half, Georges was promoted from community organizer to manager of the volunteers and projects.

Peter Puxley was going back to university or something. Once his job was open, I applied. The interviewers were saying, you know, you don't really have all of the skills, you're not as good as you really think you are. I said, Yeah, I am. If you're telling me I got lots to learn, of course. But right now, I know exactly how good I am. There's nobody you're going to bring in from anywhere else in Canada that's going to know my community up here better than I know. Nobody is going to be able to know the projects that are going to work with our people.

Prior to Georges's arrival, the CYC had attracted other Dene who wanted to get things done — James Wah-Shee, Joachim Bonnetrouge, Raymond Sonfrere, Mike Canadien, and Charlie Charlo for example. Among the work CYC members set to was the creation of the Tree of Peace, a community centre conceived by Phoebe Nahanni and incorporated in the summer of

1970. As we will see in a later chapter, Phoebe Nahanni would go on to become a consequential Dene scholar, geographer, and cartographer. In 1970 she had plans to go to the University of Western Ontario and was looking for someone she could entrust with her vision.

Phoebe came to me in the spring and said she had an idea of creating a friendship centre and a community organization called Tree of Peace. And I was so busy, the last thing I needed was more work. At the end of the summer, she convinced me to take over. It turned out to be one of the ideas that still stands and carries on to this day.

Georges wanted the Tree of Peace to be a development tool. He knew that how "the Tree" was established mattered. It was going to need to be recognized and used by the local people, particularly the Dene. First, the Tree of Peace would need a home. An older building near the original Hudson's Bay, in the Old Town near the bridge to Latham Island, was not being used. Georges went to the owner and convinced him to sell it. "I was very grateful that he was open to the idea. It was ideal for our purposes at the time." Second, the centre would need money. Georges met with Government of the NWT Commissioner Stuart Hodgson to request funds for the building and renovations. Hodgson tried to convince Georges that it was unnecessary to purchase a building, but Georges dug in and prevailed. He then got word out about the organization, inviting the community to help out with carpentry, drywalling, and painting. "Thankfully we had seed money to pay some local people and any contractors, like electricians or plumbers, that we needed." The interest was high. Soon folks were coming to the drop-in centre to congregate, discuss, and work.

At the same time, Indigenous people were returning to their cultural roots in large numbers. The political battles were, for many, spiritual as well. Georges recalls an annual conference that drew First Nations people from far and wide.

In the early 1970s several First Nations Elders from both Canada and the United States began holding conferences at Morley, Alberta, hosted by the

Stoney Nation. I had become aware of the unique gathering of both Traditional First Nation Elders and members of the Christian clergy when Ian Mackenzie and Bob Thomas had come to Yellowknife on their way to travel down the Dehcho or Mackenzie River. My uncle Jim Erasmus from Behchokǫ̀ and my dad, Fred Erasmus, had gone to an early steering committee meeting in Rough Rock, Arizona, amongst the Navajo (or Diné) and Apache. They both came back talking about the upcoming conferences in Alberta, Canada, which ended up being on the Morley reserve.

The event was open to anyone that might want to attend, set in a natural setting that looked untouched by man, with both trees and open areas, near a beautiful river and amongst the foothills of the Rocky Mountains. Everyone camped in their own tents or could sleep in teepees that were already set up. We would regularly see the local community members riding beautiful horses in the surrounding areas. Chief John Snow hosted the conference throughout the 1970s. In the morning you would wake up to Ernest Tootoosis from Poundmaker, Saskatchewan. He had a loudspeaker system set up to his truck with which he would drive through the whole camp telling everyone it was time to start the day. There would be traditional pipe ceremonies and prayer to greet a day full of Ceremony, storytelling, and, later, powwow dancing.

There was an open gathering or meeting place for those that wanted to participate in an ongoing discussion and storytelling about First Nation Spiritual beliefs and world view, and how the Christian churches had disrupted our traditional beliefs. Many Christian clergy just came to listen, but some did speak and shared the reasoning behind the early Christian efforts to Christianize the Aboriginal peoples of Turtle Island. Some openly talked of how they now knew it was wrongheaded and should not have occurred in the way it did. But the main attraction was opportunities to be with traditional Elders who still knew their language and original Spiritual Beliefs — people like Elder Albert Lightning, who always had a following of young people and others who wanted to hear what he had to say and to be part of any ceremonies or healing he might perform. Sometimes these opportunities with an Elder took place in gatherings or sometimes in private in a teepee or elsewhere. First Nations from different parts of the continent came to share their culture, ceremonies, stories, history, and plans for the future. Elders were given centre stage the whole ten days or so that the event happened. There were many young people from many nations that were sharing with other young people and discovering that we shared a common history with regional differences.

This was a wonderful occasion for any young people searching for an understanding of their background or to understand the values and beliefs of their peoples to hear it firsthand from traditional Elders. Indigenous youth from all over Turtle Island came to Morley, and it was wonderful to see how they became more and more confident of who they were year after year. There were different events put on like traditional round dance or powwow dancing at night and even a lacrosse game put on at least once. Elders wore their traditional clothing and young people started to wear traditional Diné or Navaho jewellery. Over time the event became like a festival or celebration of First Nation culture. There was much storytelling and sharing from people from many parts of Canada and the United States, even members of the Creek from Florida. It was fascinating to hear the differences and similarities in all our histories of being colonized and sent to residential-type schools run by the Christian churches and funded by governments. But it was the survival stories that we wanted to hear and how the culture still existed with its original spiritual beliefs and world view today. Over time people made friendships from all over Turtle Island that carried on long after the conferences ended. There were many traditional Sweat Lodge ceremonies over the period of the conference and the Native American Church held Ceremony with the sacred peyote. Many Nations, and many traditions and ceremonies.

I decided we needed to provide a way for the Dene from Denendeh to attend the Indian Ecumenical Conferences, so we bought a used bus that would provide free transportation to and from Morley, Alberta. The Tree of Peace bus would start in Yellowknife and make stops in Behchokǫ̀, Fort Providence, and other communities until we had a full bus. Many people drove their own vehicles, which they filled with camping gear and food, to the event. We had so many people from the north that we had a section of the campsite that resembled a Dene community, with many tents and campsites. The first year travelling to Morley was a bit of a shock. We discovered that nights in the Alberta foothills are very cold, even in mid-July. None of us brought our heavy winter bedrolls, which were needed in a land that did not have midnight sun.

We had the hot summer days that we were expecting, but the very cold nights were a surprise for those of us not used to living in the mountains. We quickly learned to bring the proper bedding in subsequent years.

Early on many northerners watched and observed the different ceremonies, but with the passing years we participated in the discussions and other events. This trip to Morley began a yearly trek that had more people participating every year and was very popular with all ages amongst the Dene. People still remember these conferences and the wonderful experiences that they shared with First Nation and Indigenous people from all over Turtle Island, celebrating their cultures and world views and ceremonies.

A funny thing happened one time when my brother Billy and I were returning from one of the conferences. Those days a large part of the Mackenzie Highway, as well as the road in northern Alberta to the NWT border, was gravel. This meant that it was a very dusty road. You did not want to be behind anyone on the highway, eating their dust. We finally got to the front of the pack on the road north, so it meant very quick stops for gas or bathroom breaks if we wanted to stay in front of the traffic. The last place to get gas and use the bathroom in Alberta back then was Indian Cabins, where we quickly stopped. Off we went and, somehow, we were still ahead of everyone else. As we were approaching the Alberta-NWT border, we saw a police car in the middle of the road with its lights flashing. We stopped and asked what was going on. The RCMP politely asked if we had stopped for gas in Indian Cabins and we answered yes, we had. He said, "Do you remember paying for your gas?" We both looked at each other and said, "Didn't *you* pay?" Neither of us had paid, thinking the other was going to pay. The policeman asked for fifteen dollars for the gas and laughed. He offered to give the money to the gas station, since he was headed that way. We were more careful to make sure one of us paid in the future.

Over the years the Tree ran numerous projects. One was a Dene language program that Cindy assisted Georges's mother, Florence, in developing and delivering. The second floor covered an area about one-half in size of the ground floor. Georges used the upstairs to house the CYC and Tree of Peace offices. For a few years, the second floor also hosted a satirical, tongue-in-cheek magazine known as the *Honey Bucket*. For Georges, the magazine was a fun way to get alternative views out to the street. Oddly enough it was popular in the civil service, a target of the satire. Maybe, Georges thought, bureaucrats need the occasional laugh too.

One day some local women representing a local community organization approached me for a sit-down meeting in the Tree of Peace. They thought it would be a good idea to have a kindergarten or preschool program in the Old Town somewhere, a program primarily for the Dene children. I listened to the very sincere and genuine concerns expressed on the community need that was not being met. The women convinced me something needed to be done. One of their points was that their organization was prepared to act on this if no one else was. I told them I agreed and that it would be our next project. They said, "Wonderful. Our job is done!"

And so we began the Tree of Peace preschool program we called a kindergarten. I wanted a bilingual, culturally appropriate program for the local Dene children and any others that would come to the school. There haven't been a lot of times that I have hired family members to fill work positions. This was one of those times, and even today I think it was the right thing to do. I hired my mother, Florence, to run this program. I came to the conclusion that Mom had raised twelve strong independent children; she could work her magic on the children that came to the school. I don't think I was wrong. I remember women from all over town trying to get their children into the school so they could spend their day with Mom and her assistant. Even to this day, Florence is remembered for her time at the kindergarten. My mom became an institution and helped create a good name for the Tree of Peace.

Georges's time with both the CYC and the Tree of Peace was rich with conversations. The discussions coalesced around a number of key issues. The White Paper wasn't the only concern of the Dene chiefs. They had long-standing land and treaty issues that they wanted resolved, and they were unhappy with the local municipal councils established by the territorial administration to displace the authority of their Band Councils. The Dene understandably wanted to administer their own affairs on their own land, and they wanted the resources they needed to do it. Perhaps most dire of all was the proposed Mackenzie Valley Pipeline and, equally important, the accompanying highway connecting the Beaufort Sea to gas pipelines in northern Alberta. Opposition to the pipeline united the Dene and Métis and put their local struggles on the television screens of Canadians from coast to coast to coast.

Over at the CYC, meanwhile, Georges was promoted to management. This meant regular trips to Ottawa for meetings with other staff from across Canada. Only one other staff member, Bob Joseph, from British Columbia, was a First Nations person. He and Georges became not just colleagues but friends. In the decades ahead, they would touch each others' lives. Later Bob would become Chief in his community, one of many roles in which he contributed to his people. Georges was president of the board at the Tree of Peace for about seven years. He looks back to that happy time with fondness, remembering all the good people. One of the volunteers he remembers working with was Rick Fader, a cameraman who was able to repair just about any equipment.

My time with the Company of Young Canadians was an amazing growth period for me personally. My management skills continued to evolve. It was also another opportunity to develop programs. I started a CYC project for ex-convicts in Hay River. I hired a vocal individual who'd been in prison. He was keen, so away we went. Over the years it was hard to know how useful this was, but we thought it was worth trying.

In the spring of 1973, a job came up with the Secretary of State, which operated the Opportunity for Youth program, OFY. It was a summer program that created jobs for (mostly university) students. Georges debated what to do. "I remember a serious discussion with Ben Batch, a senior staff member with the CYC. He thought I should take the job and not look back." And that's what Georges did, for a short time becoming a federal civil servant. Although lasting only from April until September, the OFY position was "really fun."

Once it became clear how much money we had for the Northwest Territories, I had to come up with a way to allocate the monies across the north fairly. This was before the division of the NWT and included the eastern Arctic. I asked an old friend, Rene Fumoleau, to give me a hand. Thankfully, the job of advertising the program across the north had been done from Winnipeg, so all we had to do was to sit down and go through all the applications for funding. There were requests for much more money than we had to give, but that was typical.

Georges and Rene established a few ground rules. They'd try to get money to as many communities as possible. A second project wouldn't be funded in any community until all the communities had a project. An exception could be made for a proposal too good to overlook. Since they were dealing mostly with high school students, the funding would cover two months. Georges would contact each applicant. In some cases, they'd moved on to other jobs or activities for the summer, so another applicant would be chosen. In later years Georges would learn that an Indian Brotherhood colleague, John Tseleie, had worked on one of these OFY summer programs.

"We had so many projects all across the North, it was impossible for one individual to get to all of them," says Georges. He hired another individual to visit and monitor projects in the western Arctic while he covered the rest. Georges recalls spotty travel in the Arctic of those days, with no advance arrangements either for transportation or accommodation, eating and sleeping in the houses of people he'd just met and then hitchhiking to the airport to get a seat on a chartered flight. At the airport, he'd ask around to see who had a chartered flight going where. If there was a charter going somewhere he had a project he hadn't yet visited, he would pay a portion of the chartered price and take the plane. This unglamorous life helped him to plug into local communities across the North. He shared in their dinner conversations and spent nights discussing their concerns, aspirations, hopes, and desires. It was no different from what Georges had known growing up in Yellowknife. People dropping by, telling stories, eating, and sharing in community life. When the evening's entertainments were done, out came the bedroll and perhaps a caribou skin (or, if you were lucky, a bed). Georges travelled light, with a sleeping bag and some clothes. He was a Dene and had no problem living this way. "I loved visiting places I'd never gone before, meeting all kinds of wonderful people. I would do it all over again."

In the 1970s, when the youngest Erasmus kids were in school, Georges was an established political leader with a home and family of his own. According to Joanne, he would return home to consult family at the dinner table. "This is what I'm working on and what I'm going to do," he would say. Then he'd wait for the response from Florence and Fred, and from his brothers and sisters. Georges made certain that the family was apprised of everything he was doing, as well as his reasoning for doing it. It was the Dene way.

Big families aren't unusual among Indigenous people. In a big family, the eldest kids typically assume a quasi-parental role in relation to the youngest. The children can split into two distinct generations. A middle child becomes the oldest of the youngest, and the first-born might well be raising a family of their own as additional siblings arrive. Georges is more than twenty years older than his youngest sibling, old enough to be her father. To Joanne, Jeannette, Sean, and Shannon, Georges was indeed somewhat like a parent.

Georges's leadership style didn't develop in a vacuum. His parents were a major influence, as was his experience of Dene decision making and problem solving. To this day he recalls the community meetings decades ago that culminated in feasts, where the people would discuss their hopes, fears, and frustrations.

One of the first stories I remember hearing was about the Dene version of Treaties 8 and 11. That we never extinguished our title, we never gave up control over the land. The land still belonged to the Dene. And so, consistently, you'd hear the story about, you know, why were people making decisions to do something on our land when we had never given up the authority? The first treaty was just before the turn of the century, and the second was in 1922. Particularly with the 1922 Treaty, there were still people alive that had gone to the signing. They were historical witnesses who had passed on the Dene view. All of this laid the historical foundation by which I approached the numbered treaties. I discovered many years later that the numbered treaties were all the same. They had been drafted before the government officials had left Ottawa, for crying out loud.

The community meetings of Georges's childhood began with the Chief, who was the first to speak. The Chief would carefully explain his position on the issues and his reasons for it. Over time, Georges drew from these events a deep understanding of the Dene leaders, coming to know what they supported, what they were concerned about, and what they valued. After the Chiefs, the family leaders would speak, as well as any other prominent people present. Then the meeting would open up and everybody else would speak. Some would weigh in a second time to add to a previous statement or to offer a counter view. What struck Georges above all was the respect shown to others. There was little drama, few angry words, and no shouting. Intense emotion would be evident when people spoke about the land, but not when they were expressing a difference of opinion. Over time a consensus would develop, as people saw a way to advance the collective interests. For this future Dene leader and National Chief, "it really created an understanding of how leadership works."

In his dealings with the federal government, Georges would see a contrasting style of leadership. He recalls an experience in 1973 that convinced him never to work for government again.

An interesting thing happened at the end of the summer; I was told by my regional boss from Winnipeg, Doug Buchett, that our minister, Hugh Faulkner, was interested in paddling the Coppermine River over Labour Day weekend. He was part of Trudeau's cabinet, and the cabinet had a bucket list of rivers all across Canada that they wanted to paddle. Doug and I were to be in a second canoe, separate from Faulkner and his assistant. Thus began an interesting adventure on the Coppermine.

We flew to Coppermine in a government plane, a small two-engine executive plane that we were to use to carry on to Inuvik after the canoe trip. We picked up the two canoes that the Hudson's Bay had transported to Coppermine and strapped them to the sides of a chartered Twin Otter from Yellowknife to take us up the Coppermine River. The night before I had asked friends around town for advice on how to paddle the river, only to find no one was dumb enough to have paddled it. I heard stories of folks from elsewhere that had paddled the river and sometimes not made it out alive. One individual had even made it through Bloody Falls once but not the second time.

I was told by the pilot from Yellowknife that he was not able to bring us ashore, as the river was moving too fast for him to beach the plane. The only option was a mid-river landing where we would have to load our canoes as best we could and then begin paddling from the side of the plane, while the pilots tried to keep the plane as steady as possible. We quickly filled the first canoe for the minister and his aid, then they jumped into their canoe and were off. In less than a minute the minister's canoe went directly into a large foam of water that was spraying about six feet into the air and disappeared. The next thing we saw was an overturned boat and two people in the water with packs and gear all over the river. My boss and I filled our canoe as quickly as possible and began paddling after all the items floating in the river. Fortunately, the current brought a number of things including the canoe and paddles to the opposite shore.

We picked up as much stuff as we could but lost numerous things, including a beautiful moosehide parka my mom had made me. Don't ask me what I was doing with it on the river. I easily could have left it in Coppermine with friends. Another of the things lost was their tent, so we offered one of ours. We continued our journey without further incident and camped by an amazing feature in the river. The river slammed into the riverbank to create an enormous ripple back on itself. We climbed up the two hundred or so feet to the top of the riverbank to look down on the enormous ripple. It seemed to create a level piece of river about three or four feet wide. Then it dropped eight to ten feet, beginning the ripple back out into the river for about twenty feet or more, before the ripple played itself out. We decided to wait until the morning to determine if we would portage this spot or try the small slice of water right along the rock as a possible passageway forward. We had no way of knowing if we would be pulled into the ripple if we tried to paddle or use that little shelf of water.

Come morning, the minister decided that we would try using the little shelf of water to go forward and that we would forgo having breakfast. I could not believe we were not given a chance to eat. Amazingly, we were not pulled into the ripple as we passed as near the rockface as possible, mainly by using our hands against the rockface. We could look directly down this steep drop as the water rushed back out into the river. I remember it was deep, perhaps as much as eight feet. The river was a joy to paddle after that early start of breathtaking excitement, mostly peaceful with a constant rushing current that would be first on one side of the river and then on the other. We would stay close to the current to get some of the benefit from the speed of the river without going into the middle of the current where we might lose control of our canoe.

Around the middle of the morning, I started getting hungry as we had not eaten. I was going to suggest that we stop for a bite when the minister's canoe hit a rock and tipped into the river for a second time. This time we were not able to save anything. The canoe became stuck on some rocks about ten feet from shore. The four of us waded out to the stuck canoe and lifted it up just to have it caught in the river current and disappear out of sight. That morning we had foolishly put all our food into the minister's canoe, which meant we now had no food and only one tent and two sleeping bags.

All we could do was carry on, which we did. Doug and I enjoyed our canoe trip while the minister and his aide walked the shoreline. We tried fishing after rigging up some kind of little hook. We were able to catch a small fish, which I cut into four reasonable portions. It took me some time, but I eventually found enough small pieces of dried wood, mainly willow, to make a fire. I returned to find that the three of them had tried to make a fire with green wood and had used up more than half our matches. I took the matches and said I would oversee them for the rest of the trip. I opened up my travelling equipment to get a little pot, which I filled with water and into which I put our four small pieces of fish. That night and the next day, the little piece of fish and the soup it made was the only food we had. That night the four of us crawled into a two-man tent and made it bulge in all directions. We laid one sleeping bag on the bottom and covered ourselves as much as we could with a mummy-type sleeping bag. It must have been quite a sight from outside. We did not catch any fish the next day.

Our final day on the river was overcast with low-lying fog. Our main concern was Bloody Falls, as we could not see more than a few feet in front of the canoe. We needn't have worried. We could hear the falls from a long way away. Additionally, the river opened up just before the falls and became a calm lake.

Two things happened very close together as we paddled to the riverbank to portage the canoe. The river opened up into this calm lake and then the sky opened into a bright sunny day. Once the minister and his aide joined us, we carried the canoe over the hill to the other side. In the distance we could see several islands with white tents and people. Before we got into the canoe, I told everyone to be very still and not to make any sudden moves. We had not eaten for a number of days at this point, so it was very easy to smell Arctic char being cooked at the campsite we were headed to. We arrived just as the Inuit families were going to share a midday meal together. As we landed, we were invited to join them. That was the best offer I had heard in weeks. Amazingly the minister asserted his role as head of our group and told the folks we needed a ride to Coppermine. Our friendly hosts said, "No problem. Let's eat first. We saw you and waited to eat." I sat at the community feast, but the minister insisted that we needed a ride immediately, so one of the community members took us to his community without eating.

I had never seen such discourtesy in my life. Not accepting a meal on the land when offered is just not done. And it was being done by the so-called Minister of Multiculturalism for Canada. I was disgusted and decided my time working for the government was done. The minister and his crew were given a house to use that was staff housing for teachers, but there was no food in the building. I watched the three of them open bare cupboards, looking for anything that could be eaten. I eventually left them to visit friends that I would stay with during my summer travels, and I had a little to eat. I found I could not consume much after so long without food. To this day I don't know what the rush was. We didn't have to be in Inuvik until that night, and it was only a short flight in the government plane provided to the minister. I let it be known my time with the Secretary of State was over. I left the government with a sour taste in my mouth as my expenses incurred in travelling to Coppermine and Inuvik were never repaid. A very petty thing, I thought. This was the experience of my one and only time as a government employee.

2

THE INDIAN BROTHERHOOD

Dene life in the mid-1970s was dominated by several issues: The Trudeau government's 1969 White Paper, aiming to dismantle the Indian Act and terminate the special legal relationship between Aboriginal Peoples and the Crown, laid out Canada's assimilationist agenda. The Mackenzie Valley pipeline threatened to undermine Dene culture, tradition, and livelihood. Then there were the changes in local governance. Following the Carrothers Commission, the Yellowknife territorial government took on provincial-like responsibilities as Ottawa devolved powers to what would become a fully elected legislative assembly. Like its federal partner, the territorial government — made up mostly of non-Native southerners with limited experience of the NWT — had little interest in Dene aspirations and instead promoted the view that everyone in the NWT was of the same cloth, and that all were northerners.

The Dene had been northerners for thousands of years, but they didn't care much for being lumped in this way. They wanted governance of their own design and a land base to govern. According to Antoine Mountain, the Indian Agents were calling the shots, "along with Ottawa." The Dene wanted the arrangement articulated in Treaties 8 and 11, where they retained rights to their land and to the governance of their own affairs. In other words, they wanted the oral version of the treaties, not the version redacted in Ottawa, which surrendered their title to the land and about which the Dene had only recently learned. The position of Canada was that Dene rights to the land had been extinguished by the treaties. The government had even gone so far as to send officials on a tour of the NWT to inquire about taking up reserves. In 1959, the Ministry of Citizenship and Immigration published the Nelson Commission report, an investigation into "the unfulfilled provisions of Treaties 8 and 11 as they apply to the Indians of the Mackenzie District." The Nelson report urged that "the rapid development of the Northwest Territories makes it imperative that the selecting of reserves should not be postponed further" and proposed "the setting aside of reserves for each band of Indians, the same not to exceed in all one square mile for each family of five." In total, the government proposed a land entitlement of 576,000 acres, or about 2,600 square miles. The Dene had other ideas.

"I was very familiar with the Dene view of what had happened with the two treaties in northern Canada," Georges says. Taught from childhood, he and his siblings heard the stories affirming that the Dene never surrendered their land or the right to make decisions. "They didn't use words like 'sovereignty,' but they very clearly said in their own language that we never gave up the right to make decisions on the land, who was going to do what, where, and when, and all the rest of it. So what we were after was a process to implement that." The federal government however had little interest in negotiating land deals and less in revisiting the treaties. Treaties were agreements made with Indians, specifying their unique legal status and rights. Trudeau didn't care much for the notion of rights granted by special status, as he later demonstrated by rejecting Quebec's demand for recognition as a distinct society. As Trudeau said after the 1995 referendum, "If Quebec is distinct, so is Ontario. You can't be distinct from somebody without somebody being distinct from you." His vision of Canada emphasized individual rights grounded in a common and equal citizenship. The problem was that the Dene didn't consider themselves to be ordinary Canadians, no different than anyone else. They *were* different from most Canadians, for historical, cultural, geographic, linguistic, and legal reasons. By 1969 the sixteen Chiefs of the NWT arrived at the consensus view that something had to be done. What they lacked was a process, not only in relation to land but in relation to sovereignty and internal governance. Somehow, they had to bring Canada to the negotiating table before the Dene way of life was overwhelmed.

The Dene hated the phrase "land claim." In their view, they weren't claiming anything, they were merely asserting their Treaty Rights.

> People are using the word "claim" ... that's something that the government would really like us to believe — that we have a claim. Our problem has been that the government of Canada has a claim on our land. We have no claim. The land belongs to the Dene.... Our problem is that non-Dene have come on our land, and they say that they have rights here. Our problem is that the Government, the non-Dene are claiming our land. They are making decisions on our land. They are developing our land. We are dealing with the problems of non-Dene claiming our land and our rights.[1]

Nonetheless, they saw the potential of a court case to put necessary pressure on government. "And that's where the so-called Paulette case began," says Georges.

> The sixteen Chiefs took Canada to court, saying that we did not extinguish our rights, and that our treaty is the oral treaty. Whatever you have on the written version is not right. This took a number of years. Part of the reason they were doing it was that they wanted to stop development, because development was starting to pick up pace. There was talk about this big pipeline coming. And all these mines were starting up. Diamonds, gold, coal, copper, lead, zinc, silver, and of course oil. So the court case goes through and forces the federal government to think that maybe they should start negotiating.

The Paulette Caveat asserted the Dene understanding of Treaty 8 and Treaty 11 and challenged the government's plans as set out in the White Paper.

The case concerned 450,000 square miles of land and was named after Chief Paulette, whose community of Fort Smith is the most southerly band and therefore the first a southerner would encounter. The Paulette challenge went to the Supreme Court of the Northwest Territories, where Justice William Morrow oversaw six weeks of community hearings to determine the understanding of the Treaty signatories. There, Justice Morrow heard the testimony of Elders who remembered the Treaty-making of 1900, 1920, 1921, and 1922. Needless to say, this testimony contradicted the government's assertion that the Dene had relinquished their land rights. The communities over and again emphasized that their Treaty was the version presented to them viva voce, and not the version drafted in Ottawa by bureaucrats.

To support the Dene position the IBNWT and the Company of Young Canadians collected the testimony of Dene Elders and published articles by academics, resulting in over two thousand pages of materials known as the Dene Rights Series. They also undertook a research initiative, called the Dene Mapping Project, to establish the use and occupancy evidence that would support their assertion of title. In the years ahead, the treaty, governance, territory, rights, and pipeline issues would all benefit from a land use mapping project that would assert Dene rights throughout their Traditional Territory. But who would lead this research? Fully understanding the potential of this work, local leaders came to the conclusion that a local expert was required. According to Peter Puxley, at the time director of Land Claims Research for the Dene,

> We needed experts who understood that research, properly handled, could be a road to rediscovery of Dene history by a younger alienated generation. It could be a means to bridge the gap between generations, raise political consciousness and develop political effectiveness. The experts we sought would give our work the credibility it required without stealing the research experience. It was not an idea we could express openly to Indian Affairs bureaucrats, for whom politicization was not on the agenda. The negotiations for funding were delicate to say the least.

Eventually a young geography student and Dene named Phoebe Nahanni was hired to lead the research. She took time off from her university studies in London, Ontario, to conduct the intensive community-by-community research necessary to determine who did what where and when. Nahanni and her team of twenty interviewed over five hundred hunters and trappers and Elders about their seasonal movements, campsites, hunting ranges, and more. The mapping team determined the traditional land base of the Dene to be 450,000 square miles.

Justice Morrow wrote in his Paulette judgment that the Indigenous people were "prima facie owners of the lands covered by the caveat — that they have what are known as aboriginal rights" and that "there exists a clear constitutional obligation on the part of the Canadian Government to protect the legal rights of the indigenous peoples in the area covered by the caveat." Morrow's ruling, which upheld the validity of the caveat, would be overturned by the Supreme Court of Canada. But the judgment in this case would concern only the technical question of whether a caveat may be filed in respect of unpatented Crown land. In the opinion of the Supreme Court justices, it may not. (As an aside, the court ruled that caveats could, however, be placed on third parties — for example, mining or construction companies — providing the Indian Brotherhood and the Chiefs a powerful tool to freeze unwanted development.)

The Paulette case nonetheless represented the first comprehensive Dene land claim, the first flexing of Dene muscles, and a clear indication that the Dene were serious about challenging Canada. The communities were committed to stopping any development that posed a threat to their livelihoods, especially the pipeline, and the Paulette Caveat was the proof. The feds now understood that a quick and easy settlement of the land issue, on terms favourable to the economic exploitation of local resources, was going to be difficult if not impossible. So they did what the government often does when confronted by a large and intractable challenge with no clear path forward. They established an inquiry.

Georges's generation arrived at just the right moment to have been surrounded by Elders with first-hand memories of the Treaty negotiations, while simultaneously being drawn to the radical youth politics emerging in the 1960s. Antoine Mountain says that "my main memory of that time was that we were full of energy, young, and idealistic. We wanted to zero in on important matters like the treaties and the pipelines. So we put all our energies in there and kind of helped to decolonize our leadership." In the 1970s, many of the Chiefs were in their twenties. They were grounded in their culture and traditions but also fluent in English and able to challenge the colonial system on its own terms. "Nobody in their right mind should be Chief at twenty-two," says Paul Andrew — elected Chief of Tulita at age twenty-two — "but what they needed was somebody who understood the documents." This generation combined the wisdom of the Elders with skills acquired from universities and books. They bridged the past and present. As Patrick Scott explains,

> One of the reasons Georges was such an effective leader must be because he was so tuned to Elders. They believe in what they value, and he's good at translating their worldview into contemporary realities. His deep sense of awareness of where Dene society has come from, what it has been, and what is important to it, enables him to put the puzzle pieces together. It takes incredible awareness and sensitivity to carve out space for traditional ways of doing things and traditional values and traditional perspectives, and you can only do that if you have an understanding of them and also an understanding of what the contemporary world is like. The Tłįchǫ have that mantra, "strong like two people." Well, for me, Georges has that. He knows the modern world, what makes it tick, but he also knows what makes the Dene culture what it is. And it's not just knowing. You've got to go past knowing. You have to care. You have to care that the culture survives to take the path that Georges has taken. That level of care makes a huge difference.

Paul Andrew, former Dene journalist and Chief, met Georges in 1974. Of that time, he recalls that

> one of the things that I think we all did is believe our Elders. They say that the treaty was a friendship treaty, that we agreed to share our land. And one of the things I know now is that they talk about as long as the sun shines and the river flows and the grass grows. As far as the Elders go, from those days particularly, that's like swearing on the Bible. It's a spiritual statement that they've made with that spiritual connection that they have. So that's what they told us. I think Georges was the first one that got us together to do those kinds of things.

Norm Yakelaya remembers his first encounter with Georges:

> There was Paul Andrew and Richard Nerysoo and Herb Norwegian. Georges had long hair and was in the middle. They were speaking for Dene rights and the issue of dealing with the governments of Canada and the Northwest Territories. I said, "Holy crap, where are they coming from?" I never heard people speak like this. That was my first experience of how powerful Georges is as a speaker, fighting for the self-determination and the rights of the people. But I wasn't there in my thinking. My mindset was on the teachings of the residential schools and the school itself, that whole way of life. You guys were from a different planet, and people were talking but they were talking good. That was an eye-opener for me.

Around this time, Georges wrote a discussion essay he titled "What It Means to Be Dene."

> Long before Europeans began looking for the east and India by travelling west across the Atlantic Ocean, there were people living on North America. In the Mackenzie Valley, we called ourselves Dene.

We had our own way of life, our own way of worship, making clothing, acquiring food, our own laws of how to live with each other. Dene laws and laws of how to live with the universe and nature.

Since the coming of the non Dene to the north, the traders, bootleggers, prospectors etc., control has been taken from the Dene.

Where once we were a completely independent people we are now very nearly completely reliant on gov't handouts and all the institutions that we are in contact with are not ours.

The struggle now is to become aware of the exact situation we are living in and continue from there.

We have a choice for the future either to just forget our past, our traditional life, our culture and just join in like everyone else, using our aboriginal rights to get us money & land by which we can get a head start.

Or we can decide to remain Dene, to remember who we are, and to settle for nothing less than a self reliant treaty with the confederation of Canada.

At every level in government we could go for control of the legislative bodies — municipal, territorial but that would not be satisfactory to either parties Dene or non Dene.

The Dene would have to compromise — to the non Dene — particularly with the passing of time & with more & more non Dene moving to the North. We would eventually find ourselves in a situation where the Dene were so out numbered that the Dene would be appeasing the non-Dene and to compensate for the balance of power would be morally obligated to be patronizing.

We must go for our own political institution — only through the possibilities of our own vehicle of self government do we have an opportunity.

The point is to protect and have potential of further

developing our culture we must control our future, through the present. We must be able to plan and direct ourselves as we please.

We can not go for assimilation because ideologically we would be committing suicide.

What it means to be Dene:

- We have our own past history
- We have our own languages
- We have our own political system
- We have our own ways of worship
- We have our own system of sharing economic wealth
- We have our own ideology, our own philosophy, as all other distinct peoples, because we have our own perspectives, our own understanding of the universe and the role of man, we also know what kind of future we want for ourselves.

The essence of being a distinct specific people is to be able to control ourselves collectively, shaping our future as you decide.

This clearly demonstrates that we must go for a separate gov't of our own.

We must work for Dene Nation self government/self determination and control of resource development with the capacity through our own political institute to decide what other kinds of institutions and deals we will make for ourselves in the future.

This will be a difficult fight — we must not be unrealistic in what we strive for. We must only fight for what we are committed to. We must plan seriously and involve our people in a struggle which we can achieve.

If we decide to go for a Dene Nation — we must be seriously committed to working for it because this land

> and the power to make decisions on this land will not be easily given to us.

Georges's work in the 1970s brought him into the orbit of other passionate Dene — among them George Barnabe, Gina Blondin, Paul Andrew, Gerry Cheezie, François Paulette, Stephen Kakfwi, Phoebe Nahanni, Tseleie brothers John and Frank, Jim Antoine, Herb Norwegian, Antoine Mountain, John Bekale, James Wah-Shee, Joachim Bonnetrouge, Freddie Greenland, Norm Yakelaya — and non-Dene southerners like Peter Puxley, Patrick Scott, Steve Iveson, and Rick Fader. The work of Georges and his colleagues at the IBNWT was grassroots political organization, social animation, and the like.

In the fall of 1973, numerous things started to happen. Right after Labour Day weekend, I left my briefly held civil servant job in the federal government. I had no immediate plans, but I somehow had no worries about the future. I thought something would come along, and sure enough it did. Steve Iveson approached me with a possible job at the Indian Brotherhood of the NWT. In my previous role with the CYC, I would occasionally advise President James Wah-Shee on different issues, but I had never worked directly with the Brotherhood as staff.

Steve offered me a job as co-director of community field staff for the Indian Brotherhood, something very similar to the community development work I'd done with the Company of Young Canadians. But now I would be doing community development work in the whole Mackenzie Valley, wherever the Dene have communities. I jumped at the chance to do this work and immediately accepted. There was a catch however: we had no money, yet. The Brotherhood staff were very confident we should be able to get money, as the federal government was providing community development money for First Nation communities across Canada. My first task was to join Steve Iveson to negotiate a contract with Indian Affairs in Ottawa for IBNWT community development staff funding.

It took many trips to Ottawa to convince the department to fund the Brotherhood, mainly because (as we later found out) the commissioner of the NWT, Stuart Hodgson, was totally against the Brotherhood having organizers or field staff doing development work in the communities. The government of the NWT was sending their own community development staff, pushing community local government councils that would be operating at the same time as Chiefs and Band Councils. This was going to create issues in all of our communities, because we were going to be having duelling local governments.

After many trips and meetings, including approaching the commissioner himself, we finally found a way forward. But it took us until Christmas Eve to get an agreement. The suggestion came from the Ottawa director of the Indian Affairs community development program. He said, "What if we changed the name of the program to Band Development instead of Community Development?" I asked if this meant any change in what we could do at the community level. He said, "Not one thing. You'll be able to run the program exactly the same way, regardless of what we call it. The commissioner doesn't want a CD program, so we won't call it community development." Steve and I delayed our return home until we had an agreement, so it ended up we were not able to fly right across the country to connect to our flight north from Calgary. We ended up renting a car to drive through the night across Saskatchewan to Calgary. Somewhere on the Prairies we ran out of gas and had to wake up the family that ran this little business to sell us some gas in the middle of the night. We made it to Calgary in time to catch our flight home, spend Christmas with our families, and start planning the launch of our staff hiring in the new year.

The decision to characterize the Brotherhood's request as band funding rather than community development did nothing to prevent suspicions of subversive political activity and, worse yet, Marxist insurgency. In the mid-1970s, the elite were up to their eyeballs in Cold War paranoia. The RCMP sat in a vehicle across the street from the Indian Brotherhood, where Georges and his colleagues worked under persistent invigilation. Alarmed by the FLQ crisis, the federal government inferred communist influence in everything the Dene did. Convinced that Indian Brotherhood staff were writing the Berger report, the RCMP raided their building in search of evidence.

As often is the case, it took the combined forces of a legal challenge (the Paulette Caveat) and oil industry pressure on the federal government to energize negotiations with the Dene. The proposed Mackenzie Valley pipeline promised a massive windfall, if only the land claims could be resolved. The Trudeau government appointed BC supreme court judge and former BC NDP leader Thomas Berger to lead a Commission of Inquiry into the construction of the pipeline. Berger decided to visit every community in the region, while the Dene recruited and trained fieldworkers to inform and organize the people, gather evidence, discuss Dene aspirations, and otherwise prepare for the inquiry. The work around the pipeline inquiry also attracted scholars like Mel Watkins, who was recruited to advance the anticolonial struggle from an academic perspective.

The work leading up to the Berger Inquiry was comprehensive and included not just the mapping project but also the full articulation of Dene rights, the case for Dene self-determination and jurisdiction, and a detailed analysis of the pipeline's detrimental effects. In its first five years, the IBNWT successfully lobbied for federal funding, created a monthly newspaper (*The Native Press*), pursued the Paulette land title case and the Berger Inquiry, hired thirty fieldworkers, and organized a broad international network of support that included student unions, labour, women's organizations, and churches. During Georges's time at the Brotherhood, "we would end up having community development workers, research workers, and finally pipeline information workers in the Dene communities." At one and the same time, the Indian Brotherhood conducted deep research into the distant Dene past, the present, and the future. John Bekale remembers being one of the Indian Brotherhood fieldworkers.

> The fall time comes, snow's falling. I want to go trapping. My boss Georges Erasmus says, "Yes, go. We need people on the land. Enjoy your time there, and if you want to come back, it's open for you." So that's what I was doing — going back on the land, coming back to work for Georges on the field work. We took some training to do a workshop, George Blondin, Billy [Erasmus], myself, and James Ross. We'd go to all the communities to facilitate workshops. It was interesting, because Georges was way ahead of us with what he could see. We'd go into the communities and I

> would say, what kind of government do you want? There was talk about food on the table, a roof over their heads. This is all they came back with. Georges is talking about running our own education the way we want it, having our own housing program, being able to own all the resources to be able to employ people. He had that dream, and we followed it as we went out.

There were great people who were fieldworkers over the years, but one always stood out because he had a disarming approach to getting acquainted with folks as he went to their homes. Neil Colin decided to use a tape recorder, which was an enormous success. He would tape one person and later have someone else listen and comment, whether on the same subject or another. He would tape everything: assemblies, community meetings, all his visits with people. Eventually he had a storehouse of material that he could play back for people. Later, he had a local radio program in Fort McPherson that was immensely popular. He was a born communicator, and we were lucky to have him working with us.

The Mackenzie Valley Pipeline (Berger) Inquiry was commissioned on March 21, 1974, to study the proposed construction of a pipeline down the Mackenzie Valley. Just under one year later, on March 3, 1975, the first hearing was held at the Explorer Hotel in Yellowknife, where Berger had taken up residence. The position of the Dene leadership and the grassroots was made clear to Justice Berger in many dozens of testimonies held in thirty-five communities: the pipeline, they insisted, should only happen with their consent, following a negotiated settlement of the land issue. On March 21, 1974, the Member of Parliament representing the NWT, a Métis from Fort McPherson named Wally Firth, rose in the House and said,

> I should like to mention something about the Indian Brotherhood in the Northwest Territories. After a meeting between the Minister of Indian Affairs and Northern Development and the president of the Indian Brotherhood

> in Yellowknife on January 18, there were some news reports to the effect that the Indian Brotherhood and the government of Canada were now ready, willing, and able to sit down and negotiate the land claims of the treaty Indians of the Northwest Territories. These reports were not exactly true. The fact is that for some time the Northwest Territories Indian Brotherhood has been trying to prepare for such negotiations. However, the Brotherhood does not have the resources to do so. The government has publicly announced support for such meetings to take place, but I say the government has not made sufficient funds available to the Brotherhood to enable them to prepare to negotiate their claims. At the present rate of progress of the negotiations between the Indian Brotherhood and the Government of Canada, I would guess that the native people of the Northwest Territories will not be ready to sit down at the negotiating table for another three to five years.[2]

Thomas Berger was the BC lawyer who in 1973 had represented Nisga'a Chief Frank Calder in the Calder et al. v. Attorney General of British Columbia land title case. Like the Paulette Caveat, the Calder case was unsuccessful in establishing the specific claims of the plaintiffs. But also like Paulette, Calder affirmed Aboriginal Title as a legal right based on occupation of traditional territories. The federal government could no longer take the position that Aboriginal Title was a thing of the past, ceded and surrendered in treaties. Combined with the intense pressure being applied by Native groups, these 1973 legal challenges compelled the federal government to develop a comprehensive land claims policy, initiate the negotiations that Native groups had been wanting for years, and create an inquiry to hear Aboriginal views on the pipeline. As Georges recalls, the Indian Brotherhood worked hard to inform and get the support of southerners.

We ended up having to lobby Canada in a big way. They came up with a comprehensive claims policy, but it was still based on extinguishment and only considered land. There was nothing about self-government in it. So we organized all across the country with supportive organizations, like labour and student unions, and so on. And it wasn't really tied together very well until we convinced the churches to fund what was called Project North. In the fall of 1975, the Anglican Church of Canada and the Roman Catholic Church joined by the United Church of Canada formed the Interchurch project on northern development called Project North. Later they were joined by the Presbyterian Church in Canada, the Lutheran Church of America (Canada Section), the Mennonite Central Committee (Canada), and the Evangelical Lutheran Church in Canada.

For well over ten years Project North had a staff of two — Hugh McCullum and his wife, Karmel — and a headquarters in Toronto. This tiny organization stitched together a loose network of individuals and agencies across the country. Any time Georges and his Indian Brotherhood colleagues wanted to have a campaign — or as Georges calls them, "huge, big blitzes" — Project North would coordinate simultaneous events in several places across the country. The networking provided by Hugh and Karmel McCullum was also invaluable for speaking tours, which would bring Georges to many church basements and universities throughout the 1970s and 1980s.

The pressures that brought government to the negotiating table also prompted the creation of the Berger Inquiry. The inquiry could have easily been a six month affair, with Berger flying to Yellowknife to hear from subject matter experts before drafting his recommendations. In a phone call, he and Chrétien discussed exactly this possibility. The inquiry's terms of reference directed Berger to consider the social, environmental, and economic impact regionally of the construction, operation, and subsequent abandonment of the proposed pipeline in the Yukon and Northwest Territories. He was also directed to stop short of deciding on the question of whether or not the pipeline should be built, a decision that would be made in Ottawa. Unsure how to undertake his mandate, Berger (who had never been to the North) and his wife, Beverly, took a ten-thousand-mile trip across the

Northwest Territories and held preliminary consultations. The testimony he heard made it clear to him that his inquiry would have to deviate from established norms.

Around this time, Justice Berger was appointed to investigate the possible building of the Mackenzie Valley pipeline. Before he began his official hearings he came north and conducted a couple of meetings where he let it be known he was open as to how he should conduct his inquiry. I was asked to speak to Berger for the Indian Brotherhood. Our message to Justice Berger that I delivered included several points: first, he had to have more than one kind of hearing; he should allow for community hearings where northerners could voice their views on the future of the north, in addition to those hearings where engineering information would be presented. We also requested monies for field staff that would provide information on the proposed pipeline to communities. He agreed to both ideas.

To begin with, royal commissions did not as a rule provide funding to participants. Berger however understood that if Native organizations were going to participate meaningfully, funding would have to be provided both to the Dene and Inuvialuit groups along the pipeline route, and they would have to be given time to prepare. This point was underscored by the fact that the energy companies had already provided the inquiry with fifty million dollars' worth of research on the project. How could there be any balance or parity to the testimony if one side of the question had resources of this scale while the other did not? Berger pitched the idea of funding the Native organizations to the minister of Indian Affairs, Jean Chrétien. The minister agreed.

Then there was the extensive travel, also unusual for an inquiry of this era. Between March 1975 and November 1976, Justice Berger heard from over one thousand people in community centres and gymnasiums and outdoor fields. Meeting in the North in summer meant that a hearing could go well into the evening and be followed by a baseball game, under the midnight sun, as was the case at Fort McPherson. The hearings were open to the general public and were held in thirty-five communities along the proposed pipeline route, as well as in ten cities in the south. At each stop across the Mackenzie Valley and Western Arctic, Justice Berger told the people that he would stay until everyone who wanted to speak had done so. In some communities he stayed for two days, in others as many as five. Everyone who spoke was sent a copy of the report — *Northern Frontier, Northern Homeland* — written in accessible prose. Berger cast a wide as possible net and became a television sensation. When the first volume of the report came out, on June 9, 1977, it was a bestseller at five dollars a copy. ("I stayed on an extra year and wrote a second volume about the conditions that should be observed if the pipeline were eventually to be built," Berger told journalist Mark Rendell in 2015, "but nobody remembers that.")

> In my report, and everybody forgets about this, I said: "Look, when you have set aside these wilderness areas, guaranteed hunting, fishing and trapping rights and settled land claims, then you can build a pipeline from the Delta to Alberta along the Mackenzie Valley," and I set out the route and the environmental safeguards that had to be taken, the measures to provide for jobs for the local people. As time passed and all of these things were accomplished, it isn't surprising that people who had once opposed it said "Alright, I think we're ready, let's do it."
>
> And of course it was approved; the Imperial Oil gas pipeline was approved by the cabinet, but it still hasn't been built. The gas is still in the ground; it hasn't gone anywhere.[3]

Paul Andrew says that "when the Berger inquiry came around, the two things that I heard were 'this is our land' and 'what's going to happen to our children and our grandchildren?'" For the Dene, Berger wasn't just about a gas pipeline. The people understood that a pipeline meant roads, and that roads would be a conduit for settlement, which would unleash rapid economic and social and political change. Without a negotiated recognition of their land and governance rights, the Dene and their way of life would be overwhelmed.

As far as strategy was concerned, Georges and his Indian Brotherhood colleagues debated three broad approaches to the Berger Inquiry: unconditional opposition to the pipeline, demand for a postponement of the pipeline until the land issue was settled, or negotiation of government and industry concessions in exchange for Dene co-operation. At this point, it was clear to the Dene and Métis that a fair settlement of the land claim required their unity. "The Elders insisted that no legislation or policy was going to divide us," explains Paul Andrew. At the inaugural July 1974 Fort Good Hope joint assembly of the Indian Brotherhood and the Métis Association of the NWT, attendees agreed to better coordinate their activities and passed a motion agreeing that Status Dene, non-Status Dene, and Métis would work together. This motion was the outcome of an emotional and lengthy assembly discussion concerning negotiations with Canada. The consensus of the Elders was that all the descendants of the Dene should be included in one agreement and that the Dene should speak with one voice.

I spent my career trying to bring us together and have just one organization. That's what our Elders had wanted, and I totally agreed. I could see the Dene all together, regardless of whether they called themselves Dene or Métis. We'd hoped this would give us the last push we needed to create one organization. Even though we ended up with a very large majority of our people to sign, some didn't. We were never able to create the one organization that the Dene Chiefs had wanted back in 1969–70, when they formed the Indian Brotherhood. What we were able to do was to open up the membership, which still was for individual members, to any descendant of the Dene that believed they were part of the Dene Nation.

Early in 1974, my wife Cindy told me she was interested in advancing her education. As she explored what she might do and where she might go, it seemed to me that our interests were taking us in different directions. Cindy eventually went south to make arrangements to attend university. I was headed to Fort Good Hope in advance of the first Joint Assembly, where I assisted the community in preparing to host the hundreds of delegates from all the Western Arctic communities. We set up a tent village, an outside temporary arbour for the meeting site, and an outside kitchen for communal meals. Gail Cyr, new to the north at the time, accompanied me. We worked long hours and collapsed in our beds to sleep, just to do it all over again. It was a very worthwhile event. The Joint Assembly was the first opportunity for all the descendants of the Dene — the Métis, Status Indians, and non-Status Dene — to speak about the kind of future they wanted. What we heard was that everyone felt they were related and basically one people. They wanted to approach the future together. As an observer of this amazing historical event, I felt honoured to be a small part of Dene history. I heard our people say they were not going to be divided by false divisions created by federal legislation like the Indian Act, legislation that gave different status to different Dene descendants. We all left Fort Good Hope on a high.

A few days after I returned to Yellowknife, Cindy returned from her trip south. I suggested we needed to have a serious talk about our future together. She agreed. I acknowledged that we had drifted apart over the past year, but if she was prepared to make a serious effort, I was prepared to see if we could make a go of it together. I suggested that we take a trip south together as a family and over the trip have a serious discussion about our future together. We drove south and spent some time together, including attending a Sundance in Saskatchewan that I participated in. I prayed during the three-day Sundance that whatever the future was for us that it be the best for everyone, including my two boys. In the end, it was clear that our time together as a married couple was over. In fact, it was clear from our first conversation after my Fort Good Hope trip. But I wanted to be sure, so we took the trip south. In early August, Cindy left for university with our two boys, aged five and two. We agreed I would send money to assist with raising the boys, and we went our separate ways.

When Cindy and I split up in the summer of 1974, the biggest regret I had of us going our separate ways was how this was impacting the two boys. I had suggested to Cindy we might do something a little different than the boys being the legal responsibility of one of the parents, usually the mother, but after she considered the idea for a while, she decided to go the classical route. I would get to see them from time to time as they grew up, mostly without me. Cindy never got in the way of my spending time with the boys; it mainly was my busy life with crazy travel requirements. When I got together with the boys, a lot of the time it would be spending time playing in the playgrounds in different parts of Yellowknife. It was never enough time for either the boys or I. Between Cindy and I living in different parts of Canada either going to school or work and my crazy travel commitments for my work, something had to give, and it ended up being time with my two boys. Thankfully, we have been able to spend more time together as adults.

Sandra Knight, a recent graduate in social work from Newfoundland, had started a new job with the government of the NWT in the local office. We had become friends over the summer, after trying to sell her on supporting the NDP in the spring federal election. I was an avid supporter of Wally Firth, a Métis from the Mackenzie Delta who was our MP for several terms. Sandra never accepted our NDP material, but she did go to the local community hall to hear our party leader, David Lewis, speak. After the meeting, I continued driving around, putting up posters supporting Wally and the NDP. As I approached the causeway leaving Latham Island, I noticed Sandra and another woman walking across. I stopped and offered them a ride uptown. Sandra said no, thank you, but her friend jumped in the front seat and said "wonderful!" So Sandra got in the back. The three of us ended up chatting about politics and the North when I accepted tea at someone's place. This began my casual acquaintance with Sandra. She never showed any interest in me at all, besides a friendly banter once in a while.

On the September 1974 Labour Day weekend, I visited her apartment. After we had been visiting for a while, I explained that an important thing had happened over the summer — my marriage had ended. Sandra came running across the room to jump into my arms. She said that was the best news she had heard in a long time, or something to that effect. I was totally surprised, as she had not expressed the slightest romantic interest in me. I knew right off that if I committed this was not going to be a casual relationship. I told Sandra I needed to think about things before we committed to anything. She said okay, that sounds fair. I went for a walk. I had not thought that I was going to get into a serious relationship so soon after Cindy and I separated. In fact, the funny thing is I had come to visit Sandra because I thought she had no interest in me.

I now knew she had a very serious interest in me and was prepared to get into a long-term relationship.

Part of my reason for taking time to sort out my plans was because I knew someone else also loved me dearly, which I thought I would possibly explore eventually once some time passed. I decided to enter a relationship with Sandra, which I knew meant saying goodbye to my other interest. I was honest with Sandra. I explained that I also loved someone else, and she should know this. She said are you suggesting a three-way relationship, and I said no, definitely not. I just wanted her to know that part of my heart was already taken. She said she understood, and she could live with that. Over the years Sandra would tease me. She would say, well, you could check and see what your other love would think or do in this situation. She turned the situation into one we both could laugh about from time to time. For a while we lived in separate homes, but eventually we moved in together. Thus began a forty-three-year relationship that ended with Sandra's passing in April 2017, after five years of living with cancer, sometimes in remission.

(left to right) Shannon, Margaret, Sean, and Sandra at Fred Erasmus's cabin, 1976.

Over the fall and winter of 1974–75, the Indian Brotherhood and Métis Association considered how to proceed after the summer Fort Good Hope meeting, characterized by Georges as "epic." Georges and his colleagues decided to put their efforts into a decolonization project focused on the Aboriginal Peoples of the Mackenzie Valley.

We concluded that part of our decolonization work should include finding a term to call ourselves from our own history, rather than terms like "Indian" given to our people by outsiders. Someone suggested using Dene as an umbrella term, and it was quickly adopted by people in both organizations. That was fine, but what recognition did we want from Canada and the Crown? Obviously, we wanted to be recognized as a Nation of People. It also quickly followed that we wanted recognition of our right to continue being self-governing or self-determining.

The question then was do we want to do this within Canada, or were we going to push for independence, like Quebec? We came to the conclusion that it was not in our interest to push for independence. We considered what it would mean to self-govern with such a small population and large land mass. The costs would be enormous and, in reality, we did not believe we could convince enough of the Aboriginal People in the North to seriously consider it. Most Indigenous Peoples are very practical. After a little time discussing it, we abandoned any idea of independence.

We decided to call our statement "The Dene Declaration." Once we had figured out what we were going to bring to the second Joint Assembly, it was simply a matter of composing the text. Someone was asked to try his hand, and I agreed to write a longer version, which, for some reason, I did in longhand. I went home and once there, undisturbed, the ideas just poured out of me. In the fall of 1975, after the Fort Simpson Joint Assembly passed the Dene Declaration, a reporter picked up a copy of the longer version and it was published as a Dene Manifesto.

The Dene Declaration

Passed at the Second Joint General Assembly of the Indian Brotherhood of the NWT and the Metis Association of the NWT, at Fort Simpson

JULY 19, 1975

Statement of Rights. We the Dene of the Northwest Territories insist on the right to be regarded by ourselves and the world as a nation. Our struggle is for the recognition of the Dene Nation by the Government and peoples of Canada and the peoples and governments of the world.

As once Europe was the exclusive homeland of the European peoples, Africa the exclusive homeland of the African peoples, the New World, North and South America, was the exclusive homeland of Aboriginal peoples of the New World, the Amerindian and the Inuit.

The New World like other parts of the world has suffered the experience of colonialism and imperialism. Other peoples have occupied the land — often with force — and foreign governments have imposed themselves on our people. Ancient civilizations and ways of life have been destroyed.

Colonialism and imperialism are now dead or dying. Recent years have witnessed the birth of new nations or rebirth of old nations out of the aches of colonialism.

As Europe is the place where you will find European countries with European governments for European peoples, now also you will find in Africa and Asia the existence of African and Asian countries with African and Asian governments for the African and Asian peoples.

The African and Asian peoples — the peoples of the Third World — have fought for and won the right to self-determination, the right to recognition as distinct peoples and the recognition of themselves as nations.

But in the New World the Native peoples have not fared so well. Even in countries in South America where the Native peoples are the vast majority of the population there is not one country which has an Amerindian government for the Amerindian peoples.

Nowhere in the New World have the Native peoples won the right to self-determination and the right to recognition by the world as a distinct people and as Nations.

While the Native people of Canada are a minority in their homeland, the Native people of the Northwest Territories, the Dene and the Inuit, are a majority of the population of the Northwest Territories.

The Dene find themselves as part of a country. That country is Canada. But the Government of Canada is not the Government of the Dene. The Government of the Northwest Territories is not the Government of the Dene. These governments were not the choice of the Dene, they were imposed upon the Dene.

What we the Dene are struggling for is the recognition of the Dene nation by the governments and peoples of the world.

And while there are realities we are forced to submit to, such as the existence of a country called Canada, we insist on the right to self-determination as a distinct people and the recognition of the Dene Nation.

We the Dene are part of the Fourth World. And as the peoples and Nations of the world have come to recognize the existence and rights of those peoples, who make up the Third World the day must come when the nations of the Fourth World will come to be recognized and respected. The challenge to the Dene and the world is to find the way for the recognition of the Dene Nation.

Our plea to the world is to help us in our struggle to find a place in the world community where we can exercise our right to self-determination as a distinct people and as a nation.

What we seek then is independence and self-determination within the country of Canada. This is what we mean when we call for a just land settlement for the Dene nation.

As we'll see in a later chapter, the unity forged to fight for Dene land would eventually crumble over the resulting Dene/Métis final agreement. By 1974 there was nonetheless a broad Dene consensus on the way forward, specifically by opposing the pipeline. In community after community, witnesses spoke of the threat to their culture and traditions and their fear of the world that a pipeline would bring. Patrick Scott records numerous inquiry statements in his book *Stories Told: Stories and Images of the Berger Inquiry*, among them a succinct and memorable summary from Yellowknife trapper Fred Martin. "Having the pipe go through our land," Martin told the inquiry, "is like driving a steel pipe through our hearts."

Berger exposed the divisions between Native and non-Native people living in the NWT, with one side speaking against the pipeline and the other for it. For many non-Natives, development was natural and inevitable, synonymous with jobs and progress and prosperity. What was the North if not a vast resource? Depending upon which side of the fence you were on, the pipeline was either a harmless straw crossing a football field or a razor blade passing through the *Mona Lisa*. The divide manifested itself in many ways. In Fort Simpson, Berger held separate hearings in separate locations for the white and Dene communities. "It was very polarized, politically and economically," recalls Patrick Scott.[4] As Georges explained in a 1978 interview, even the attitude toward the North was polarized. "The one from the South has been to look up and to say there's a frontier. And that's where a man can go and he can pioneer things, he can be courageous, exploring, making new areas for man to conquest. And people who've always been living here don't see it as a wilderness. It's our home. And everything around us, we've always used the way it exists now."[5]

The perceived intransigence of Native people over the pipeline led to rumours in the non-Native community that the Dene were being manipulated. The story went around that they were being told what to say by outsiders. The rumours eventually reached leaders like Paul Andrew. "If we were angry before, we got even more angry. Phillip Blake and Jim Antoine — really nice, good, decent human beings — started talking about blowing up the pipeline." A December 20, 1975, *Toronto Star* article by Hugh McCullum, titled "However, If We Are Forced to Blow Up the Pipeline ...", records these words of Dene social worker Phillip Blake, delivered to Justice Berger at Fort McPherson:

> Mr. Berger, we have never tried to conquer new frontiers or outdo our parents or make sure that every year we are richer than before. We have been satisfied to see our

> wealth as ourselves and the land we live with. It is our greatest wish to pass this land on to our grandchildren in the same conditions we got it from our fathers. But, Judge Berger, if your nation chooses to continue to try and destroy our nations, then I hope you will understand why we are willing to fight so that our nation can survive. It is our world. We do not wish to push our world on to you, but we are willing to defend it for ourselves, our children and our grandchildren. If your nation becomes so violent that it would tear up our land, destroy our society and occupy our homeland, by trying to impose this pipeline against our will, then of course, we will have no choice but to react with violence.

The idea that the Dene were unable to think and to speak for themselves was an injury wrapped in an insult. Needless to say, the media picked up on the anger and made headlines of it. As far away as Toronto, an August 8, 1975, headline declared, "Indians Warn They'd Blow up N.W.T. Pipeline." Not only were the Dene capable of thinking and speaking for themselves, they were doing it with force and clarity.

Strong though the Dene were, by 1975 the Indian Brotherhood of NWT had a problem. That problem was their president, James Wah-Shee. Some of the Chiefs, among them Paul Andrew, had begun to doubt his ability to successfully lead the Dene in the fight for their land and way of life. According to the Aklavik Chief, Freddie Greenland, "James was saying that the territorial government was the government of the Dene. We didn't agree with that." James Wah-Shee was bright and articulate, but he was unpredictable. Mainstream media characterized him as a moderate, in contrast to "radicals" like Georges. One example of Wah-Shee's unpredictability concerned Dene self-determination. From a practical and strategic standpoint, the Dene could assert themselves in one of two ways: they could leverage their majority population to take as many seats as possible in the NWT territorial council, or they could reject the colonial system altogether. After much discussion, the IBNWT chose the latter.

The discussion at one of these strategy sessions held at Drum Lake was about how do we prove that the government of the Northwest Territories is not our government? After all kinds of discussions among the Chiefs and Elders, somebody came up with the idea to tell our people not to run for office. It's not our government, so let's not send our people there. There was a territory election coming up in the fall, so the decision was "Okay, that's what we'll do. We're going to tell our people not to run." We came out of that meeting and we told everybody no one's going to run, because it's not our government. All of a sudden we find out that James Wah-Shee, our president, who is supposed to be implementing this policy, has put his name in to represent the Tłįchǫ region in the Territorial Council. What the hell! We'd just told everyone if you're a Dene don't run! All of a sudden we had a crisis.

Dene assembly opening prayers, Yellowknife drummers, late 1970s.

I'd become fairly close with James over the years, and I couldn't believe what I was hearing. I went to his home to talk to him directly. "Are the rumours true?" He didn't answer. A civil servant advising him spoke on James's behalf. "Yes," he said. "Papers were filed, and why shouldn't they be? It's an easy win for a member of the Tłįchǫ like James." I asked once again, and this time James conceded that he'd filed his papers. I asked him about the decision we'd made not to field candidates. He had nothing to say.

The inexplicable behaviour of their president forced the hand of the IBNWT board. James Wah-Shee was stripped of his powers and a December assembly was called in Fort Rae (Behchokǫ̀). "That assembly tore the Dene apart," Georges says, "as James still had a lot of support." At one point in the assembly James tendered his resignation. The next day he tried to retract his resignation, but the chair would not allow him to do this and insisted the assembly vote. The assembly debated and voted, with near 60 percent of the assembly accepting the resignation. "Had he not resigned," Georges says, "the vote would have been tougher. We would have needed two-thirds to remove him, but to accept the resignation, we only needed 50 percent plus one." James Wah-Shee was replaced by Vice-President Richard Nerysoo until an election for president could be held at the July 1976 Indian Brotherhood Assembly.

The question now was "Who could beat James?" Because everyone expected him to seek the presidency again. I'd never wanted to run for office and had turned down being the Indian Brotherhood vice-president back in late 1971, when Vice-President Ed Bird had died in office after being shot by the police at his home during a domestic incident. After going through possible candidates who might run against James, someone suggested that I consider running. It didn't look like anyone else was able to beat him, so I agreed.

To this day Georges wonders how it could have worked, having the president of the Indian Brotherhood also a member of the legislative assembly, when the official policy was not to run candidates in GNWT elections. In June 1976, Georges replaced Nerysoo (who at age twenty-two was

Georges Erasmus and George Barnabe, Indian Brotherhood election campaign, June 1976.

considered too young for the role) as president and George Barnabe of Fort Good Hope became his vice-president. "I found it hard to be vice-president," Barnabe says. "I wasn't used to office work and that type of stuff, I was more used to being in the community and discussing the broad picture, not so much specific things." Georges however was grateful to have Barnabe as his partner. "Barnabe had strong support from his community and region when he ran for the territorial council. We needed to show that I was part of a team, and, as much as I liked Richard Nerysoo, I explained to him that we needed someone older and with more experience. Richard very graciously agreed to step back and let George run as my running mate." Nerysoo would go on to a long political career including premier of the NWT.

In the spring of 1976, Georges and George announced their joint candidacy and began their campaign. Georges was very lucky to somehow get the support of the Elders from the Tłı̨chǫ community of Behchokǫ̀. Elder Nick Black put together a group of Elders that Georges says "basically won

Tłı̨chǫ drummers at Dene assembly.

the election for me." The campaign chartered a plane to take the Elders, George Barnabe, and Georges to communities such as Délı̨nę (known as Fort Franklin until June 1993), a Sahtu territory on the western shore of Great Bear Lake. Georges would explain to the assembly why they were there, and the Elders would then take over, explaining in their language who Georges and his family were, and that they had been in Behchokǫ̀ before moving to Yellowknife. The Elders affirmed that they'd observed Georges's work and supported him for the leadership of the Indian Brotherhood. Georges and George worked the phones and had a good idea how much support they had heading into the Fort Norman (Tulita) election. Then, not long before the Fort Norman-Tulita assembly, James Wah-Shee announced that he would not be seeking the presidency after all. A couple of his supporters ran against Georges, who received a strong mandate with over 70 percent of the vote.

Georges became president of the Indian Brotherhood during the pipeline inquiry, in July of 1976. A stocky twenty-seven-year-old, Georges looked like a rock star. (In fact, he was once mistaken for a member of the band Kiss, whose waiting limousine driver opened the door when Georges emerged

Georges just elected as Indian Brotherhood leader, July 1976.

from the hotel where he and the band were staying.) Of seeing Georges for the first time, people recall above all else his long hair — "a Jimi Hendrix kind of hairstyle," as Herb Norwegian described it — and his fringed leather jacket. "I felt kind of intimidated by him," says Patrick Scott, "but intrigued as well." Georges tooled around Yellowknife in a blue Bronco, frequenting Dene meetings where issues and strategy were discussed. By this time Georges was articulating a comprehensive Dene agenda that included political, economic, and territorial self-determination. The Berger Inquiry gave Georges the opportunity to deliver his first public presentation as Indian Brotherhood president. Also, 1974–76 were critical years. As Patrick Scott puts it, "The Mackenzie Valley Pipeline inquiry was a profound opportunity for the Dene to stake their place and start their decolonization. Georges, at the end of the Dene Assembly in Behchokǫ̀, talked about the Berger process being a decolonizing process. When the Berger Inquiry began, people were Indians. When it ended, they were Dene."

One of the first items on Georges's agenda as president was to come up with a plan for how to deal with Canada. "We had a strategy session that summer to discuss our next move. We concluded that we should hold an assembly to build on the Dene Declaration with a more detailed negotiating position that we would bring to Ottawa to present to Canada." The Dene had done their homework. They'd researched the treaties and mapped out their land and prepared for Berger. They'd had many, many "long, incredible, powerful and engaging sessions," as Herb Norwegian describes them, about decolonization, identity, culture, political aspirations, and strategy. They'd built institutions and political networks. They were no longer Indians; they were now the Dene. On October 10, 1976, about two hundred delegates to the Fort Simpson assembly voted in favour of a proposal for how to go about negotiations with Canada. The Dene proposal rejected extinguishment and sought negotiations for land title and political independence. The vote was unanimous and was followed by cheering and applause.

Georges and his colleagues came to Ottawa with a document titled "A Proposal Presented to the Government and People of Canada on 25 October 1976." Ironically this assertion of political power came at a time when Indian Brotherhood funding was in short supply.

> Our funding for the assembly in Fort Simpson had been cut off, for one reason or another. So that event was actually covered by Oxfam and by the Anglican and Roman Catholic churches. We didn't have enough money to do this ourselves. When we organized this trip to Ottawa, in 1976, we took a lot of the Chiefs. But we couldn't afford to stay in a regular hotel. We had Gina Blondin and Debbie Delancey operating out of an office for us in Ottawa, and they found us a place to stay, a cheap way to do it.

The churches also provided emergency funds to get the Dene leaders to Ottawa, where they would present the negotiations framework approved at Fort Simpson to the minister of Indian Affairs. As it happened, Georges and his Indian Brotherhood colleagues lodged in a former jail turned into a youth hostel, located in the ByWard Market area of the city. "The walls

Georges Erasmus, president of the Dene Nation, 1976–83.

were about three foot thick," recalls John Tseleie. "Just straight rock. No fancy hotel — straight to jail. We slept on death row, I think." Word of this arrangement got around to Noel Starblanket, President of the National Indian Brotherhood, who said, "You can't have your people in this old jail" and offered to fund better accommodations. The presentation went well, and talks were positive.

As with every other Dene effort, the Dene Declaration was seen by many white people as the work of left-wing consultants. Even more dismissive, Judd Buchanan (the minister of Indian Affairs at the time of the declaration) called it gobbledygook and said that a high school student could have written it. Now, a year later, the prime minister had shuffled the cabinet and Warren Allmand was the minister. Unlike Buchanan, he was sympathetic to Dene and Métis aspirations. Allmand accepted the Dene research and negotiating position, which was based on nationhood and self-determination within Canada. "Without blinking an eye," Georges says, "he told us he would review our documents with interest." Direct negotiations between Georges and Minister Allmand ensued. "We were trying to lay the foundation for more detailed negotiations in the future."

Nineteen seventy-seven started out with several things going our way. We had direct negotiations with Minister Warren Allmand on a possible political agreement with Dene on Land and Governance, without extinguishment. Then Berger delivered his report on April 15, 1977, recommending a ten-year delay in the construction of the Mackenzie Valley pipeline to allow for the negotiation of new agreements between the Dene and the Crown on land, Aboriginal rights, and self-determination. Again, these negotiations would be based on recognition, not extinguishment. Berger also recommended strengthening the renewable economy on which Indigenous people relied. This included hunting, fishing, and gathering. It was a clear victory for the Dene.

In June 1977 over one thousand people attended an assembly at Fort Fitzgerald, where the Dene passed a resolution on a political model for the Western Arctic called the Metro Model. Allmand took the position that the Metro Model fit into the traditions of Canada. Unfortunately, Warren Allmand's time at Indian Affairs would be brief. According to Georges, "The NWT commissioner Stuart Hodgson and his territorial

Georges chairing a Dene meeting, late 1970s.

executive were terrified by the negotiations that we were very publicly having with Minister Allmand. I also naively fed into that fear. I didn't realize how strongly Hodgson feared what was going on. These fears were fed to Ottawa and no doubt to the prime minister. Before long Warren Allmand was moved to another portfolio."

Accepting the Metro Model would be one of the last things Allmand did for the Dene. After exactly one year, he was replaced by the less sympathetic Hugh Faulkner, Georges's old Coppermine River paddling companion. The new minister of Indian Affairs would ask for a meeting in Yellowknife not long after his appointment. In the summer of 1977, Faulkner told the Dene he was cutting off their funds, putting a stop to the negotiations Georges had been having with Warren Allmand. This, Faulkner said, would be the last meeting he would have with the Indian Brotherhood. "True to his word," Georges says, "I was never to have another meeting with him." (Dene talks with the federal government would be paused for another four years, until 1981.) The minister's next stop was Inuvik, where he announced that negotiations would take place with the Inuvialuit. In sharp contrast to the

(left to right) François Paulette, Georges Erasmus, and George Barnabe, summer assembly, mid-1970s.

Dene model, these negotiations would be based on extinguishment and would have no provisions for self-government. Instead, they would produce a Regional Corporation.

Once our funding was terminated from the federal government, we started looking elsewhere for funding. With the help of Hugh and Karmel McCullum from Project North we applied for assistance from the Special Fund to Combat Racism operated by the World Council of Churches from Geneva. In August of 1977, we were approved for funding from the Special Fund to Combat Racism. In addition, the World Council of Churches published an education pamphlet called *No Last Frontier: Dene Nation, the Struggle of Canada's Internal Colony for Self Determination*. It told the story of the Dene struggle against major pipeline projects and our efforts to achieve self-determination in Canada.

The June 1977 Fitzgerald assembly was attended by a member of AIM, the American Indian Movement, who informed Georges and the others that the United Nations Non-Governmental Organizations, or UNNGOs, were holding a conference in September to discuss the possible recognition of international Indigenous rights. He recommended that Georges and his colleagues attend. This was the beginning of what became the UNDRIP, the United Nations Declaration on the Rights of Indigenous Peoples. The UNNGO conference in Geneva turned out to be a wonderful opportunity for Georges and François Paulette to tell the world what Canada was doing — cutting off existing negotiations with Indigenous people and opening new rounds based on extinguishment with no opportunity to negotiate self-government and self-determination.

We didn't get much opportunity in Geneva to give our story, but immediately after the conference we had an opportunity to travel to different countries in Europe with support organizations that were going to create public speaking venues in major cities across Europe. François and I decided to tour Germany for three weeks and were joined by AIM members Russell Means and Clyde Bellecourt. We spoke in front of thousands of people interested in what was happening to Indigenous populations in the Americas and received a lot of

Voting at the assembly in Fort Franklin/Délı̨nę, March 1978.

Assembly in Fort Franklin/Délı̨nę, March 1978.

Drum Lake Dene Nation strategy session, 1978.

Dene Nation summer assembly, 1978.

publicity. We also created long-term contacts to assist us in the future, just as we had support organizations in Canada. Over time these organizations were very useful for support activity and arranging events for us.

Over the years a network of churches, labour unions, students, and NGOs would produce letter-writing campaigns, petitions, demonstrations, and other forms of direct action. Whenever Georges asked for it, the help would pour in. "If we hadn't had that kind of support, we wouldn't have been able to put the kind of pressure on Canada that we did." The Anglican, Roman Catholic, and Pentecostal Churches provided funding and coordination support, while the unions and students put direct pressure on governments. The work of Hugh and Karmel McCullum, at Project North, educated Canadians. And then there was the solidarity of Canadians in general. Time and again, the federal government took notice of the winds and, having exhausted all the alternatives, did the right thing. The good news is you can make things happen if you make a big stink. The bad news is you have to.

Georges chairing summer assembly with mother, Florence, sitting behind him as translator, 1978.

According to Herb Norwegian, "One of the changes that we wanted was to get out of calling ourselves the Indian Brotherhood, because we are a nation, and we always have been a nation. We needed to change the name to reflect that." In the summer of 1978, the Indian Brotherhood of NWT became the Dene Nation. Georges remembers it as a very happy but also heavy moment, and "quite sobering to answer the phone with the words 'Dene Nation' rather than 'Indian Brotherhood.'"

In 1979 Georges decided he would seek the federal NDP nomination in the upcoming election, with conditions. The Indian Brotherhood had decided a few years earlier not to participate in the territorial elections, asserting that Canada's colonial governments were not theirs. Now, here was Georges, chasing a seat in the federal government. On its surface this may seem a contradiction, but the point in both instances was to assert the Dene right to self-government. Georges's goal was to insert self-government into the federal negotiation process. Pressuring the government from the outside had got the Dene nowhere. Now Georges was trying to change the system from within.

We would take years getting negotiations to resume. It would take the Liberals losing power to Conservative Joe Clark in May 1979, then returning to be government in February 1980, before the conditions were in our favour again. We spent part of that time doing southern support work, with the help of Project North, an organization funded by seven Christian churches. We knew we needed the support of Canadians if we were going to convince Canada to modify the Comprehensive Claim policy to be based on recognition not extinguishment and to include self-government and self-determination.

At one point in 1979 it looked like a minority government was likely at the federal level. A new idea was thrown into the mix at one strategy session. What if we could win the federal seat in the Western Arctic with a minority government and the NDP being the balance of power. That was how we had ended up with Justice Berger, with a minority government; maybe we could

Georges and interviewer, February 1979.

do it again, but this time to change federal policy. We decided that I would seek the NDP nomination for the May 1979 federal election, if I could convince leader Ed Broadbent about a few things we wanted from the government.

The NDP leader Ed Broadbent and I had a meeting, and we discussed changes to the Comprehensive Claims policy that Canada had been using for negotiations with Indigenous groups. I said that the Dene wanted the extinguishment of rights dropped and replaced with recognition. Ed Broadbent asked for a clear and complete reason, which I provided. I then said we wanted to negotiate self-government, not only land. After I answered all his questions, he said he could support our position. Given the opportunity in a minority government, he would include these items in the positions that the NDP wanted.

When the spring election was called in March 1979, Georges was in Nova Scotia as part of a national campaign organized by Project North to tell Canadians why the Comprehensive Claims policy being used by Canada had to change. Georges made it clear that the negotiations must include self-government and be based on the recognition of rights rather than extinguishment. Aboriginal organizations from Yukon, BC, and the NWT

Vote for Georges: On the NDP campaign trail, May 1979.

(including Inuit) joined the coalition. Across the country public speakers appealed to Canadians to pressure the federal government. It took a long time, but eventually this effort bore fruit.

Georges returned to Yellowknife to seek the nomination. It was contested but he ended up winning. The campaign sent him across the North in a private plane owned by an NDP supporter. The vote was split three ways, was very close, and was interfered with by the spring breakup of the ice. Six hundred and seventy-three votes separated first and third place, with Georges coming in third. "I'm still thankful for that," he says. "If I'd been elected, I wouldn't have seen my house for years." The Trudeau Liberals were defeated, and Progressive Conservative leader Joe Clark headed what was to be a short-lived government. While the Dene Nation's discussions with Clark's Indian Affairs Minister, Jake Epp, were moving

Drum Lake Dene Nation strategy session, 1979.

in the right direction, the Dene Nation was unable to convince him to resume negotiations.

Within six months the Clark government was brought down in a non-confidence vote.

Georges decided not to seek the NDP nomination for the February 18, 1980, election. Instead, he swapped places with Wally Firth, who had worked hard on behalf of the 1979 Erasmus campaign. Despite Georges's efforts, Firth received nineteen votes less than the victorious PC candidate Dave Nickerson. The Trudeau Liberals returned to power with a big majority. In preparation for a Trudeau victory, Georges had made several trips to Ottawa to lobby the deputy minister of Indian Affairs for a meeting with the incoming minister as soon as the cabinet was announced. The deputy minister agreed that Georges would get a meeting early on the first day.

Immediately after the 1980 election Georges flew to Ottawa, where Prime Minister Trudeau announced that John Munro from Hamilton was the new minister of Indian Affairs and Northern Development. Sometime after supper, he met with Georges. "I pressed our case," says Georges. "I said that it was time the Dene Nation return to the negotiating table with the Crown, that good work had been done with Warren Allmand, and enough time had been wasted by negotiations not happening." Munro had many questions, and the meeting carried into the night. Georges was struck by how tired he looked. It was obvious he'd campaigned long and hard to get elected. "I finally suggested that we have another meeting after he had some time to sort out his new position. It looked like he seriously needed to go to bed."

Around this time the possibility began to surface of an oil pipeline from Norman Wells to Alberta, connecting to the existing pipeline network. Georges had continued to lobby Minister John Munro to resume funding and the negotiations on land and governance. He invited the minister to the assembly at Fort Good Hope to discuss the possible Norman Wells pipeline and the resumption of negotiations. This was an election year for the Dene Nation. Stephen Kakfwi decided he wanted the job of president and challenged Georges. The July 1980 assembly was going to be held in Fort Good Hope, Kakfwi's hometown. According to Georges, "It was quite emotional

Dene assembly at Fort Good Hope attended by federal minister John Munro, 1980.

to have Steve run against me. Over the years, working together at the Dene Nation, we had become friends." Georges was elected for another term at an assembly whose big event was a visit from John Munro, who had slipped in the shower and broken his jaw. Able to speak, but not without pain, the minister engaged in a very serious discussion over the Norman Wells oil field, whose ownership Georges insisted had to be on the table when negotiations resumed. This discussion went well into the evening and continued the following day. Munro promised that the government, which held a one-third stake, would take a serious look at Dene ownership of a portion of the Norman Wells oil field.

We were working close with the Métis Association at this time. President Jim Bourque and Vice-President Bob Stevenson were among the delegates at this assembly. On our return to Yellowknife, I spent some time considering that we needed to do something different from once again fighting to stop the construction of a pipeline. This time it was an oil pipeline, completely different

Assembly at Fort Good Hope. (left to right) Federal minister John Munro, Georges, and Métis leaders Jim Bourque and Bob Stevenson, 1980.

from the gas pipeline, and it only went halfway up the Mackenzie Valley. After discussing a possible new strategy with the Dene Leadership, who were all coming onboard, I organized a meeting with Jim Bourque. I said, "Jim, I think it's time for a new strategy for the proposed Norman Wells pipeline. We should consider supporting the construction on certain conditions." He liked the idea. I suggested we jointly ask for a meeting with the executive of the Territorial Government, to see if we could get them onside. No doubt they were surprised, but interested, so a meeting was arranged between me, Jim Bourque, and the GNWT executive.

Georges proposed the Dene conditions: First, ownership of a portion of the Norman Wells oil fields had to be on the table at the land and governance discussions with the Dene and Métis. Second, there needed to be a three-year delay of construction so that Northern and Aboriginal businesses could participate. Third, social impact funds were needed for communities to deal with the negative effects of the construction phase of the pipeline. Fourth, economic development monies allowing the Dene and Métis to directly participate in the pipeline construction were an imperative. Fifth, skills-training dollars should be available to anyone who wanted a job on the pipeline. The territorial government executive accepted everything except the three-year delay, which they wanted changed to two years. All agreed and a trip was planned to Ottawa.

One of the Dene demands was funding to enable the Denendeh Development Corporation to be involved in the Norman Wells project. "Esso was very cute," Georges says. "They wanted to build man-made islands in the middle of the Mackenzie River, and they wanted to drill from there, rather than drilling from a barge. They basically took a look at us and said, if you guys want in, you're gonna have to take the risk with us. You're gonna have to drill from these man-made islands." Together the three parties created a joint venture called Shehtah Drilling Limited, 50 percent owned by Esso, a quarter owned by the Dene (through the Denendeh Development Corporation), and a quarter owned by the Métis.

Minister John Munro met with the delegation and was generally onside. Georges recalls this as "the one and only time that I could say

Chief Johnny Charlie, Sandra Knight, and Georges, assembly at Fort Rae/Behchokǫ̀, July 1980.

the Dene, Métis, and the government of the Northwest Territories presented a solid front. Ottawa couldn't divide us." Ottawa acceded. The Norman Wells pipeline would be built. "There were hiccups," Georges says. "Some communities didn't feel they benefitted enough from the project. But compared to the usual economic ventures on Dene land, we did reasonably well."

Another thing happening around this time were meetings on the political evolution of the NWT. Inuit in the east and high Arctic were negotiating a territory of their own. In the western Arctic, discussions concerned what might happen if a division of the NWT occurred, removing half the territory. The Métis Association, headed by Jim Bourque, got together with the Dene Nation to draft a discussion paper with a possible government model of the new NWT. The *Public Government for the People of the North, Denendeh Government Proposal* was released and public meetings were held to discuss the ideas.

In the final year of Georges's term as Dene Nation president, the Dene-Métis negotiation process was finally about to begin and a chief negotiator was required. Georges convinced Bobby Overvold to accept

(left to right) Sam Raddi (president, Committee for Original Peoples' Entitlement), Georges, and Jim Bourque, 1981.

the position. Georges announced he would not be seeking another term. "Some Elders asked me to reconsider. A Tłįchǫ Elder named Alexis Arrowmaker came to my house. He told me that my work with the Dene was not done and that I needed to stay until we had our claims fully negotiated with Canada and the Crown. I thanked him for his comments, but my mind was made up." In 1983, at the age of thirty-four, Georges resigned as the president of the Dene Nation. An assembly to elect a new leader of the Dene was held at Fort Resolution. Herb Norwegian and Stephen Kakfwi were the contenders. The election took place on day two, and Kakfwi prevailed. Georges was surprised. "Herbie Norwegian was the vice-president, and I assumed that, as vice-president, he had a good chance of winning."

On day three of the assembly, Georges no longer had a role to play with the Dene Nation. He flew home to Yellowknife, where his in-laws were visiting. "For some strange reason, a delegate from the Delta made disparaging remarks about me leaving early. To this day I don't know what brought that on." A September 13 Canadian Press article — "Dene Nation's Leader

Leaves Post in Disgrace" — asserts that "Erasmus sneaked away at dawn … after the election of a rival" and cites internal criticisms of his handling of the land negotiations (now ten years along) and his decision to make the Dene Nation a business partner with Esso Resources Ltd. of Calgary. The fact was that, after seven years, a desire for change was in the air. The new president, Steve Kakfwi, came in promising a more accommodating style, excoriating Georges for demanding a new country with "total control over everything."

Well, there's no history without irony. Within months, Kakfwi would ask Georges (to his surprise) to represent the Yukon and NWT as the Northern Regional Chief at the Assembly of First Nations. As a December 26 *Toronto Star* article puts it, "To say he went out in disgrace, as a Canadian Press story did at the time, overstates the matter and overshadows his contribution to Dene causes." A more fair assessment is that Georges was adapting to increasingly complex challenges in ways that were certain to displease at least some of his fellow Dene. Georges's reputation of being an angry radical overlooked his ability to be flexible and pragmatic and thoughtful. In 1982, Esso offered a partnership in the Norman Wells project, and Georges accepted. This decision to support the development of an oil rig and pipeline shocked and outraged some.

We brought down the Mackenzie Valley pipeline, and Berger came out with his recommendation that nothing be built in the Mackenzie Valley. And then we turned around when we wanted to build a little oil pipeline. We said, you know, we can do this. This is smaller. We were able to negotiate a deal. It's the only pipeline that has ever been built North of 60. The ironic thing is I'm the guy who everybody thinks is anti-development, and also I'm the one that put together the coalition that put this package in place and gave it the go-ahead — the coalition that came up with the development corporations that are still in existence.

A surprise ending to the story of Georges's Dene Nation years, but then again the world is full of surprise. Now arguably the most well-known and well-respected Native leader in the country, Georges wanted some time off to finish building his house in Yellowknife and maybe even go to university.

In the fall of 1980, my wife Sandra Knight and I were driving around. I remembered that a piece of property was up for sale near one of my aunts. We decided to look at this property, which overlooked Yellowknife Bay eastward. We fell in love with the property. We'd been looking for something with a view of water and enough land to build a house plus a garden, and this had it all. It bordered on some green space and was a bigger lot than most. We tracked down the owner and inquired about the land. We were told it had not sold yet as the individual that wanted the land was having trouble putting the money together. At the same time, Sandra and I said, "We have the money!" Well, he said, I can't just sell it without giving the fellow one more chance. He said come back next weekend. If he hasn't been able to get the money, I'll sell you the land. It was an anxious week as we waited for the weekend. Saturday morning we were back, asking if he had sold the land. No, he said, it's yours if you want it. We said yes, definitely.

That winter we started discussing the kind of home we wanted to build. We both wanted a super-insulated house, perhaps with some passive solar capacity, that would be energy efficient and had wood-burning capacity. I began drawing house plans to fit into the rock and small hill. The house would face east, south, and north, where the views were. After I had spent much time on the kind of home we wanted to build, I came to the realization that I didn't have the time to learn about, and draw, the structural, mechanical, and electrical schematics that would have to pass inspection. We looked at building magazines for plans we could modify, and we made our selections. We also acquired plans from one of the prairie provinces on double studded homes that allowed the builder to put as much insulation as was desired into the walls. In the spring we went to the city with our plans and, once we had approval, we began construction.

Sandra and I had bought a little house in the core of the city several years earlier and had spent several years renovating. We had added windows, insulated the walls, put new flooring down, and installed a wood stove. This gave us the confidence to try building our own home. We asked George Mandeville, a local Métis carpenter, to assist with the concrete footings, which he did. Because of the unusual shape of the house, he had the corner posts of

Friends with Georges and Sandra raising front walls, 1981.

Raising the walls.

Raising the walls.

(left to right) Sandra Knight, Herb Norwegian, and Dennis Crane.

the footing surveyed. We began construction in spring 1981. We arrived at 5:00 p.m., right after our office jobs were done, and began hammering and sawing, going well into the night. We had hooked up a typical construction electrical power supply, which allowed us to use power tools. We were so excited to be building our forever home that we would forget the time, working under the midnight sun.

One evening one of our neighbours-to-be came up to see the progress. We had just finished putting the plywood down on the first floor. Our neighbour was either the mayor or deputy mayor at the time. He said a number of admiring things about our project, the view, and the work to date. Then he said, Georges, do you know what time it is? I looked at my watch: it was past midnight. I had been using my power tools, making noise that was way too loud for that time of night. I apologized and shut down the operation for the day.

We set up an interesting routine, where Sandra and I would construct the walls (which were double studded and between eighteen and twenty inches deep) then leave them for a group lifting. Friends from the Métis Association, including Métis president Jim Bourque, and from the Dene Nation, like Fred Gudmunson and Dennis Crane and Vice-President Herb Norwegian, would all come to assist in putting our big thick walls into place.

There were few super-insulated houses in Yellowknife in those days. It became a curiosity. People came to look at it. Some even helped with the wall lifting. Rene Fumoleau was a regular at our construction site, doing an assortment of little jobs. I remember I had somehow made a miscalculation on one of the very tall two-story side walls, with perhaps a 45-degree angle at the very top. Rene climbed to the top and repaired my mistake, walking the eighteen-inch width of the wall.

Sandra and I ended up getting help from all kinds of people. It was heart-warming. One guy, a local architect, was also building a home for himself and was very helpful, getting cedar siding that he ordered directly from a mill in BC. The costs ended up being less than half of materials sourced locally, so we decided to join the four other home builders that Lorne Matthews, the architect, had brought together to share the costs of the truckload of cedar siding. Lorne also sold us our first set of kitchen cabinets. He installed them too. Another friend, Dan Prima, was an electrician and offered to wire our home for free.

Dan also found some cheap Gyproc for our walls. He was working at a school that had extra drywall, which was being offered to the workers on the job. He offered to purchase it for us if we were interested. We ended up with all the drywall we needed for the whole house.

Sandra and I were making good progress when, in the fall of 1981, I was called by Phoebe Nahanni from Ottawa. We were now on the roof, shingling the last portion of the job before we could leave the work of finishing the house until next spring. Phoebe said I needed to get down to Ottawa as fast as possible, because Section 35 of the constitutional package that Prime Minister Trudeau was going to bring to London had been dropped, and some other changes (like having a Notwithstanding Clause in the Charter) had been added to appease seven premiers. "The Night of the Long Knives," as Quebec politicians would call it, had just happened. She wanted me to begin a lobby campaign to put Section 35, the Recognition of Aboriginal and Treaty Rights, back into the constitutional package.

I immediately put down my tools and headed for Ottawa, where I spearheaded a campaign with many others to bring back both the Equality and Aboriginal and Treaty Rights provisions. We had a loose coalition that included the Inuit, the Native Women's Association, the Métis, and some First Nation Leaders. The Native Friendship Centre let us use their facilities. We demonstrated every day, joined by thousands of Canadians, especially women. We travelled back and forth across Canada, speaking at events, many times jointly with women who were lobbying for the Equality clause to be put back into the constitution. Finally, after many weeks of demonstrations and enormous publicity, the premiers and the prime minister blinked. The Equality clause was returned and the word "existing" was added to the section recognizing Aboriginal and Treaty Rights. We saw this as a clear victory for the Aboriginal Peoples of Canada. One of the leaders who joined me in this lobby was Chief Gary Potts from Bear Island. We became lifelong friends.

I returned to Yellowknife to finish getting our new home ready for winter. The shingles still needed to be finished, but now we didn't have any sunlight after office hours. I was wondering how Sandra and I would be able to finish shingling the roof. To make things more difficult, we had snow on everything and it was cold. I was totally surprised when I was met at the airport by my

Chief Paul Wright of Fort Norman/Tulita congratulating Georges on reinstating Section 35 of the constitution, fall 1981.

staff, who drove me to a local hall. I was given a hero's welcome for my work on the constitution.

Sandra and I resumed shingling the last part of the roof by climbing on the roof through a skylight and sweeping off the snow. We had a cold northeast wind to deal with as well as brittle shingles that threatened to break. We had to take our gloves off to hold the roofing nails. We worked by the light of lanterns. Not a fun job, but we both kept at it until we had the roof totally shingled. We then put in the skylight and boarded up the door with plywood to leave the project until the weather warmed up.

A funny thing happened sometime in January. I ran into our neighbour, the deputy mayor. He said, "Your house is occupied." I said, "How? We have no heat." Ravens had taken to spending the night in the house. We'd decided to add two more windows on the second story, facing Yellowknife Bay. The openings had been left open. Sandra and I decided to leave the cleanup job for the spring (the ravens had been pooping everywhere) and we closed the two open window holes.

About a month later, I ran into the deputy mayor again. This time he told me that, just before dark, the ravens would complain that they couldn't get into the house anymore. In March, we entered the house with shovels and garbage bags and cleaned up the droppings. It was quite a mess. We resumed work in the spring, mainly inside, having the plumbing done by a plumbing company and the electrical work by our friend Dan Prima. We insulated and put drywall on the walls, built the stairs, and closed in all the rooms. One of my brothers, Guy, was working with the city at the time. He recommended that we have insulated water and sewer pipes — advice that we took. Guy also helped me hook up the sewer line to the city system.

We moved into the house in September of 1982 with much work to be done inside. This allowed us to sell the little house on 46th Street in the centre of town that we had owned for several years. We were then able to put that money toward continuing the interior finish work. One of the parts that needed completion was the large living/dining room cathedral ceiling. We needed deeper ceiling space for our three batts of six-inch insulation to achieve R60. We lived with three tiers of scaffolding for our first winter in the house while we finished lowering the ceiling, insulating, then adding cedar board. At Christmas, we used scaffolding to decorate a tall northern Christmas tree.

In the middle of the winter, frost could be seen on the roofing nails in the ceiling. I would be teased to no end by Sandra, as I got ready to travel for work, that I would be sleeping in hotel rooms with no frost on the ceilings. She was extremely understanding and supportive of the work I did while we were together. We lived in a construction site for years, as we could only get to the building when I wasn't travelling. We would have to take a break from continuous work and just enjoy where we were living. We began landscaping and gardening as soon as we could get time to plant and bring soil to our rock outcrop.

At the national level, Prime Minister Trudeau called a First Ministers' Conference for March 15 and 16, 1983, to be held in the old Ottawa Conference Centre, which included the national Aboriginal organizations: the Assembly of First Nations, the Inuit, the Native Council of Canada, and the Métis. The Native Women's Association was part of the AFN delegation. We had many internal meetings planning what we should present to Canada and the premiers. One of the things we wanted to add to Section 35 of the constitution was a clause that would recognize land claim agreements as modern treaties, and this was supported by the other national organizations. I was selected at the AFN leadership meetings to be one of the AFN spokespersons along with leaders from different parts of the country. The national Aboriginal organizations agreed on an extensive agenda, including self-government; removing "existing" from Section 35; recognizing the rights of modern treaties; clarifying that Aboriginal and Treaty Rights are equal to men and women; a land base for Métis; a consent clause, meaning that no section of the constitution could be changed without consent from the national Aboriginal organizations; and much more. In the end, we were able to get the recognition of modern treaties and equality of Aboriginal and Treaty Rights for men and women, but we were not able to get the consent clause we were after. However, we did get agreement that a clause would be added to the constitution "that section 91:24 would not be changed without a First Ministers' Conference that included the national Aboriginal organizations and at least two more First Ministers' Conferences over the next few years."

One of the things I arranged in my last year in office as Dene Nation president was to hire a chief negotiator for the Dene-Métis negotiation process that was finally getting off the ground. I convinced Bobby Overvold to accept the position of chief negotiator.

I had spent ten years at the Indian Brotherhood, which became the Dene Nation. I spent three of those years as staff, running fieldworkers, and seven years as president. While there was lots to do both in the north and at the national level with more First Ministers' Conferences promised, I truly felt it was time for a change in leadership. I always believed in collective leadership, and this was me putting that belief into practice. I enjoyed the work and I look back and realize how lucky I was to always be able to find great people to work with. I have fond memories of my time at the Dene Nation.

3

THE ASSEMBLY OF FIRST NATIONS

Not long after Georges retired as president of the Dene Nation in 1983, his successor, Stephen Kakfwi, asked him to be the Assembly of First Nations Regional Chief representing the NWT and Yukon. Georges had taken on contract work and offered a part-time commitment, to which Kakfwi agreed. Around this time Stephen Kakfwi and others decided to create an organization that would challenge misinformation coming out of the animal rights movement. Among the efforts of these activists was an attempt to create a ban of the leg-hold trap, a staple device that many Dene trappers (and other Indigenous people) were still using. Kakfwi wanted Georges to lead the Canadian part of an organization called Indigenous Survival International (ISI), as co-chair of Indigenous Survival International Canada. "Okay," said Georges, "I'll do it."

The first order of business was to secure funding. Georges applied for government funding for travel, lobbying, a small office, and an educational campaign telling the story of traditional activities on the land and of Indigenous respect for the animals harvested for food, clothing, tools, and sale. "We wanted to tell the story of how it was the most traditional of Indigenous people who were still harvesting wildlife," Georges says, "either by hunting or trapping, and that this was a continuation of a lifestyle that went back thousands of years, albeit with some modern tools." Canada was very receptive. Georges set up shop in 1984 and began attending international conventions like CITES, the Convention on International Trade in Endangered Species of Wild Fauna and Flora. ISI executive director Dave Monture recalls that

> there was kind of a game being played in those international forums. Delegates from many Third World countries had their way paid to these international conferences, providing that they would vote against trapping. I know that was going on at the IUCN [International Union for Conservation of Nature] in Costa Rica. It was all a huge lobby effort. There was a lot of money being raised and put into these attempts to ban trapping with CITES with IUCN and so on.

One of the fears at ISI was of a possible ban on fur caught with the leg-hold trap. Another was the effect that a halting of the Newfoundland seal hunt would have on Inuit seal hunting. The campaign focused on the harvesting of baby seals using a club. "They still use this image in the twenty-first century," says Georges, "even though it's been decades since a seal has been clubbed. And the thing was, that was an instant kill. And the seals are hunted when they're older, they're not baby seals. But it's such a money-maker for some of these organizations." The baby seal campaign was affecting all seal harvesting, even the traditional harvesting of seals by the Inuit. Canada was working hard to replace the leg-hold trap with the less cruel alternative, the quick-kill trap. Over time, all traps in Canada were replaced with quick-kill traps. ISI participated in lobbying and in explaining that the whole animal was used by Indigenous Peoples and that they were not exploiting the wildlife they lived with. Rather, Indigenous Peoples have always considered all life sacred.

ISI moved into AFN office space after Georges became the National Chief. They had a small staff, but many were interested in helping with the campaigns. The James Bay Cree, many of whom were active hunters, were very much involved in ISI. The James Bay Northern Québec Agreement (JBNQA) with Canada and Quebec provided support for activities on the land, the only provision of its kind in Canada. Thomas Coon, of the James Bay Cree, was very active and a wonderful spokesperson of traditional life on the land. He and Georges made several international trips together.

Greenpeace had targeted trapping and the seal hunt, and ISI wanted their leadership to understand how this was affecting the lives of Aboriginal people. In 1976, Greenpeace had started a campaign against the commercial harvesting of marine mammals, in particular the East Coast seal hunt. In 1984, ISI went to Edmonton to see Patrick Moore, Greenpeace co-founder and president. The executive director of the World Wildlife Fund, Monte Hummel, helped set up the meeting. "I remember the conversation with Patrick Moore was frustrating," Georges says. "He took the position that it was time to move on to a different lifestyle. He couldn't see the continuation of the harvesting of animals for their fur or food." Georges and his colleague Thomas Coon patiently explained that they were talking about the most traditional of their people, and that this way of life was thousands of years old. And while the income from the selling of fur was only very modest for most, it was a large part of the income of many.

As frustrating and infuriating as it was to have to explain how Indigenous Peoples lived, Georges took the necessary time. He explained the Indigenous emphasis on living in harmony with all other living things, and in a fully sustainable and balanced approach to managing the harvesting of animals, big or small. The Indigenous approach included fish and roots and berries and everything else. Moore gave his ISI guests the time necessary to say everything they'd come to say, and the meeting was polite and cordial. Georges left uncertain of what if anything had been accomplished.

ISI proceeded to their next move. "We requested time at Greenpeace's board meeting, and I got on a plane for London, England," Georges says. To his great surprise, Georges discovered on arrival that the Greenpeace board had already discussed the issue he had come to talk about, and they had already decided. Greenpeace was getting out of the animal rights movement and instead was going to deal with other matters like climate change.

Dave Monture led the staff at the ISI offices. "We were very lucky to hire him," Georges says. "He was fully committed to our project, and he worked hard to accomplish our goal of protecting the traditional lifestyles of Indigenous Peoples." At ISI, Dave organized a December 1987 educational exhibition at the British Museum, called *The Living Arctic*. The exhibit presented a true picture of how Indigenous Peoples lived in some of the harshest climates on earth, as well as how traditional lifestyles created a balanced, sustainable, and fully respectful approach to the environment and to all living things in their territories. "Trapping was an essential part of the local economy," Monture explains, "enabling people to buy basic foodstuff. So a lot of our positions were very down to earth and practical."

ISI's contact at the British Museum was Jonathan King, who went out of his way to be completely accurate in his presentation of the Inuit, Dene, Cree, and Métis lifestyles depicted in the exhibition. "He built an Eastern Arctic bungalow right inside the British Museum, to show the typical Inuit

Dave Monture (back, second from left), Cindy Gilday (front, left), and George Blondin (front, right) at the Indigenous Survival International (ISI) British Museum exhibit *The Living Arctic*, London, U.K., December 1987.

home setting," recalls Dave Monture. "It depicted seals being butchered right on the floor. Skidoos had to be brought in from Canada and Jonathan had to smuggle some antique firearms into Britain because of the British gun laws. It was quite an adventure." Georges recalls a "beautiful interactive computer game" also featured in the exhibit.

> The game had a variety of traditional camp settings, tents and such. There were pictorial stories about traditional life on the land and Indigenous values. You'd go on, say, a caribou hunt. The game would ask how many animals you were going to take, and why. If you didn't know the answer, you could ask an Elder. The point was to teach young people that you only take what you need, and you use everything. The Elder would tell the player that the goal of trapping, hunting, or traditional fishing was not to see how much harvest was possible, but rather how much was needed by the family and how to harvest it with respect, giving back to the land. It was really wonderful. Later, we consulted with Jonathan to see if this game was something that youngsters enjoyed. And it was, obviously, one of the keynotes. It was always being used. Whoever came up with the game was brilliant.

The British Museum exhibit opened with Inuit throat singers, Dene drummers, a hoop dancer as master of ceremonies, and the London Philharmonic Orchestra led by Mohawk conductor John Kim Bell. ("It's about time we had an Indian pulling the strings," quipped the MC.) The exhibition was so popular it was given an extended stay.

Some of the other, wonderful people who were involved in the work of ISI included Louis "Smokey" Bruyère (then president of the Native Council of Canada), Cindy Gilday (a Dene activist from Yellowknife), and Jim Bourque (a Métis from the north whose varied career included wildlife officer, deputy minister in the GNWT, and president of the Métis Association of the NWT). Georges fondly remembers travelling to Brussels in the mid-80s with Smokey Bruyère and lobbying members in the European Parliament, including members of the upstart Green Party. Smokey arranged for some of the most skeptical members of parliament to visit a northern Manitoba trapline in the middle of winter and on Ski-Doo.

A piece of cake, one of them decided, using modern tools like a Ski-Doo. Smokey soon changed his mind. Dave Monture describes it like this:

> I remember one of the Dutch members of the European parliament. He almost starved during World War Two, as a child under the German occupation. And of course, like many Dutch he had a lot of respect for the Canadians who were part of taking back Holland. He was a real tough nut for us to crack until Smokey got him on a modern trapline. He just about froze to death. He came to realize that this wasn't an easy life at all. It was a tough but dignified life, and it was associated with habitat preservation and conservation of the species. He was turned around and became an ally.

Through ISI, Georges and Dave and others were able to begin making the changes that would protect Indigenous lifestyles. Over time, the leg-hold trap was completely replaced in Canada. Today, Dene and other Indigenous trappers are using quick-kill traps. The European Parliament allows the traditional harvesting of seals while banning the much larger commercial seal hunt. The campaign to educate the world on the traditional lifestyles of northern Indigenous Peoples continues. Greenpeace has become an ally of Indigenous Peoples and of Indigenous lifestyles also, including the traditional harvesting of wildlife.

When Georges was elected Northern Regional Chief of the Assembly of First Nations, in 1983, the country's constitution was the big deal in Indigenous politics. There was nothing especially new about Trudeau's proposal to patriate the Canadian constitution, completed on April 17, 1982, with the signing of the Constitution Act. As early as 1927, Prime Minister William Lyon Mackenzie King had proposed domesticating the British North America Act (BNA), Canada's founding document. The effort to patriate the constitution, which began with Trudeau's 1980 re-election, wasn't even *his* first attempt. Many attempts had tried and failed to bring the constitution home from Britain. The rub was getting all the provinces to agree on an amending formula. Patriation would require the accommodation of diverse interests, including Quebec's, and to a large degree it was Trudeau's federalist solution to the ongoing crises of separatist referenda.

Indian, Aboriginal, Indigenous — whatever term one prefers, Trudeau had no intention or plan to entrench these rights in the Constitution Act. To begin with, he was allergic to the notion of group rights. And as the White Paper had made clear, assimilation of Indians into the body politic had been his preferred course. On the matter of rights, Trudeau asserted that all were equal under the law and that no one could claim special status. At the time of the White Paper, he famously said that "we can't recognize Aboriginal rights because no society can be built on historical might-have-beens."[1] Confronted with the White Paper, Indigenous people rose up in indignation and Pierre Trudeau relented. It would be the same with the constitution. To his credit, Trudeau changed his mind when it was made clear to him that he was in error.

Across the country the focus was on getting Indigenous people at the negotiation table, and they were making a mighty noise. On November 24, 1980, two trains departed from Vancouver's Pacific Central Station bound for the capital. There, the one thousand passengers on this "Constitution Express" protested the lack of Indigenous consultation and involvement in Trudeau's proposed constitutional framework. There were demonstrations on Parliament Hill. Initially, Aboriginal self-government was included in the wish list, as was a consent clause allowing for the involvement of Aboriginal Peoples in any section of the constitution dealing with their rights. Some First Nations wanted to stop the process until all the treaties were implemented.

As for settling treaty issues before agreeing to discuss the constitution, Georges could read the writing on the wall. "Patriation was going to happen. So we had to make sure that whatever we had in the constitution that referred to Aboriginal people, the term we used back then, had to be as strong as possible." Others did not support the BNA being brought to Canada, because many of the treaties were with the British Crown, leading to worries that this might diminish Treaty Rights. Organizations including the National Indian Brotherhood sent entourages to London, England, to lobby on behalf of Indigenous people. Joe Miskokomon remembers being one of those people.

> The National Indian Brotherhood didn't have any money, so the Union of Ontario Indians sent Dennis Martell to England to help me with press releases and communications to the British parliament. And he didn't have any money either. We went down to Fleet Street, where the newspapers are, and we pitched editorials. Along that whole street is a number of print shops. We gave them the National Indian Brotherhood logo and we said, we'd like fifty copies of this printed on envelopes and letterhead, and we'd have to have them approved by our manager before we place the order. So they would run off, whatever, thirty to forty sample copies for us to get approved. We used the samples to type our letters on and send them to Parliament.

The purpose of going to England was, as Pat Madahbee puts it, "to make sure that, if the Constitution is patriated, the rights and obligations of the Treaties remain within the Crown in right of Canada and the Crown in right of the provinces." From 1980 to 1982, the critical period when Aboriginal rights were put into the Constitution Act, Del Riley was the elected leader of the National Indian Brotherhood, the Ottawa-based lobby organization that would become the Assembly of First Nations. As Del recalls,

> The constitutional talks were coming up. Trudeau wanted an amending formula, because for him it was embarrassing to have the constitution in England. He was fighting the provinces, trying to get them to agree on what was the best formula. In the meantime, things were happening. The Calder case, land claims, whatnot. I was trying to pull

> all the leaders across the country together. I was telling them, "Look, we've got to get moving on this stuff. I'll put us in the constitution." That was my platform when I ran for national leader. We did a massive lobbying effort in Ottawa. I probably met every cabinet minister and the Prime Minister multiple times.

The eventual outcome of the lobbying, grassroots activism, and mass protests was Section 35 of the Constitution Act of 1982, recognizing and affirming "existing aboriginal and treaty rights":

> 35. (1) The existing aboriginal and treaty rights of the aboriginal peoples of Canada are hereby recognized and affirmed.
> (2) In this Act, "aboriginal peoples of Canada" includes the Indian, Inuit and Métis peoples of Canada.

Section 35 began as a much larger document proposed by the National Indian Brotherhood — "about nine pages," according to Del Riley. At the time of patriation, it consisted of the first two clauses, which affirmed existing Aboriginal rights and included in the term "Aboriginal" — "the Indian, Inuit and Métis peoples of Canada." But what exactly were "existing" rights? Were they rights that existed prior to the Constitution Act or rights determined to exist by the courts? The word "existing" was first proposed by Alberta and, according to Del Riley, "was all about resources."[2]

Alberta did this because of a case with the Māori in New Zealand in which the court determined that "existing" meant only from the time it went into the constitution. But when it got to the court here in Canada, "existing" included everything.

Section 35 was a huge victory for Indigenous people, but it was a qualified victory. As would become evident in the years ahead, inclusion of Aboriginal and Treaty Rights in the constitution provided a foundation for future battles. That was the good news. The bad news was that many battles would be necessary and that these battles would be long, exhausting, brutal, and expensive. "With Section 35 in the constitution," says

Konrad Sioui, "for a moment we thought that we had it made. We thought that we were winning something. But then we realized that it was a ticket to go to court ... with millions and millions of dollars spent and lots of pain and misery."

While Section 35 may have been a ticket to go to court, Section 37 of the Constitution Act was a ticket to go to the March 1983 Federal-Provincial Conference of First Ministers on Aboriginal Constitutional Matters. Section 37 specified that a constitutional conference should be called within one year of the act coming into force, on April 17, 1982, and that the conference should include Aboriginal representatives and "an item respecting constitutional matters that directly affect the aboriginal peoples of Canada, including the identification and definition of the rights of those peoples, to be included in the Constitution of Canada." The agenda for the meeting comprised six items, among them the Charter of Rights of the Aboriginal Peoples, amending formula revisions, self-government, and the planning of additional conferences. Georges attended in his dual functions of Dene Nation president and AFN spokesperson.

Georges and Chief Gary Potts at First Ministers' Conference, Ottawa, 1980s.

These were exciting times at the AFN, as we were in the midst of First Ministers' Conferences on the Canadian Constitution, looking at how we might improve and clarify what was already in Section 35. I became very involved in the constitutional process, travelling regularly across the country to attend ministerial meetings, internal AFN strategy sessions, assemblies, and lobbying meetings with provincial government, premiers, and attorneys general. We had total and complete support from New Brunswick premier Richard Hatfield, and we had good support from Ontario premier Bill Davis and his attorney general Roy McMurtry. It was surprising in some ways that we had a better relationship with the Davis government, where we had a generous and friendly partnership, than we did with the Liberal Government that followed. Ian Scott became the attorney general in the David Peterson government and was a bit of a thorn in our side.

Another strong ally was the Manitoba government of Howard Pawley, whose attorney general was Roland Penner. "We could always depend on their support," says Georges. The Assembly of First Nations took the position that Section 35 of the Canadian Constitution already recognized Aboriginal self-government and self-determination, and that what they were after was an inventory of the contents of the constitutional box. In the AFN's view, the box was full. It was a view not supported by all governments.

Indigenous people had less than a year to prepare for these talks. The AFN set up a Constitutional Working Group, or CWG, coordinated by a Kanien'kehá:ka (Mohawk) named Arnold Goodleaf. The CWG had one representative from each province. "We did a lot of traveling and a lot of meeting," says the AFN's CWG representative from Newfoundland, Marilyn John, a member of the Miawpukek (Conne River) First Nation. "Behind the scenes, we were doing the work and presenting it to the political organizations for their consideration." The AFN also collaborated with the constitutional working groups of the other national Indigenous organizations, who would also attend the First Ministers' Conferences: the Native Council of Canada, the Métis National Council, and the Inuit Tapirisat of Canada. "I'm not sure how many times [the Inuit, Métis, and First Nations] all met as a group," says Nancy Hall, who worked for the

Inuit Committee on National Issues, the Inuit equivalent of the AFN's Constitutional Working Group. The meetings, she says, "were fascinating. I remember the tension between the treaty and the non-treaty land claims folks, and trying to work with that."

"We had very seasoned people on the constitution," says Marilyn John. The list of folks working on the constitution talks, behind the scenes or otherwise, from the national Aboriginal organizations includes Billy Diamond, Smokey Bruyère, Melody Morrison, Dorothy Wabisca, Bill Wilson, Charlie Watt, Mark R. Gordon, Clem Chartier, Jim Gosnell, Mary Simon (the future governor general), Max Gros-Louis, Gord Peters, Grant Wedge, Gary Potts, Joe Miskokomon, Pat Madahbee, Harry Daniels, Wally McKay, and Marcia Smoke, "the key coordinating person" according to Nancy Hall. The initial background meetings took place with lower-level government bureaucrats and elected officials, and eventually worked their way up the chain. Georges, for his part, travelled the country to gain support for specific constitutional amendments.

By the time the national Indigenous leaders (David Ahenakew, John Amagoalik, Jim Sinclair, Smokey Bruyère, and their respective lieutenants) sat down with premiers, in the old train station that is today the Senate of Canada building, dozens of preparation meetings involving hundreds of people had taken place across the country. The March 15–16, 1983, First Ministers' Conference on Aboriginal Rights covered a broad range of topics, from securing a land base to the systemic gender discrimination of the Indian Act.

The first day of the talks were tense. The Indigenous participants were unable to agree on a draft Statement of Principles of Aboriginal Rights and requested a number of amendments. Clem Chartier, of the Métis National Council, requested "the two following principles — the principle that there must be recognition of a land base for the Aboriginal Peoples and, as well, a principle dealing with fiscal arrangements." Charlie Watt, representing the Inuit at the meeting, added the principle that "the Aboriginal Peoples of Canada have the rights to the land and water and to the resources which have served as [the] basis for the self sufficiency and the development of Native community." Allan Williams, British Columbia's attorney general, pushed back: "I'm concerned that if we attempt, around this table, to begin to add and subtract that we will lose what we agreed upon last night."[3]

The provinces signed a document that produced three constitutional revisions: at least two more conferences would be held, all present and future successful Aboriginal claims would be protected by the constitution, and Native women would have equality of rights. Clauses (3) and (4) would be added to Section 35:

> (3) For greater certainty, in subsection (1) "treaty rights" includes rights that now exist by way of land claims agreements or may be so acquired.
> (4) Notwithstanding any other provision of this Act, the aboriginal and treaty rights referred to in subsection (1) are guaranteed equally to male and female persons.

The conference also produced this memorable exchange between Pierre Trudeau and Bill Wilson, the father of future attorney general Jody Wilson-Raybould:

> **Bill Wilson:** I have two children in Vancouver Island, both of whom for some misguided reason say they want to be a lawyer. Both of whom want to be the prime minister. Both of whom, Mr. Prime Minister, are women.
> **Pierre Trudeau:** Tell them I'll stick around till they're ready.
> **Bill Wilson:** Mr. Chairman, I'm informed by the government of British Columbia that one of them could be out here on a plane this evening.[4]

While the first round of constitutional talks yielded few gains, the mood at the end of the conference was optimistic. Even Trudeau felt compelled to say that the Aboriginal participants were "doing pretty well." In fact, they were stealing the show. Bill Wilson's exchange with Trudeau exemplifies both the optimism of the day as well as the one-upmanship. David

Ahenakew, the AFN National Chief, concluded that there was enough goodwill and trust "to go forward in developing our relations." It's a beginning, said Inuit leader John Amagoalik. "We recognize the fact that provinces are very reluctant to agree to anything that they don't understand, but this is nothing new to us. We have had a long history of educating European Canadians of what Inuit are, and we're prepared to keep doing that. And we're prepared to sign this accord."[5]

In early 1984, an all-party House of Commons committee led by Keith Penner came forth with a report. The Penner Report supported the position that Aboriginal Peoples in Canada already had the constitutional right of self-government. Canada therefore could not *give* this right to Aboriginal Peoples, it could only *recognize* it. Many political leaders came out in support of this view, and needless to say the Aboriginal organizations agreed also. If only the prime minister took to this view. Trudeau called a second First Ministers' Conference on Aboriginal Rights in 1984, at which time his government proposed negotiations on "Self-Government Institutions" that would be created through provincial and territorial legislation. Only Ontario, Manitoba, and New Brunswick supported this idea. The AFN delegation also deliberated this proposal, which became known as "contingent self-government."

Trudeau talked about "institutions of self-government" rather than the self-government of Aboriginal Nations or Peoples. It was like he couldn't bring himself to say we had this right. Since this proposal had the support of only three provinces, it fell far short of the threshold required for a constitutional amendment. It wasn't going to happen, and Trudeau made little effort to make it happen. Also, like Mulroney's later proposal, these institutions of self-government would be contingent, which is to say subject to future negotiations with the provinces. Nothing was there until it was passed by legislation, provincially and federally. So you're actually emptying out Section 35. At least Mulroney's proposal, which actually acknowledged the right of self-government and had the support of seven provinces, was an improvement on the Trudeau offer.

There were plenty of arguments at the AFN and elsewhere against getting involved in the constitutional talks. To begin with, some wanted to settle treaty issues before supporting patriation. The involvement of the provinces in the talks was another stumbling block, since only the Crown had jurisdiction in Aboriginal matters. Opening up the negotiations around Aboriginal matters also risked the incursion of hostile provincial agendas. Why should anyone care what Alberta has to say about the Crown–First Nations relationship? Ahenakew, whose thinking was much along these lines, had taken the position that the AFN should withdraw from the constitutional negotiations, three rounds of which had taken place by the 1985 election. People around Ahenakew had become so concerned that the AFN executive set out to limit his role and was even careful not to let him negotiate with Mulroney unaccompanied.

Mulroney comes in and we have our first First Ministers' meeting with him in April 1985. Ahenakew is still there. And Mulroney has this package for the self-government resolution that is dependent on, you know, successful negotiations and all the rest of it — "the contingent resolution," the contingent self-government kind of approach which we were against. And we were also kind of concerned that Ahenakew was going to agree to it. So we wouldn't let him go to the meetings with Mulroney by himself. I guess Mulroney could sense what was going on, because he was looking at me more than he was looking at the National Chief in these meetings.

The AFN had two seats at the constitution talks. A roster of presenters took turns occupying one of the seats, while the other seat was mostly reserved for the National Chief. For instance, when the debate took place with Trudeau over Aboriginal Title, the AFN had agreed that Georges would vacate his seat to allow the Nisga'a leader, James Gosnell, to present on Aboriginal Title. Miles Richardson recalls the background of this decision:

> At a two-day meeting in Vancouver, Bill Wilson and AFN reps like George Watts and Joe Mathias explained that we had to get ready for the question of Aboriginal

> Title to come up at the First Ministers Conference. They said, "we need to appoint somebody from BC." We spent two days debating what should be said and who should say it. The whole room enthusiastically appointed Jim Gosnell, President of the Nisga'a Tribal Council. After the vote, Bobby Manuel and the Union of British Columbia Indian Chiefs decided they didn't support it and created a little bit of discomfort. But when that moment came — when Prime Minister Trudeau asked, "What does Aboriginal Title mean?" — James Gosnell made his famous speech, our ownership of this land is "lock, stock, and barrel." There was a week of preparation to answer that very question.

The AFN compiled lists of people who would be attending the conference site. "There were only so many seats behind each group," Georges says. Some seats were even farther back, in the foyer, where screens allowed attendees to watch the proceedings. The occupants of the seats behind the two AFN spokespersons would also rotate. Ontario would have so many seats for a time, and then these seats would be yielded to Alberta or Yukon or the NWT and so on.

Georges regarded the AFN's Treaty–Aboriginal Rights schism as both misguided and unnecessary. Weirdly, a rumour was spreading across Indian Country that Georges Erasmus not only supported the constitutional negotiations, but that he was against the treaties.

There were these strange stories going around about me, that I was against the treaties. These Elders would want to meet with me, so I remember going to Edmonton. I explained to them that I come from a place where there are two numbered treaties, 8 and 11. I said, maybe what's going on is that we have an oral treaty in Canada and the Crown has a written treaty which we never agreed to. We never agreed to give up any rights to govern ourselves. So maybe that's what's being misunderstood. I'm not against the treaties, I'm totally in support of our oral treaties. It took a while to get the people to kind of turn around, to see that I was in fact a supporter of the treaties, so I had to build support.

Unfortunately, not everyone at the AFN was in unity mode and, in the spring of 1985, a faction calling itself the Prairie Treaty Nations Alliance broke away from the AFN and sought an independent seat at the April 2–3 first ministers' constitutional conference. The PTNA further threatened to negotiate directly with the federal government, not only over the constitution but in other areas where the AFN was active. In a further affront to the principle of unity, nearly one hundred Ahenakew supporters left the

Georges at First Ministers' Conference, with Indigenous leaders showing support, Ottawa 1980s.

assembly after Georges's victory to hold a meeting in another part of the building, where they discussed the development of a rival organization.

Although Prime Minister Brian Mulroney's March 1985 self-government proposal was better than Trudeau's, it was still contingent upon negotiations with the provinces. It didn't take long for the AFN to decide. "In our meeting with Prime Minister Mulroney," Georges says, "he tried to make us understand that, as much as he would have loved to do better, this was as far as he could bring the provinces. We thanked him for his efforts, but we made it clear the AFN could not support this amendment." In the end all the national organizations took the same position, making it clear that they could not accept a contingency clause. They all wanted a clear statement that Section 35 included the inherent right to Aboriginal self-government.

Former AFN National Chiefs Phil Fontaine and Ovide Mercredi both have positive recollections of Georges's performance at the constitutional talks. One of Ovide's favourite memories of Georges is his leadership "in the

Georges and Smokey Bruyère at First Ministers' Conference with Prime Minister Brian Mulroney, Ottawa, March 1987.

early period, 1982 onwards, with the first round of discussions we had after patriation, after the employment of section 35." Phil Fontaine thinks that "the most significant thing that Georges did was to represent us at the constitution talks. Georges was seen as the person that was the best and most articulate in representing the positions of what became known as aboriginal people, including Inuit and Métis, and everyone wanted him to speak first. I mean, there was no one bigger in our community than Georges at that time, for sure."

Over time, the constitution talks boosted the political status of the AFN. In the years ahead people would begin to speak of the "Thirteenth Premier," referring to National Chief Georges Erasmus. The First Ministers' Conference pushed the AFN to think more deeply about its future and the kind of leadership it required. Gord Peters, a former AFN Regional Chief from Ontario, says that "we left those early constitutional meetings in the frame of mind that we had to have more clarity about what we wanted and what the process is going to be. By the time the Assembly of First Nations election of 1985 rolls around, we clearly have Georges as our leader, the one that we want as our spokesman. Georges wins that election, and he heads to Ottawa. On his own credit card. Because there is no money at the AFN."

Georges was a week from his thirty-seventh birthday when he was elected National Chief of the Assembly of First Nations, on July 30, 1985. "I never had any plans to run for the AFN," he says. "By this time, I'd been attending National Indian Brotherhood and Assembly of First Nations meetings for over ten years, as Dene Nation President or Northern Regional Chief. I wasn't excited or convinced." Much of the senior leadership of the AFN however was. As Gord Peters notes, Georges had the skills and vision to lead the AFN through the constitutional negotiations. He also had a record of running effective organizations, and the AFN was in desperate need of good management. By 1985, the conclusion arrived at by a number of Chiefs, Georges included, was that things were a mess. Under David Ahenakew, the organization was burdened by unsustainable spending and a debt of more than two million dollars, over 20 percent of its total budget. Every month, far more money was going out than was coming in. Worse yet, much of the money coming into the AFN wasn't even funding its operations. Funding would temporarily land in the AFN account and then flow to the Federation of Saskatchewan Indian Nations (FSIN), where Ahenakew had been president from 1968 to 1979, via a contractor called SINCO (the Saskatchewan Indian Nations Company, a holding company owned by roughly forty Indian bands). Under the Ahenakew business model, the AFN was largely a sub-contracting agency distributing resources to the National Chief's favoured people and entities.

A culture of cronyism had set in, with Ahenakew favouring his inner circle — people including Max Gros-Louis, Sol Sanderson, and Noel Starblanket. According to Joe Miskokomon, "There was a tremendous amount of Western-based influence, which was primarily headed up by FSIN. And David Ahenakew had come from there — his roots, his origin, his background. The AFN didn't represent the assembly as a whole but was representing one or two provinces. And that became very difficult to stand by and watch."

Georges and his colleagues had tried to work with Ahenakew. They'd drafted an executive resolution asking him to reduce spending so that the organization could cover its costs and avoid going further into debt. "Didn't do a damn thing," says Georges. Next they tabled a resolution at a confederacy meeting, with the same result. No amount of petition was making a difference. Even assembly resolutions were being ignored by the National Chief.

There were criticisms of the National Chief even beyond financial mismanagement, favouritism, and corruption — such as Ahenakew's poor management (as some AFN colleagues saw it) of the constitution talks. By 1984 AFN regional Chiefs like Gordon Peters and Konrad Sioui, and other prominent leaders like Harry Allen and Joe Miskokomon, could tolerate National Chief Ahenakew no longer. The AFN executive was left with no recourse but to try a vote of non-confidence, which might well have happened had an election not been scheduled later in the year. Replacing Ahenakew was the last, best option.

Joe Miskokomon tells the story like this:

> It became evident that we couldn't have Ahenakew serve another term. And so the view was, well, who do we get? What do we look for? And it became clear to us that Georges was the person we needed to have as a leader to advance our constitutional discussions. We needed a stronger, more articulate person at the table. And so the campaign was on. I think it was spring 1985. Gord Peters and I were at the Westbury in Toronto. And that's where we sat down and first made the pitch to get Georges. It was a good discussion. A lot of questions by Georges. He was very reluctant. He didn't necessarily want the job, but we had thought it through. And we made our arguments, which I thought were compelling

Georges, AFN campaign, July 1985.

Pre-election vote: (standing, left to right) Chief Eddy John, Georges, Simon Lucas, Vancouver, July 1985.

> arguments, and eventually he agreed. And that's where we begin the campaign.

As time went on, Georges realized that he might have the best chance of winning. So Georges and his fellow regional Chiefs went beyond merely watching. The race for National Chief was on. The group set to ousting Ahenakew. With an election only weeks away, the National Chief established CREDA — the Committee to Re-elect Dave Ahenakew. With a nod to a certain pop group from Stockholm, Joe Miskokomon responded in a counter campaign he called "ABDA" — *Anybody But David Ahenakew*. Georges and his team took to the road and to the phones and used every economical means available to impress upon the Chiefs just how desperate things had become. Their message was that it was time for a new leader and a new approach — a new regime that was honest and fair and open and transparent. Support for Georges was strong in the North and in much of British Columbia, as well as in Ontario and eastern Canada. The support of fifteen Chiefs was required for a nomination. Ninety-eight Chiefs signed letters of support for Georges.

AFN election speech, Vancouver, July 1985.

AFN National Chief elected. (left to right) Eddy John, Konrad Sioui, Gord Peters, Georges, Joe Miskokomon, and Neil Stirrett, Vancouver, July 1985.

The election took place in Vancouver on July 30, 1985. The winner would need 60 percent of the vote. Georges had made a deal with a rival candidate, the Hesquiaht leader, Simon Lucas. Whoever came second of the two on the first ballot would drop out of the race to support the other. On the first ballot, Georges finished in first place with 198 votes. According to journalist Ian Mulgrew's July 31 *Globe and Mail* article, when the first ballot was counted "Mr. Ahenakew [...] could muster only 169 votes and was clearly shaken by the outcome." Having got 39 percent of the votes cast, Georges confidently advanced to the next round. According to Mulgrew, he talked between ballots "as if he had already been declared the winner." As agreed, Lucas withdrew in order to support Georges. On the second ballot, Georges captured 271 or 54 percent of the 505 votes cast, failing to reach the 60 percent threshold. Joe Miskokomon remembers that the vote went to a third ballot. "Georges picked up a few more votes, while Ahenakew's support melted away." Georges crossed the 60 percent threshold in the third ballot, becoming the AFN's National Chief.

David Ahenakew and Georges Erasmus couldn't have been more different. Fifteen years Georges's senior, David was of a different generation. Furthermore, their personalities and leadership styles and backgrounds differed greatly. One was from Saskatchewan and the other from the Northwest Territories. Georges was reserved and thoughtful, David brash and outspoken. Georges was less a political creature than he was an effective problem-solver, consensus builder, and strategic thinker. David was a political creature through and through. Georges was big-picture in a way Ahenakew wasn't. According to Konrad Sioui, "He had a global view about Indigenous Peoples of the world and about our place in the constitution, and he had a very clear agenda on where we should be going." Georges had long been known for his fabulous rock 'n' roll hair, while David was known for hair that hadn't changed since his days in the Canadian Armed Forces. It's weird that these two, of all people, ended up competing for the top job in Indigenous politics.

In Vancouver, Georges told the audience of Chiefs that political unity would be the first priority of his term. "The assembly has gone back into the hands of the Chiefs of this country," he said. "I see this as a vote which means that we intend on unifying ourselves across this country." Since its inception in 1982, the Assembly of First Nations had been divided into two factions, the Treaty Group and the Aboriginal Rights Group. The former conceived of the AFN as a vehicle to enforce and to build upon the existing agreements with the Crown, as articulated in the Numbered Treaties, while the latter group wanted to pursue negotiations around Aboriginal title and rights. This led to disagreements over strategies and priorities, as internal schisms concerning the constitutional talks illustrated. The group aligned with Georges believed it was crucial to get involved in the constitution talks and, as Gord Peters says, "used to call ourselves the BFN."

Now the BFN was running the AFN, and the BFN meant to clean house. According to Lyle Sayers, it started like this: "I was playing baseball. I was out in left field. I see somebody coming into the field. I look and here's Brian Shawana. He says, 'Come on, you gotta go.' He says he got a call from Joe Saunders. There's a new Chief, and he wants us to go and change the locks. So that was the beginning of my term with Georges, changing the locks at midnight at the AFN."

I remember telling my wife Sandra Knight that we would not have to move to Ottawa for me to do the job as AFN National Chief. She asked how that was possible and I said much of the work is travel to different parts of Canada, what does it matter if I start travelling from Yellowknife or Ottawa. Plus, I had just finished watching David Ahenakew work mainly from his home in Saskatchewan. It became apparent by Christmas that I was needed in Ottawa a lot more then I originally thought. At Christmas, Sandra and I decided that she would ask for a couple years leave from her job as social worker with the GNWT beginning April 1 and we would move to the Ottawa area. In March we went house shopping; we decided to buy even though we were only going for a couple years. I had no intention of seeking a second term. We had friends living in the country on the Ontario side that wanted us to live near them, so we spent some time looking there but neither of us found anything that we liked. We wanted hills, which we found on the Quebec side, so we purchased in

Chelsea near the Gatineau Park. Our two-year move ended up being a sixteen-year stay, which we mostly enjoyed. We took up cross-country skiing, which we could do from very near our home so long as there was enough snow. We were able to use trails in our neighbourhood that hooked up with the park trails. We would buy season's passes, which we always used. The house we bought in Chelsea had a Jøtul wood-burning stove on the second floor and, on the first floor, a very large, open on two sides, living room fireplace and a custom-made insert that also opened on both sides. It was so deep we could almost put four-foot pieces of wood inside.

One of the very interesting things for me coming from northern Canada was burning hardwood. Ironically, we had just finished putting down hardwood flooring in Yellowknife before we began to rent it out. The closest thing we have to hardwood in the NWT is birch, none of the oaks or maples that I eventually used for burning in Chelsea during my sixteen-year stay.

At Christmas we had decided to move at the end of April because we knew we needed time for us to finish the house enough to rent it. We ended up asking Sandra's parents, Tom and Margaret Knight, to come help us finish the list of things that needed doing. They willingly came and the four of us took on different projects to get everything done. One of my big jobs was to finish putting our Bruce hardwood flooring down. It was one-inch thick, random length and width, with three coats of flooring wax baked in. I had few tools like I have today for a challenging floor pattern. We have a living room–dining room area that starts at around thirty-eight feet and widens to forty-four with a fireplace in the centre. I was able to cut all my flooring with a simple skill saw and created tight seams, which I am still proud of today. What really took a long time was hand-nailing in the flooring, as I did not own or was unable to rent a flooring nailer. I had to rig up a system to press the flooring together, very labour intensive without the proper tools. When I tell the story about how much effort went into getting ready to leave Yellowknife, I normally say I was nailing down the last piece of Bruce hardwood floor as I was backing out the door. It is not too far from the truth.

My father-in-law Tom built the railings on our second-story landing or balcony and put clothes hangers in our closets and several other projects that needed doing. One of Sandra's jobs was to oversee what could be put in our shed while we were gone for a few years and to clear my home office. Unfortunately, I had tons of paper, some still in envelopes from the AFN Constitutional Working Group that had been sent out by our co-ordinator Arnold Goodleaf. A lot of the time the material that would arrive at my home I already had from the meetings I had just attended, but Arnold would not take a chance that we didn't have our material so he would make sure we would all get copies mailed to our homes. It took Sandra a very long time to sort through the material. In the end, between the four of us, we were able to get ready to rent our house. We decided that we would allow pets as we knew how tough it was to find accommodation for family pets. It did not take us long to find someone to rent the house. Over the sixteen years we lived in Chelsea we had many different people rent our home.

Georges found the return to Ottawa "very sobering." So much had to be done to repair the damage done to the organization. The AFN was now $3.6 million in debt. On his return, he faced one of his most difficult tasks ever, having to dismiss "many wonderful staff to reduce the AFN's daily costs, so we would stop going further in debt." He took pains to explain his decision at a staff meeting, but there was no good way to tell people they didn't have a job anymore.

By the fall of 1985 an audit of AFN's finances was complete and a clear picture of Ahenakew's spending habits was taking shape. Details first appeared in an October 6 *Toronto Star* article, "Ex-leader used assembly funds in bid for re-election, chiefs told." In the weeks preceding the election, at a time when the AFN was deep in debt, Ahenakew spent $32,000 on campaign charter flights and $5,000 on meals. Manny Jules recalls eating at a hotel restaurant during the campaign. "Dave paid for my meal. It turns out he was buying everybody meals. He was flying by helicopter to virtually all of the communities between Prince George and Prince Rupert. That's a hell of a lot of communities." In the week preceding the election, he spent over $18,000 on hotel suites. Then there was the $199,000 research contract with a Saskatchewan consulting firm that had close ties with Ahenakew. Nothing of any value came of this contract, as Georges soon discovered. Ahenakew and his people had been living large on the organization's dollars, making up for the operational deficits by taking dollars from things like the AFN's education research budget. Ahenakew countered that the expenditures were for legitimate business and, in any case, he wasn't accountable to the government's rules. "That's what Indian nationhood and Indian government are about — to do it our way, not what the government wants us to do."

As National Chief, Georges inherited a political agency deep in debt and split down the middle. To make matters worse, the majority government of Brian Mulroney, elected the previous September, was keen to reduce its expenditures wherever it could. The Assembly of First Nations got its money from the federal government, and the government was now in a mood to cut. Never mind lavish hotels — even the basic expenses of the AFN had to be re-evaluated. "We immediately decided I had to lay off a whole bunch of people," Georges says. "We looked at what it would take to bring the monthly bills under control." Then there was the money owed to consultants and contractors and First Nations organizations. Georges trimmed AFN's operations and was candid about the state of the AFN's finances. To his surprise, a number of organizations forgave debt. "It was wonderful how everybody pulled together. And, I mean, we had to work with the organizations to do that. They would say, you know what, maybe we can get away with $60,000 and write off the other $40,000. That really helped."

Georges took the same approach at the bank, with a different result. "We laid our cards on the table, thinking it was better being honest than trying to hide. The bank gave us notice: by the end of the day, go find another banker." (By the end of the day, Georges had.) Ironically, the bank had said and done nothing throughout the reckless Ahenakew years, but now the AFN was under a new management team committed to transparency and accountability, and the bean-counters wanted nothing to do with it. Georges set to trimming expenses, and the National Chief's office rediscovered the rustic charm of travelling alone, in coach. The AFN's financial problems challenged the new leadership in many ways, but the changes were welcomed by regional Chiefs like Konrad Sioui: "Georges was very honest, very honest. And that pleased me, because I was from the same school, and we were on a mission. We were not talking about 'I' — what's in it for me. We were talking about us, the *nous*, the we. Collective rights would be the first

Tom Knight (front, left), Sandra Knight (back, left) Harry Allen (back, right), and Doris Allen (front, right) in the Yukon, summer 1987.

reasons we would be sitting there, and not what's in it for, say, Saskatchewan. We didn't play those kind of games."

During the constitution talks, one of the issues to emerge was gender discrimination within the Indian Act. According to amendments of the act made in 1951, male children born out of wedlock to Status Indian men could register for Indian Status, while their female children could not. Most notorious of all was the so-called marry-out rule, which deprived First Nations women (and their children) of Status upon marriage to a non-Status man, while conferring Indian Status to the wives of Status Indian men. Pressure from Indigenous women, coupled with the equality provision of the Canadian Charter of Rights and Freedoms, gave rise to further amendments of the Indian Act. In 1985, Bill C-31 amendments removed all sex-based distinctions affecting entitlement to Indian Status. These amendments also restored Indian Status to women who had married non-Status men. Bill

C-31, however, kept in place measures to curtail the number of individuals entitled to Status. The second-generation cut-off rule in particular ensures that over time the number of Status Indians will decrease as a result of Status Indians marrying out. The child of an Indian and non-Indian is 50 percent Indian, and the child of that child is 25 percent Indian, assuming another generation of marrying out. Under Bill C-31, the third generation is not entitled to register for Indian Status.

There's almost two hundred years of history behind the Indian Act. The 1850 "Act for the Better Protection of the Lands and Property of the Indians in Lower Canada" was an early effort to determine who could be considered an "Indian" for the purpose of residing on Indian Reserves. In the mid-1800s, the definition of an Indian was broadly based and generally sex neutral. It included all persons of Indian blood, all persons married to an Indian, all persons residing amongst Indians whose parents on either side were Indians, and all persons adopted in infancy. In 1869, authority shifted from the colonial administration to the Canadian government. The Gradual Enfranchisement Act of 1869 was followed by an 1876 consolidation of all laws pertaining to Indians and Indian lands into the first Indian act. This act narrowed the definition of who is an Indian and introduced a sex-based registry outlining rules of descent through the male line. The government's scheme contradicted the matrilineal form of social organization used in many First Nations. First Nations children, for example, get their Clan membership from their mothers and are not allowed to marry someone of the same Clan.

By the 1980s, First Nations women had been fighting the Indian Act and its definitions of their identity in many ways and for many years. Sandra Lovelace, a Maliseet from the Tobique reserve, had lived her whole life as Maliseet. Then for a few years she was married to a non-Indian. When she returned to Tobique after the marriage to buy a home on her reserve, she was disqualified from doing so by provisions of the Indian Act that removed her Indian Status and therefore her membership in Tobique. Sandra fought this all the way to the UN Human Rights Committee, which ruled in her favour. She was one of many women who fought the discrimination of the Indian Act.

By June of 1995, Bill C-31 had reinstated the Indian Status of 95,429 individuals, 57.2 percent of them women. Under the post–Bill C-31 Indian Act, no one now gets Indian Status through marriage. "The discussion that got lost in the rush," says Georges, "was the termination provisions of the legislation."

A sort of blood quantum was introduced with everyone already registered being considered at 100 percent. From now on, if someone married out, their children would be regarded as being 50 percent. And if those individuals married a non-Status person, their children would be said to be at 25 percent for the Indian Status registry. If any individuals at the 25 percent level in the registry married out, their children would not have Status. Since approximately half of our people were marring non-Status people every year, it was a clever way to get support for a bill that would at some point clearly mean there would be no Status Indians left in Canada. To anyone that took the time to read the act, it was a "Termination Act" that would rid the Canadian Government of having to provide federal programs to Status Indians, because there wouldn't be any left.

Georges was the Northern Regional Chief between 1983 and 1985, when the discussions resulting in Bill C-31 were taking place. The discussions began during the Trudeau Liberal government and continued into the Mulroney Progressive Conservative government. "I had very good relations with the Native Women's Association leadership," Georges says, "and I tried to explain that this would affect all of us and our descendants down the road. But my words fell on deaf ears."

After being denied Status for so long, the women were so happy that reinstatement was happening that they didn't want to look a gift horse in the mouth. I pointed out that all we had to do was get a good accountant or mathematician to look at when we would be losing members again. We could probably be given a rough date when we would see the last Status Indian. It was simply a matter of time.

Speaking at the Dene Metis AIP signing in Behchokǫ̀, NWT, September 5, 1988.

Georges predicts that we will be hearing about a lot more women and men fighting to have their children recognized as Status Indians. Even as this book was in the final stages of production, he heard a story about a Dene woman who was fighting the Indian Registrar (the official in charge of the Indian Register and First Nation membership lists maintained at Indigenous Services Canada) to get her child registered as a Status Indian, without success. She was pregnant with a second child who she expected to fight to get registered also. According to Georges, "She married an Indigenous person from South America, which didn't help her with the Indian Act registry."

Education was a major issue during Georges's tenure as National Chief, sharing top priority with unity. The biggest project the AFN had was an education study by Rose-Alma "Dolly" McDonald, a work that Georges calls "timeless and still important." Harry Allen was the AFN's executive member in charge of the study and also replaced Georges as Regional Chief for Yukon and the NWT. The AFN received six million dollars to revisit the National Indian Brotherhood's 1972 report, *Indian Control of Indian Education*. "What we found," says the AFN's Director of Education at that time, Dolly McDonald, "is that not much had changed."

McDonald's 1988 follow-up study was titled *Tradition and Education: Towards a Vision of Our Future*. The themes of the study were quality, management, resourcing, and jurisdiction. "When I came in as director of Education," she says, "they had five rooms of data that had been collected for the *Indian Control of Indian Education* study. And one room was a mega lit review on *Indian Control of Indian Education*. And then there was another room that they researched models of First Nations jurisdiction over education, because during that time, we started to use the words First Nations jurisdiction over education." The report's release, McDonald notes, was timely. "Fifty-four recommendations came out of the study. The fourth volume was 'A Declaration of First Nations Jurisdiction over Education.' Right around the same time that we were releasing this, everybody was going crazy. There was demonstrations on the hill."

"Education was one of the issues that we held many protests over," says Georges. "Education funding meant employment for our people. It was a no-brainer." The demonstrations had to do with changes to funding introduced by the Mulroney government and set to go into effect April 1, 1989. The government plan was to freeze the $130-million budget for post-secondary education (an investment that, as Georges liked to point out, was already far less than the $350 million spent on welfare) and to reduce the number of months students could receive assistance. The AFN registered its displeasure in a forceful full-page ad, signed by Georges and published in the April 4, 1989, edition of the *Globe and Mail*. The letter begins:

> Dear Mr. Prime Minister:
> Your Minister of Indian Affairs, Mr. Pierre Cadieux, has announced that the Government will implement new guidelines for First Nations citizens for Post-Secondary Education effective April 1, 1989. The Minister is being ill-advised by his education officials. You yourself as

> Prime Minister made this public commitment to the First Nations on April 18, 1985: "Current funding levels of programs designed to correct the serious inequities which exist for Native people and Native communities will be maintained. Policies regarding Aboriginal people will be made after open, public consultation, especially at the grass roots level." While the department claims to have consulted over 500 Chiefs, educators, and associations, it is shocking that our students have been given only 11 days notice for changes which will adversely affect their education and curtail it for many of them.

The letter goes on in great detail, itemizing the social ills faced by First Nations, the "deliberate policies to destroy our culture, tradition, values and family life," and the worsening outcomes "since [the Mulroney] Government was elected in 1984." The remaining eight paragraphs lay out the case for reversing course.

> The citizens of the First Nations have no wish to be a burden on the Canadian economy. On the contrary, we are striving for self-government (to which you say your government is committed) and self-reliance. We wish to be masters of our own destiny. To achieve those ends we need to have our young people and even our adults educated and trained so that we may not only control our own lives but operate our own economies to the benefit of Canada as a whole. We wish to create jobs for our Peoples, to build them better housing, to obtain for them better health care … The key to that future is education … We ask you and your colleagues to set aside the new Post-Secondary Education guidelines which were implemented on 11 days notice. We are willing to meet with your Minister at the earliest possible date to review the situation and to arrive at solutions which would enable our young people to become

> productive citizens and better contributors to their own First Nations and to Canada.

To make matters worse, both the minister and deputy minister of Indian Affairs took the position that education was not a Treaty Right. Two paragraphs of the letter abuse this notion while further paragraphs note the wastefulness of the bureaucracy and the need for training and skills in the coming free trade era. The letter concludes, "The time to talk is now."

An indication of how things were going arrived on April 15. "Gord Peters and I led the occupation of Indian Affairs at 10 Wellington Street," says Lawrence Courteoreille. "They came in and arrested us around midnight, and they closed it down. Later on, all the charges were dropped." Gord Peters also remembers "going to that meeting where we were supposed to be a handful of people, meeting with Pierre Cadieux, who was the Minister of Indian Affairs." The handful of people turned out to be around eighty in number. More assembled out front of the building in a show of support. "People from communities all over wanted to be a part of that," says Peters.

> Everyone was screaming across the country. You would think it's a no-brainer. They keep talking about getting our people employed and getting them out to work, and all that. Firstly, you don't have to worry about welfare, because they're in school. I mean, give me a break. Fund every last one who wants to go, for God's sakes.

The protests, sit-ins, and hunger strikes had begun on March 22. Indian Affairs offices were occupied in Thunder Bay, Regina, Sioux Lookout, Edmonton, Lethbridge, and Winnipeg. On April 20, 1989, the *Globe and Mail* quoted Beth Brown (of the Canadian Federation of Students) saying that "department officials are clearly 'scared out of their minds' by the protests … and the widespread publicity they have garnered." Six students in Thunder Bay went on a hunger strike that was in its twenty-fourth day when they joined the April 15 Indian Affairs occupation. One of these six was future National Chief RoseAnne Archibald. "She was one of the students in Northern Ontario going to university," says Georges, "demonstrating for

Georges Erasmus

Outspoken Chief of Canada's Indians

by Kirsty Jackson

Georges Erasmus moves towards the microphone in front of the Parliament Buildings, as a fine drizzle begins. It's September 24, opening day of the Canadian parliament in Ottawa.

Article in First Air magazine *Above and Beyond*, December 1990.

more money for post-secondary education. The students were demonstrating in numerous places, and they went on a fast. We eventually brought them to Ottawa, because we were concerned for their health." The AFN issued a statement in which the National Chief expressed grave concern about the health of the protestors, watched over by an Ottawa doctor named Pierre L'Hereux, two Elders, and Linda Jordan of the Native Women's Centre.

Opposition leaders Ed Broadbent and John Turner pounded Cadieux, who in turn complained that he was being "held hostage" by the "unreasonable pressure tactic" of hunger strikes.[6] On April 24 the Liberal and NDP parties forced a special debate on the Conservative government's funding cap, thirty-five days into a hunger strike still being observed by Confederation College students and sisters Debbie and Melinda Sault. For weeks, Georges put pressure on Mulroney to intervene, tying a red ribbon around the sleeve of his suit jacket as a symbol of solidarity with the hunger strikers. By now, however, he was also telling the students, for whose health he feared, that they had done their part and that it was time to let other forms of protest take place.

On April 14, Minister Cadieux agreed to an April 18 meeting with the six Thunder Bay student protestors who'd given up their hunger strike, on the advice of Elders, and with Georges and other Chiefs. (The Sault sisters maintained their fast.) A spokesperson for the students, Eric Johnson, was quoted in the April 18 edition of the *Toronto Star* explaining the media were missing the point of the hunger strike. "It is not just over college and university funding for Natives, he said, but over the whole federal attitude of dictating terms to Canada's Aboriginal people, whether they agree or not. 'We're just not taking what is being handed to us any longer.'"

This quotation is a good reflection of the mood in late-1980s Indian Country. A book released by the Assembly of First Nations at this time, titled *Drumbeat: Anger and Renewal in Indian Country*, contained this paragraph in an introduction written by Georges:

> Sadly, as we head towards the 1990s, we, the people of the First Nations, have to admit that our relations with Canadian government have never been worse. Our rising expectations of recent decades, our hopes for a better future, have unfortunately turned out to be illusory, shattered by the grim reality that governments, whether Liberal or Tory or NDP, are still not ready to work honestly with us to resolve issues that have been outstanding for centuries.

By 1989, Georges was speaking candidly about the likelihood of violence across the country. In a June 7 *Toronto Star* article, Georges says that "the frustration of our people is continually rising. There are a lot of leaders who probably will not resort to violence, but who knows what leaders will do in the future." And then there is the famous speech, "Deal with Us Now," delivered by Georges after his 1988 re-election as National Chief in Edmonton:

> We say, Canada, if you do not deal with *this* generation of leaders, and seek peaceful solutions, then we cannot promise that you are going to like the kind of violent political action that we can just about guarantee the next generation is going to bring to you.[7]

Considering that the Oka Crisis was only a couple years into the future, these words may seem prophetic. But the fact was that the evidence of unrest and pent-up rage was already everywhere one cared to look. "I never thought that the blockade in Kanesatake was much more than many other situations where our people were demonstrating," Georges says. "I personally had participated in many demonstrations as National Chief — supporting fishing rights in the Atlantic, border crossing rights of the Jay Treaty, post-secondary rights to education, stopping the Meech Lake Accord — the list goes on and on." From west to east to north, Indigenous people were employing direct action to register their frustrations. The Haida blocked logging machines in British Columbia, while the Lubicon blocked roads in Alberta, and the Teme-Augama Anishnabai prevented the building of the Red Squirrel logging road in Northern Ontario. In retaliation for a police raid of their community, Akwesasne Mohawks took over the Seaway International Bridge at the U.S.-Canada border and Kahnawà:ke Mohawks shut down the Mercier Bridge at Montreal. The Mi'kmaq and Maliseet defied hunting and fishing restrictions in Nova Scotia. The Wet'suwet'en and Gitxsan fought for their title to the land; the Innu of Goose Bay, Labrador, protested the NATO low-level flights that threatened their hunting and health; and the Algonquins occupied Parliament Hill. Oka was simply another in a series of events, even if it happened to capture the country's attention in a unique way. In 1988, Georges was only saying what was obvious to Indigenous people across Canada.

It had taken numerous protests and a hunger strike to get the attention of Cadieux. Eventually he yielded to the pressure and signed an agreement to stabilize post-secondary education funding and to support communities that had run deficits trying to manage their education programs. "That was huge," says Peters. "I think it was probably one of the last times we've had real significant change to the post-secondary funding program. That was a biggie that Georges got to sign off on that agreement. We got to be able to pressure government to be able to create the change."

Meanwhile the constitution talks of March 26–27, 1987, focused on treaties and the constitutional amendment on Aboriginal self-government, a concept unresolved in the April 2–3, 1985, First Ministers' Conference, the first of the recently elected Conservative government.

> Mulroney came in with a big majority. We have two First Ministers' Conferences still promised. Mulroney, I must say, worked like a dog. And, you know, he got these really redneck premiers on side, seven provincial governments all in agreement. [The constitutional amendment formula required the agreement of seven provinces with 50 percent of the population, known as the 7/50 rule.] The proposal was an amendment of the constitution that said in Section 35 the inherent right to self-government was there, but that we needed to negotiate it. This was the "contingent self-government" proposal. And we turned the proposal down. So the next meeting, in 1987, was just a formality. He was saving all his political cards, because he'd already planned to deal with Quebec.

According to Georges, the March 1987 meetings "achieved nothing beyond speeches." It was a completely different story, however, when the premiers met a few months later to discuss Quebec's place in the constitution. Quebec was now under a Liberal government led by Premier Bourassa. He very much wanted to be the agent of Quebec's reinstatement into the Canadian family. Mulroney made it clear that no one was going home until there was a deal. The man who had taken the provinces as far as he could, when it came to the constitutional status of Aboriginal people, suddenly found the mettle to take them much further. For Georges "there was much to the Meech Lake Accord which was a slap in the face to Aboriginal Peoples." To begin with, Meech would now require unanimous approval from all the provinces if a new province were to be created in Northern Canada, where Aboriginal people are majorities. Another slap was the recognition of Quebec as a distinct society after failing to affirm the distinct status of Aboriginal Peoples. Georges was enraged by how little effort had been made to find solutions on Aboriginal issues in the four conferences.

On the bright side of things, Mulroney's self-government plan gave rise to the unity Georges had spoken about in 1985. Graham Fraser's *Globe and Mail* article of March 30 said that Georges was "visibly relieved that the federal proposal was so far from Native demands that all four groups could reject it unanimously." And reject it they did. Yvon Dumont, of the Prairie Métis, asserted that Native leaders achieved an unprecedented degree of unity at the March conference, "and that appears to be solidifying."

As early as February of 1987 the chances of an agreement appeared low. A February 20, 1987, *Globe and Mail* headline announced, "Talks on Native Rights Held up by Differences." At a two-day preconference meeting in Toronto, Nova Scotia tabled a compromise position and bureaucrats from the federal Department of Justice worked through the night to produce a document that could bring the parties closer together. The meeting only managed to show how divergent and irreconcilable the positions were. With the western provinces united against Native self-government and Quebec refusing to participate, Ontario held the power to make or break a deal. Ian Scott, the province's attorney general, rejected the Nova Scotia compromise and called on the Native groups to back away from their position and to withdraw their plan to define self-government in the courts rather than through negotiations.

The position of the Indigenous negotiators was that the right of self-government was an *unconditional inherent* right and didn't have to be negotiated at some unspecified future date with the provinces, who would be inclined to bleed the concept of force. And they pointed to the fact that Section 35 already recognized and affirmed "existing aboriginal and treaty rights," which surely included the right to self-government. Opening up these rights to further negotiation would only jeopardize them. In the end, they argued, the federal proposal didn't entrench any rights into the constitution. All it entrenched was a negotiation process. An editorial that ran in the March 27, 1987, edition of the *Globe and Mail* set out the position of the four national Indigenous organizations and concluded by asserting that "We will not accept a constitutional amendment which makes our aboriginal rights unenforceable in the courts and contingent upon reaching future agreements. Would the *Globe and Mail* accept an unenforceable contingent right to freedom of the press? We think not."

The federal and provincial governments held to the position that Aboriginal rights to self-government had to be contingent on political negotiations. Having arrived at this impasse, the constitutional discussions became an exercise in futility. Ontario premier David Peterson (who introduced a failed compromise, recognizing Native self-government as a constitutional right while also protecting the jurisdiction of the provinces) told reporters that it would be pointless to have another First Ministers' Conference when Native groups and western provinces were so far apart. "It wasn't as bad as when we first met with Trudeau," Georges says, "but we were just going through the motions."

The media coverage of the First Ministers' Conference on Aboriginal Rights accurately characterized the event as a failure. On March 28, 1987, the *Globe and Mail* reported that "a constitutional amendment would have established self-government as a right. Now that the hope for a protected right is gone, it leaves Native governments open to any changes insisted upon by the federal Government and vulnerable to pressures from provincial governments." The hope for a protected right was gone because the constitution provisioned a five-year commitment to talks, ending on March 28, 1987.

As Georges further notes, Mulroney saved his political capital for the push to bring Quebec into the constitution. "He basically said, I'm not going to let you guys out of the city until you agree on Quebec and the distinct society clause." The result of Mulroney's gambit was the Meech Lake Accord.

The Meech Lake Accord was a behind-closed-doors affair described by many observers as "eleven men in suits." On April 24, the leaders of the four national Indigenous organizations — representing Treaty Indians, Inuit, Métis, and non-Status Indians — wrote to Prime Minister Mulroney insisting on their participation in the meeting. In the letter, Georges said that "it is incredible that Brian Mulroney and the premiers can contemplate such major amendments to Canada's Constitution without us, especially when most of the agenda items affect us." The prime minister's office said in response that the immediate interests of Natives were not being discussed at the meeting. Smokey Bruyère, president of the Native Council of Canada, shot back that "Senate reform, federal proposals on a new amending formula and a variety of other items on various provinces' constitutional agendas will affect Aboriginal and Treaty Rights."

Georges was enraged by Mulroney's display of mettle when it came time to accommodate Quebec. Where was this resolve when they were discussing a constitutional amendment on Aboriginal self-government? A June 25, 1987, *Toronto Star* article reporting on the AFN's annual general assembly in Toronto stated that "more than a dozen chiefs condemned the recent accord to amend the Constitution as evidence that while the federal and provincial governments will take legal risks to bring Quebec into the country's top law, they will do everything possible to reject any similar leap of legal faith on behalf of more than 500,000 Indian, Métis and Inuit people."

On June 3, 1987, the premiers signed the "1987 Constitutional Accord" negotiated at Meech Lake on April 30 and at the Langevin Block (a government building that houses the office of the prime minister and Privy Council) throughout the night spanning June 2–3. This Meech Lake Accord proposed seven amendments to "bring about the full and active participation of Quebec in Canada's constitutional evolution." Most notably, Meech recognized the province as a "distinct society." There were also further commitments in the accord to Senate reform and fisheries. As for Aboriginal rights, too bad, so sad. Their distinct societies would have to wait for another day.

By December, the approach used at Meech Lake was being considered for a future self-government conference — not the strategy of locking everyone into a room until they agreed, but rather of a preconference negotiation of principles and a draft proposal that could become the basis for agreement. That month, government and Indigenous leaders met to discuss the possibility of another First Ministers' Conference on the business of entrenching the Native right to self-government. After his December meeting with Justice minister Ray Hnatyshyn, Georges told a *Globe and Mail* reporter that "the possibility of starting up the process again looks reasonably good," a quotation that appeared in the December 29, 1987, edition. But the reality was that the pressure to negotiate had dissipated and would not be revived. There was now a deal Mulroney could sell to the country, and the prime minister was all about selling deals. A former labour lawyer, Mulroney prided himself on being an effective negotiator. And like most politicians, he had a competitive streak. At Meech Lake, Mulroney did what his predecessor Pierre Trudeau couldn't. He cut a deal with Quebec.

For Indigenous people, the years 1988–91, roughly from Meech Lake to Oka, were angry, ugly, mean, and relentless. At a press conference launching the Canadian Bar Association report *Aboriginal Rights in Canada: An Agenda for Action*, lawyer James O'Reilly stated that "we are sitting on a powder keg." No wonder. The report itself concluded that Aboriginal Peoples have been subjected to widespread racial prejudice and injustice. Pressing another explosive metaphor into service, Liberal MP William Rompkey asked the House of Commons, "Is it the intention of the government of Canada to allow the ticking time bomb of Native rights in Canada to deteriorate to ugly situations?" An October 20 *Globe and Mail* headline warned, "Push on the Verge of Coming to Shove."

On May 31, 1988, Georges was re-elected National Chief at an AFN Edmonton assembly. His "Deal with Us Now" victory speech electrified the audience and got the attention of national media. Here, for example, is an exchange aired June 2, 1988, on CBC's *The Journal*.

> **Host:** Have you reached the point where you think violence is the only way?
> **Georges:** The point I was making, we come from a tradition of people where we warn our enemies. And normally we give them three warnings before we get to that point. And if Canada is going to look to what I said a couple of days ago in any logical way, the way they should look at it is, the Assembly of First Nations and the First Nations in Canada have given Canada the first warning. Now let's sit

> down and resolve things before we have to go any further is the point that we were making.[8]

The Chiefs were now united. A motion tabled at the gathering concerning Justice Minister Hnatyshyn's offer to finance preliminary self-government talks between the provinces and Native leaders (in essence, talks about potential future talks) was unanimously rejected. Nothing but electioneering, Georges told the assembly. Worse, he concluded, the offer would "put all the pressure on us to continue to lower our expectations." George Watts of the Nuu-chah-nulth Tribal Council thought Georges's speech was an understatement: "I think the days of pure negotiations are gone."[9]

The bitter taste of Meech Lake was still in Georges's mouth when he was invited to an October 1989 VIP meeting in Ottawa to discuss the celebration of Canada's 125th anniversary. One by one the attendees weighed in with their shiny ideas, but Georges had other plans. "I gave an off-the-cuff speech that was later called 'Nothing to Celebrate,' where I made it perfectly clear how displeased we were with the Meech Lake Accord and the general situation of First Nation Peoples in Canada." Georges's improvised speech lit the room on fire. So much so that an eight-minute excerpt was broadcast on CBC Radio's *Morningside* on October 16, 1989. Host Peter Gzowski introduced it like this:

> A conference held in Ottawa last week hosted by the Department of the Secretary of State listened to a wide assortment of Canadians talk about how, if at all, we should celebrate 1992. Nineteen ninety-two marks a number of anniversaries, from the founding of Montreal to Columbus's first trip overseas, to of course Confederation, which will be 125 years old. Each of the speakers at the conference — an impressive list that included Maureen Forrester, Lincoln Alexander, Antonine Maillet, among other people — talked eloquently and with some passion, many expressing important concerns: Maureen Forrester, for example, on the need to fund and recognize the arts. No speech, though, made

a stronger impact than one that wasn't celebratory at all. It was made with no notes so far as one could tell by Georges Erasmus, National Chief of the Assembly of First Nations. Here's an excerpt from that speech …

What are *we* going to celebrate? Are we going to celebrate that it took until 1959 before we could vote in this country? Are we going to celebrate that it took until 1968 that we could vote in Quebec? What are we going to celebrate? Are we going to celebrate the fact that our Aboriginal languages are not considered important enough in this country to be regarded in any legal way? Are we going to celebrate the fact that there's not a single court in this country, where if the only language you speak is an Indigenous language you don't have any legal rights there? And you will be forced to operate in French and English.

What are we going to celebrate? I don't like what has happened over the last 500 years, 125 years. I couldn't do a lot about it. Let's say the majority of the people in this room and this country couldn't do anything about it. But what are we going to do about the next 500 years? What are we going to do about the next 10 years? — so that when the year 2000 comes around, there are some differences.

What are we going to do about poverty amongst Native people. We don't like it when Canadians are unemployed. We're concerned when we're around 10 percent and more. We're concerned when there's a million people in this country that are unemployed. What about when 90 percent of your people are unemployed? I don't think we have a solitary thing that we should be celebrating about, unless we're going to do something different in the future.

It's really time for some change. It's really time that the European people and their descendants, and the rest that are here that are now Canadians, seriously begin to address the basic relationship they have with this land and the people that were here first.

We can do things differently in this country. We can be leaders for the world.

We criticize Africa, Southern Africa, and the racism that is seen there. And yet we have no examples at home. The problem they're having in South Africa is descendants of European people trying to wrestle with how they are going to live with an Indigenous population. In that case, the Indigenous people are the majority. And so there's paranoia in that white race that's there. But what's your paranoia? *We're* the minority here. Why can we not deal here with the problems that we criticize South Africa about?

Why can we not have a situation here where Native people have enough land and enough control over their lives that they can have some dignity? We have no reason to criticize anybody else. We have no examples to show the world. But it can be different, and it *must* be different, or the next couple of decades will not be the French-English problem. That will not be your problem.

You cannot continue to have a situation where people are lined up to get to the negotiating table, and maybe in thirty years, maybe in forty years, they will begin to negotiate. You cannot continue to contain that situation. What we have now in the way land is being dealt with in this country, we have treaties that are hundreds of years old, that are supposedly protected by the highest law in this country, the Constitution. And we have not yet fulfilled the land requirement in those constitutional legal documents.

Can you think of any other people amongst us that we would have that kind of legal document and we would still 100 years later be talking about whether we should fulfil that? It only could happen — it *only* could happen to Native people. It certainly would never happen to the

> Anglos. And the time has come, and thank God to them that they have the power now, it would not anymore ever happen to the French.
>
> It was an insult to the First Nations when the premiers and the prime minister of this country could walk out of a room that they were locked into long after midnight and they were going to tell the world that there were two founding peoples, that there was two distinct societies. My God almighty, those men were the same men, the majority of them for the five years previous, that people like myself had been meeting with. And yet they had the audacity, or the ignorance, to come out of there and not recognize that Canada … nowhere else, nowhere else in this world do the Indigenous people from here call home. And if we are not distinct here, where in the hell are we distinct?
>
> I believe we can do something different. We want to do something different. We are sick and tired of coming to events like this and being your conscience, absolutely sick and tired of it. We'd love nothing more than to be able to go around and dance and feel good about ourselves.
>
> But by God, we have too many real things to be concerned about.

The only thing left was to ratify the 1987 Constitutional Accord in Parliament, and in the legislatures of the ten provinces, by the June 23, 1990, deadline. Since polls showed that the agreement was popular with Canadians, how hard could that be? Quebec was the first to ratify, on June 23, 1987. As the June 1990 deadline approached, the remaining premiers committed to shepherding the agreement through their respective parliaments, with the understanding that matters such as an elected Senate, an amending formula, and Aboriginal issues would be sorted out at a later date.

Only, Georges hadn't said in his 1988 re-election speech "deal with us at some later time." For Native people, Meech Lake was simply another affirmation of Canada's willingness to build a nation that leaves Indians out in the cold. And it pissed them off. A good indicator of the mood was the June 22, 1988, *Globe and Mail* headline that read "Become More Militant, Natives Told at Protest." At a June 21 rally in Toronto, in support of the Teme-Augama Anishnabai blockade, Georges told an audience of about three hundred people that it was time to "stand up and be counted, even if it means acts of civil disobedience. We are saying to Canada, we are saying to Mulroney, 'We've had enough! We are going to change the rules of the game, and we are going to win at this game!'"

In an allusion both to the politics of Quebec and to the government's change to post-secondary funding for First Nations, Georges declaimed that Natives were losing patience with a government "that can spend a billion dollars to win a by-election in Quebec, yet cannot afford to send Native youths to university this fall."

The Meech Lake Accord included changes to the way that Senate appointments were made and provinces were created. Amendments of this order require the unanimous consent of the federal Parliament and the provinces, a very high bar over which to leap. Still, the Mulroney government could take comfort in the fact that Meech was well received at the time of its announcement in 1987. The problem was that a day is a lifetime in politics, and the deadline to ratify the Accord was 1,095 political lifetimes away. This gave critics plenty of opportunity to build up a resistance. Could this happen to the Meech Lake Accord? As Georges said about violent political action, you could just about guarantee it.

Sure enough, the critics attacked. The first among them was Pierre Trudeau, who objected to the special status given to Quebec and what he saw as the weakening of federal power in deference to the provinces. As time passed and the June 12, 1990, ratification deadline approached, support for the Meech Lake Accord began to unravel. What no one anticipated was that the eight-year constitutional highway would encounter an impassable roadblock manned only by a solitary Oji-Cree politician from Red Sucker Lake.

That Oji-Cree politician was, of course, Elijah Harper. According to Ovide Mercredi, he and Phil Fontaine "had a meeting with [Manitoba NDP leader] Gary Doer. There were other NDP members who wanted to say no, but our request was for the leader not to allow the other MLAs to say no, although they could have, and to have just Elijah be the one who voices that negative voice against Meech Lake." Today Indigenous people remember Harper as a hero, courageously holding up his eagle feather on behalf of all First Nations, Métis, and Inuit people. But behind the scenes, Elijah was anxious. "We had breakfast at the Charter House," Fontaine says, "and he was worried about his seat, because he was going to be challenged by George Hicks, another Aboriginal person for the NDP nomination."

> He wanted to be sure that he was doing the right thing. I told him history would prove him right, that he was on the right side, and that Meech was a bad deal. We had the last First Ministers' Conference and they didn't even really make an effort — and then, a couple months later, the prime minister rounds up all the premiers and he's not gonna let them out of town until they have an agreement. He brings Quebec into the fold. But they were throwing us out the door on the other side. So I knew that killing Meech was absolutely the right thing.

A series of accidents and technicalities uniquely positioned Elijah Harper to torpedo the plans of a prime minister and ten provinces. The ratification process required public hearings, which the province now had no time to undertake. The only way around this requirement was the unanimous consent of all the legislature's members. One dissenting voice was all it would take to prevent debate, and therefore a vote. Every day the Meech Lake resolution was brought forward by the Speaker, and every day Harper held up an eagle feather to signal his objection. "He was in the right place at the right time to represent us," says Georges, "and we were so pissed off with that agreement hanging over us." Georges could see that now was the chance to do something about it. "I reinforced with Elijah that he was on the right track, because he could have changed his mind in any one of those votes. And the thing was, it was set up so that they could avoid debate. The Speaker was asking for unanimity in the house. And so all you needed was one member to say, 'no way.'"

The Meech Lake Accord never reached the debate stage in the Manitoba Legislature. The Meech Lake Accord was dead. Newly elected Premier Clyde Wells therefore cancelled the proposed vote in the Newfoundland Assembly. Ironically, an exercise in national unity and nation-building set loose a number of centrifugal forces. Indigenous people were scandalized by their exclusion from Meech Lake and took to the streets. As commentators at the time noted, the relationship between Aboriginal and non-Aboriginal people seemed worse than ever. Indigenous objections to the 1987 Constitutional Accord tanked the deal, providing fresh oxygen to Quebec's separatist movement. For reasons that went beyond constitutional matters but which doubtless included them, Mulroney plummeted in popularity. ("Interest rates are higher than Brian Mulroney's polling numbers," Chrétien joked at a campaign rally.) The 1990s were a decade of reflection on the often brutal historical relationship between Canada and Indigenous people, beginning with the Royal Commission on Aboriginal Peoples and ending with the establishment of the Aboriginal Healing Foundation. As it happened, Georges would lead both.

The Kanesatake land dispute known as "The Oka Crisis" had its origins in a seventeenth-century French habit of stealing Mohawk land. The first missionaries in New France were the Récollets, who were soon tossed out by the English. Around 1630, the Jesuits arrived. But the business of ruling the affairs of Indigenous people truly got underway in 1721, when the Sulpicians established a mission at Oka and imposed the "seigneurial" system, a French word meaning "we're the boss of you."

The Seven Years War put an end to French domination of New France, and the Mohawks of Kanesatake saw their opportunity to dispute Sulpician claims to their land. They petitioned their allies, the British, to no avail. Over and again, the Mohawks appealed to the colonial authorities and engaged in acts of civil disobedience. The most famous instance happened in 1869, when a Mohawk Chief named Joseph Onasakenrat challenged the Sulpicians' exclusive claim to timber rights by felling an elm tree. Noting that their eloquent letters to the authorities went nowhere, the Mohawks took to shaking things up and burning things down. The Mohawks even issued an ultimatum to the Sulpicians, giving them eight days to leave town or else. In his later years, a mellowed Chief Joseph Onasakenrat lobbied his people unsuccessfully for peace. In 1910, the Supreme Court of Canada affirmed Sulpician title to the land, much of which had already been sold off to establish French settlements.

One of these settlements, Oka, became the occasion for yet another violent eruption at Kanesatake in 1990. There were actually two sets of events that led to the crisis. The first and better-known was the proposed expansion of the Oka Golf Club into a parcel of land called The Pines — known also to the locals as "The Commons." Kanatiio (Allen Gabriel) was at The Pines throughout the Oka Crisis and explains the events of 1990 as follows.

> In the late 1950s, the municipality and the province expropriated part of The Commons, which we know as The Pines today. People limit their knowledge of The Pines to the lacrosse field where the shootout happened. But to our people, The Pines or The Commons is a larger area that covers more territory than that. It includes the existing golf course. That's where our people used to pasture their animals. They took part of that, then they built the private nine-hole golf course, which opened in the early 1960s. In 1989 the golf course and the municipality announced a plan to expand to eighteen holes and to cut down the rest of the forest across the road from where I lived. The plan included a condo development, because the rage in Quebec was to build a golf course with condos or a ski hill around it, and then charge a whole lot of money. So it was going to be a high-end condo development. They announced those plans, and our people said No.

On April 1, 1989, three hundred Kanesatake members and non-Indigenous allies marched through Oka, and in August protestors crashed a press conference where a symbolic tree-cutting was planned. A frustrated municipal council agreed to meet with the Kanesatake Band Council. They talked, but nothing was resolved. On March 8, 1990, the Mohawks occupied The Pines and established a camp one day before the Oka municipal council voted to proceed with the golf course expansion. Word got around the community that a contractor was coming to cut down the forest, so a group of Kanesatake residents moved a fishing shack into a clearing at The Pines. The Mohawks barricaded a road leading into the forest, and soon there were other barricades, the most infamous at the Mercier Bridge linking the Island of Montreal with Kahnawà:ke. The municipality issued two unsuccessful injunctions against the blockades, and on July 11 they called in the Sûreté du Québec (the province's police force) who attacked the barricade with tear gas and concussion grenades. The seventy-eight-day Oka Crisis had begun.

The other set of events began at a Mohawk community called Akwesasne. According to Mike Kanentakeron Mitchell, a long-time Akwesasne Chief,

> Oka actually started in Akwesasne. The police were confiscating, aside from cigarettes, other criminal things that went across the border. It became a duel between the newly-formed Warriors and the police. When the illegal casinos open up, in the late 1980s, the Warriors become hired bodyguards to watch over the casino operations. And one of their first duties, I guess they made it their duty, was to go after the police on the Canadian side, the Akwesasne police. The community residents set up blockades to the casino entrances, and in the fall of 1989 this led to a Mohawk civil war, the confrontation between the Warriors and the anti-casino people. The result was that the external police, who were supposed to be the backup for law and order, were afraid to come to their support in any level.

You may be wondering, how on earth did Akwesasne end up in a mess like this? To make sense of it, there are a few things you need to know.

The first has to do with location. The answer to the question "Where is Akwesasne?" is that it's everywhere. Five provincial, state, and international borders cut through the community. Part of the community is in Quebec, part of it is in Ontario, and part of it is in New York State. (The "American" side of the community is called St. Regis.) In Akwesasne, a drive to your local grocery store can and does involve crossing provincial, state, and international borders, with all the headaches that this implies.

For decades Akwesasne fought for recognition of their Jay Treaty right to unhindered movement across the U.S.-Canada border, and for years the residents of Akwesasne were subjected to searches, duties, and confiscations as they went about their everyday errands. Add to this the assertion of Mohawk sovereignty (which by the late 1980s was being enforced by the armed Mohawk Warriors), and you have the elements of a jurisdictional nightmare. Akwesasne was the perfect place to create and exploit a law-and-order vacuum in which to move drugs and cigarettes and guns and just about anything else. The Mohawk Warriors emerged to take advantage of this opportunity. With the law enforcement agencies of five jurisdictions hesitant to take on the Warriors, the community devolved into violence and chaos as Akwesasne morphed into a narco-state. Residents were shot and killed, cars and homes were set on fire. "It was a massive, ugly period of our history," says Mike Kanentakeron Mitchell. As the death toll mounted, it became untenable for outside authorities to stand by. One particularly bad weekend in Akwesasne, from April 30 to May 1, witnessed the firing of three to four thousand rounds of ammunition, burning houses, an attack on an RCMP patrol boat, and two community deaths.

Requests for help went out to Prime Minister Brian Mulroney and Minister of Indian Affairs Tom Siddon. Hardest of all to move was the governor of New York, Mario Cuomo. The Grand Chiefs on both the American and Canadian sides of the border requested his intervention. One of them, Harold Tarbell, observed that "it was very clear that the Canadian government understood the threat to public safety, while Cuomo just shrugged." According to Grand Chief Mitchell, Governor Cuomo was finally persuaded to act. Together with the premiers of Ontario and Quebec he assembled an occupation force and for six months Chief Mitchell's community became an occupied police state.

The Warriors fled Akwesasne and went into hiding at Kanesatake. They were defeated and disgraced, regarded by many of their fellow Mohawks as little more than drug-dealing thugs who'd dragged the community into a needless and bloody civil war. Then, in the summer of 1990, they saw an opportunity to rebrand themselves as defenders of the people. Once again they would take up arms in a confrontation with the police, but this time, they surmised, the Warriors would be regarded as heroes. As Mike Kanentakeron Mitchell puts it, "The Warriors became the emblem of standing up. Their image, of the fast money grabbers to the defenders of Mohawk sovereignty, happened quickly."

When the shooting began at Kanesatake, Georges was in Yellowknife to oppose the final agreement on rights for the Dene and Métis of the NWT.

I quickly returned to Ottawa to get closer to the events. We were right in the middle of the situation I'd warned about in my 1988 AFN election victory speech in Edmonton. I could see that it would be impossible to continue with the status quo of extensive and protracted negotiations, or worse yet, simply ignoring poor housing, unsafe drinking water, poverty, poor health, high crime rates, and so on. Something had to give. At some point, a First Nation community somewhere was going to say, "Enough is enough." We were seeing it play out right before our eyes.

Georges knew exactly what was going through the minds of First Nations people across the country as they watched what was happening at Kanesatake: This could easily be us. AFN meetings among the Chiefs and executive became more and more emotional. Roadblocks went up across the country. One of Georges's sisters called from Yellowknife. "Guess where I'm calling from?" she said. "The regional Indian Affairs offices. We've taken them over!" Georges was in shock.

She'd never participated in a peaceful demonstration before in her life. Then she says, "Dad is outside, demonstrating." Dad? At a *demonstration*? That was a clear signal to me that the whole country was watching and was involved.

There's only been one other time when First Nation people from coast to coast to coast felt they were all together emotionally and started acting out, and that time was when it became apparent that thousands of children were buried far from home in unmarked graves. Catholic churches were put to the torch. Someone even started a fire in the Catholic church in Yellowknife. The fire was extinguished before much damage had been done. First Nations leaders came forth, asking for an end to these actions, but unfortunately after a short pause the fires have continued.

The Deputy Minister of Indian and Northern Affairs contacted Georges on behalf of the federal government. Canada wanted him to appeal to the Mohawks to end the blockade. "I made it clear that the AFN didn't support the use of weapons, but we were totally in support of the right of the Mohawks to defend The Pines and the graveyard." Georges was not impressed by the deputy minister's presumption. "I was insulted that he would even think that we would ask a First Nations community to abandon their efforts for proper treatment and remedy of their situation." Over the next couple of months, Georges would make many public statements and participate in demonstrations supporting Kanesatake and Kahnawà:ke.

Konrad Sioui was the Quebec and Labrador Regional Chief and the first point of contact at the AFN. "Every day I would go to the media," Konrad says, "and try to be as good as possible as a peacekeeper." The reality was that the entrance of armed outsiders — the Sûreté du Québec, the Ontario Provincial Police, the Royal Canadian Mounted Police, and the Mohawk Warriors — into a local dispute over land set the conflict on a new trajectory. During an August AFN meeting in Kahnawà:ke, ten thousand protestors took to the streets in neighbouring Châteauguay to demand the end of the Mercier Bridge blockade. "We arrived on the bridge," Konrad Sioui says, "and there were war songs. On the other side of the bridge, we could see them in Châteauguay hanging the effigy of a warrior. Every night at seven o'clock, they would burn a warrior. And I went out on the front and the warriors were armed, ready to shoot to protect the people in the back."

There wasn't much that the AFN could do, and in fact there wasn't much their contacts at Kanesatake wanted them to do. On his return to Ottawa,

Georges sent Ovide Mercredi, Gord Peters, and Lawrence Courteoreille to Kanesatake to find out how the AFN could help.

The people the AFN executive spoke to at Kahnsatake didn't want the AFN to be the face of their cause. According to Gord Peters, "They asked us for food and for support across the country." AFN Regional Chief Lawrence Courteoreille remembers that "we had a number of discussions, and we wanted to show our support. We showed the community that we were behind whatever they were prepared to do. And to us, to me, that was the most important thing that needed to be heard, because I've been to a number of blockades. And we always wonder if the support is there nationally. I think we encouraged them to continue their struggle and that we were there to support them in whichever way we can."

"I forget who led the talk," says Ovide Mercredi. "But they didn't really want our intervention of any kind. They just wanted some stationery, some supplies. They weren't keen to have the AFN in any way represent their cause. They just wanted us to be supporters, which I think is what essentially we did." The support took many forms, as Georges recalls.

At one point, the Confederacy of Nations decided that we should find ways to show support for the Mohawks in our different communities and territories through local demonstrations. Across the country, First Nations, supported by many Canadians, organized peaceful demonstrations. The BC First Nations decided to rent a large meeting space in Vancouver and present their culture rather than blockade roads. I attended this all-day event at BC Place, and it was inspirational to experience. It showed the world that the First Nations of BC were alive and well. I loved the positive manner in which support for the Mohawks was shown.

On August 6, the Canadian Forces were deployed at Kanesatake and Kahnawà:ke. Operation SALON involved 4,500 personnel, rivalled Canada's troop deployments in the Korean and Cold Wars, and exhausted the country's barbed wire supply. As the conflict dragged on with no resolution in sight, there were calls for Georges to act as an intermediary. The Bourassa government put pressure on Konrad Sioui to end the barricade.

Although support for the Mohawks had been strong across the country ("The number of calls of support that came into the AFN was just incredible, absolutely amazing," recalls Phil Fontaine) they could see public opinion turning sharply against them in Quebec. Patience was depleting and some in government wanted the army to put down the resistance. Kahnawà:ke called for an emergency meeting. The AFN pulled together the meeting and sent a contingent to the community. Ovide recalls the discussion at Kahnawà:ke as "probably the closest I've come to a meeting where people were getting militant about their relationship with the country."

Everyone was determined to make sure that the Mohawks were not defeated and that the use of the army was not going to go unchallenged. "They asked us to take action with them and support them," says Gord Peters, "so we did that." Asked about the country-wide demonstrations by a reporter, Georges responded that "we're rattling our chains. Perhaps the authorities have forgotten that all of Canada's major roads, railways, hydro lines, and water shipping lanes run through First Nations land." Georges added that it was bad enough that First Nations people started off with small reserves. Any time that land was needed for development, First Nation reserve land was taken. "That means we don't have far to go to create a roadblock on a major highway or railway." In Ottawa, Georges gave a widely covered speech in which he threatened to shut down the country from coast to coast. He pointed out that much of the country's critical infrastructure was near a Native community and vulnerable to sabotage. The next day, five hydro transmission towers went down in Southwestern Ontario. Georges was shaken, as he suddenly understood the scale of violence and destruction his words could provoke. From that point on he chose his public words with more caution.

When the military were called in, things got crazier. There were scenes of soldiers and Mohawk Warriors staring down each other in a face-to-face standoff. Every day and night CBC, CTV, and other news networks covered the events. We were connected emotionally to this little community, surrounded and under siege. Most of the AFN staff worked well into the night. Day and night, the calls poured in, one right after another. Canadians told us they didn't support what the military were doing. They said that they felt ashamed. Some were crying and wanted us to know that they totally rejected what they were seeing.

Georges appealed for a resumption of the talks, but the political consensus on the non-Indigenous side was that the Mohawk demands were unreasonable (Prime Minister Mulroney described them as "bizarre") and that, unless immediate lifting of the barricades and the end to the standoff were on the table, further negotiations were pointless. On August 29, the Kahnawà:ke Mohawks reached an agreement with the government and the Mercier Bridge reopened. On September 2, the army dismantled the barricades at Kanesatake. The roughly twenty Warriors who had remained on the barricades absconded along with sixteen women and six children to the Onen'tó:kon Healing Lodge, a drug and alcohol treatment centre that was known simply as "The Treatment Centre." On September 13, the Canadian Army prohibited deliveries of food and other supplies and cut off telephone service. On September 25, 1990, after twenty-six days without supplies, the last of the participants in the Kanesatake resistance relented. They were arrested, and journalists, whose attempts to send reports to the outside world had been obstructed by the army, were interrogated. In the chaos of people fleeing to avoid arrest, a soldier stabbed fourteen-year-old Waneek Horn-Miller with a bayonet.

The night the hydro towers and lines came down in a remote part of Ontario, I knew immediately, even before I was told by a Quebec Chief, that I had no authority to threaten Canada and that I had to modify my statement. Too many of our people were emotionally connected to the daily drama that was happening at the Treatment Centre and were looking to the AFN leadership for direction. It became abundantly clear that we were so connected as First Nation people with the Mohawks. People felt helpless and wanted to act, to punish, to fight back. They, too, were behind the barriers. If I called for an escalation, or for more actions like this, they would fulfill the request. I didn't retract my statement, but I made it clear that taking up the gun which we all had for hunting, and then using it for war, was not the way forward. I asked for peaceful demonstrations in support of the Mohawks. Together we watched as one night they came out of the Treatment Centre. In the chaos, a young Mohawk woman was stabbed by a bayonet. Thankfully that was the only physical damage to the folks that had resisted for seventy-eight days.

The Oka Crisis was over, and nothing had been resolved. Gord Peters says that "the federal government promised us that when Oka is over, we're going to sit down and we're going to hammer out a new process. Instead, they announced the four pillars." Peters is referring to Brian Mulroney's plan, announced on September 25, 1990, that the Aboriginal agenda would henceforth have four aspects: land claims, the economic and social conditions on reserves, the relationship between Aboriginal Peoples and governments, and the concerns of Aboriginal Peoples in contemporary Canadian life. As for Mulroney's view of self-government, "I will be very clear on this point: Native self-government does not now and cannot ever mean sovereign independence. Mohawk lands are part of Canadian territory, and Canadian law must and does apply."[10]

The events of 1990 prompted Prime Minister Mulroney to promise a royal commission, but for Georges it was too little too late. "I'm sure that, for those behind the barricades, it sounded like a joke. We were all glad that no one was fatally hurt coming out of the Treatment Centre and from behind the barricades, but I'm sure we all felt stabbed when a fourteen-year-old, Waneek Horn-Miller, was bayoneted in the chest, even though it was an accident." After Oka, the AFN was inundated with speaking requests. Everyone wanted to know more about what had happened, and why. People were now really interested in Aboriginal people. The AFN provided speakers, including Georges, to events across the country. This was, for Georges and others, a wonderful opportunity to educate Canadians.

Looking back, Kanatiio says that

> there was a time when we were working together. In The Pines, everybody would gather in the morning, we'd burn tobacco, and we'd come to decisions by coming to one mind. Eventually that started unravelling, because there

> were hidden agendas at play. The Warriors had their own agenda that involved cigarettes, and for the rest of us, it was just about land. There was one very powerful group in The Pines that was determined to have a shootout with police, as we found out later on. They had a specific agenda in mind. Then July 11 happened. It was the shootout, and we got locked down. And then everything just went from there. Everything we fought for, we gave up in the end. Today my people are destroying The Pines, tree by tree.

Something of great importance happened just prior to the Oka Crisis, at a June 1990 AFN assembly held in Whitehorse. Georges had agreed to convene this assembly earlier than usual, hoping that he "could perhaps have an easy summer, where I might take holidays." Instead, it would be a summer of battles that would culminate in the death of the Meech Lake Accord. "We had a good meeting in Whitehorse and, amongst other things, we heard for the first time about the effects of the Indian residential schools on our people when the Grand Chief of the Assembly of Manitoba Chiefs, Phil Fontaine, disclosed that he had been sexually abused at a residential school."

The context for this disclosure was a wide-ranging discussion of the AFN's future work. First Nations wouldn't be able to move forward effectively, Fontaine argued, until they'd dealt with a matter that was "a black cloud, and a plague in our communities." As Fontaine says, "I recall quite clearly a couple of women Chiefs coming to me afterward in tears. They told me what I'd said had brought back so many memories about their own experience in residential school. The National Chief, Georges Erasmus, came to me and praised my efforts on that day. But then I encountered another Chief who chastised me for raising such an issue. As we talked, I discovered he had been abused himself. That was the reaction of a number of people: denial. Even those close to me."

Phil Fontaine left Whitehorse for home. He knew he'd raised a sensitive topic at the assembly and that the silence over residential schools would have to end. What he didn't know was that a conversation intended for the AFN

Chiefs was soon to reach a much bigger audience. In October, Fontaine made a business trip to Ottawa. In a Toronto airport, he was approached by a journalist and a conversation that he says "was supposed to be off the record" ensued. The reporter had been at the Whitehorse assembly and wanted to hear more. Fontaine obliged, going into more detail about the abuses he suffered in the Sagkeeng and Assiniboia Indian residential schools. He also told the reporter what he was going to do about the issue of residential schools as a political leader. On October 31, 1990, back home in Winnipeg, Fontaine discovered that his story was on the front page of the *Globe and Mail*. "It hadn't been said to create a story," he would later reflect. "Now when I think back, this one issue overshadowed everything else."

For many of the people who were there, Georges's AFN years were a high point in Native politics. Gord Peters says that the period from 1988 to 1991 was the most memorable. "That's a critical era for me, and I think it's a critical era for many people. So many people would say that's probably one of our most productive eras that we went through. Because it became about us. It didn't become about what the federal government wanted. It didn't become about what the provinces wanted. It became about us and what we wanted. It was a great time of civil unrest for our people. To me that was huge."

"The time Georges was around, he was a real force in our lives," says Phil Fontaine. "And I'm not saying this because I need his vote for my next election." According to Konrad Sioui, "We had the best National Chief ever in Georges Erasmus. He was a very high-skilled diplomat, and so we felt secure with our National Chief. He had a lot of authority in front of anybody, lots of authority. And that's what we needed. He was never there for his own purpose. Georges would always say, 'Well, you invited me to a feast, make sure that everybody eats before you would serve me a plate. If there is some food left, I will eat. Otherwise, feed the people before me.'"

Joe Miskokomon recalls an era of "a unique blend of talent," the talent of great orators like James Gosnell and Joe Mathias. "There were young men and women just coming out of law schools and higher education that were eager to assist, and there was great energy around a sense of mission, a duty that we had. All of this focused energy, and a certain degree of calming of this energy. Georges brought that kind of atmosphere to the table." According to Pat Madahbee, Georges was a great strategist who brought things down to a common-sense level. "He was very adept not only at strategic thinking but at harnessing the strategic thinking. Georges wasn't a one-man show. He listened to everybody, which I think was one of his strengths."

Georges describes 1988 to 1991 as "a daunting time" but also a time that set a "really strong direction for people at the community level." At this point, it became clear to Georges that the work of the future was not going to be done at a national level, but in the communities. When Georges stepped down from the AFN, in June of 1991, his political career came to an end.

4

THE ROYAL COMMISSION ON ABORIGINAL PEOPLES

The horror of what became known as the Oka Crisis convinced Brian Mulroney that a royal commission was necessary to study the present and historic relationship of Canada and Indigenous Peoples, a fact affirmed by Minister of Indian Affairs Tom Siddon, as reported by Susan Delacourt and Rudy Platiel in the *Globe and Mail* on April 24, 1991: "Asked whether all this would have been taking place if the crisis had not occurred at Oka, Que., last summer, Mr. Siddon said: 'The summer events, I think, brought Canadians face to face with the absolute imperative of dealing honourably and generously with these questions.'"

A year later, in September 1991, Georges was the Royal Commission on Aboriginal Peoples' co-chair. Canadian Press announced on Saturday, August 3, 1991, that Brian Dickson planned to recommend a list of commissioners to Prime Minister Brian Mulroney "as early as Tuesday," and on August 26, 1991, Dickson's sixteen-point mandate was made official through an order-in-council formally establishing the Royal Commission on Aboriginal Peoples (RCAP). When Georges received the call from Brian Dickson, he had no plans or intention to take on new work. But here was an opportunity he couldn't refuse.

In early June of 1991, Georges resigned his position of National Chief at the Assembly of First Nations. He'd been elected in 1985, at a point when the AFN was divided and more than $3.5 million in debt. Year after year, the Conservative government of Brian Mulroney had imposed severe funding cuts on the organization, yet Georges had been able to bring the balance sheet back into the black. Now he felt it was time for a slice of retirement. As he often did, Georges retreated to Newfoundland, where Sandra had been raised, and set to working on a cabin for his mother-in-law, Margaret.

Georges didn't know it yet, but his next job, his next challenge, and his next change had already been set in motion. The first act of the newly elected AFN National Chief, Ovide Mercredi, was a breakfast meeting with Brian Dickson on the morning of June 12, 1991. The election for National Chief had stretched well into that morning when, at two o'clock, Ovide was finally declared the winner after four rounds of voting. Ovide wanted to talk about the scope and composition of RCAP, as well as about the kind of work it was going to do. "After the election I went to sleep around four o'clock and met Brian early in the morning. And when I met with him to review what he'd decided so far about RCAP, he'd decided to have a judge from Quebec to be the chairman of the process. I couldn't understand why he'd chosen a non-Aboriginal person, least of all a non-Aboriginal person from Quebec, when what precipitated the whole thing was the crisis that we now know as Oka. I rejected that idea, and I told him that it was important for a First Nations person to lead the commission. And so, we came to this conclusion that Georges would be one of the people to lead the process."

Georges has always felt privileged. Though work frequently and for a long, long time took him away from family, looking back he now concludes that the benefits of that work far outweighed the drawbacks. Georges and his wife at the time, Sandra, never had the retirement they had originally planned. They'd said that once the work was done, there'd be plenty of time for retirement. In the meanwhile life was exciting, it was challenging, and it was always changing. Each job brought opportunities to learn. The Royal Commission on Aboriginal Peoples would be particularly challenging.

I let it be known many months before my second term was up that I would not be seeking a third term as AFN National Chief in 1991. Not because I didn't love the job, but because I've always been of the opinion that no leader should overstay their welcome in a political position. Particularly if their role is part of a movement. It was my opinion that the First Nation struggles for self-determination, self-reliance, and a fair land base in the Americas, be they struggles for treaty recognition or recognition of Aboriginal title, are movements of the First Peoples. These movements needed to have many leaders over the generations. To keep relevant and strong, the struggle must continue to renew itself with new, young leaders taking over the mantle and taking us to new places and means of achieving our collective goals.

I approached the Winnipeg AFN Assembly in June of 1991 with satisfaction that I'd done a good job in the office of the National Chief. This was a very

Georges after AFN departure, working on the Newfoundland cabin, summer 1991.

well-attended assembly, as this was an election year and there were going to be discussions with the Chief Justice of the Supreme Court, Brian Dickson, on a Royal Commission on Aboriginal Peoples. I had a number of meetings with the chief justice after his appointment by the prime minister to recommend the terms and possible members of a Royal Commission on Aboriginal Peoples. I let anyone and everyone that asked know that I wasn't looking to be on this commission. I wanted some time out. The previous year I had promised my mother-in-law, Margaret Knight, that I would come to Newfoundland in the summer of 1991 and build her a cabin on the lands where she had spent her early years with her parents. They called this land "Beachy Cove." Once I was free of the obligations of the office of AFN National Chief, Sandra and I headed to Newfoundland, and we built the cabin.

Beachy Cove cannot be reached by road. It is situated on a large high headland that pierces out into the North Atlantic. It has hills on three sides, including the north, giving it a sheltered twenty to twenty-five acres of beautiful farmland. It has beaches on two sides that we used to access the site of the cabin. I bought cut lumber from a local sawmill and began to build a two-story cabin very near the edge of one of the beaches. Twillingate could be seen in the distance from our deck and windows. I hadn't worked solely with planks before. It was a delight to buy, transport, and haul the wood up the hill, and then to hand-cut the boards to size before nailing them into place. Sandra and I built the cabin all that summer, assisted by her mom, Margaret, and when available her brothers, Ted and Ken. From time to time her dad, Tom, also pitched in. We had no plans or power tools. We did everything by hand. Against the sound advice of her father, Tom, we built right on the edge of the cliff. Tom was suggesting we build where the old family home used to be, just below the south-facing hill, so the cabin would have maximum shelter from the North Atlantic winds. We wanted the view that the spot chosen by Sandra gave us. So Tom did everything he could to anchor the cabin on our chosen spot.

In late August, I returned to the Knight family home to find a message from the office of Chief Justice Brian Dickson. I called the chief justice and we had a conversation. He was calling to inform me that my name was amongst the co-chairs to be appointed to the Royal Commission on Aboriginal Peoples.

Tom Knight at the Newfoundland cabin, summer 1991.

Sandra nailing down the roof on the Newfoundland cabin, summer 1991.

Georges and Sandra sitting on the roof of their Newfoundland cabin, summer 1991.

I reminded Justice Dickson that I had told him, and everyone else, that I wasn't interested in the role. He laughed and told me that Ovide Mercredi, the National Chief of the Assembly of First Nations, had given him one name only: Georges. I said that I didn't know anything about that, but I guess I don't have much choice. He said I'd be getting a call from Prime Minister Brian Mulroney. Sure enough, not long after the phone rang, and it was the PM's office. The prime minister and I had a very friendly chat. He said, "I'm giving you a day job, Georges." He informed me that I was going to be working with Justice René Dussault. "He's not like us, Georges, used to the rough-and-tumble of politics. But he's a great guy, and you'll enjoy working with him." I must say, the prime minister was right. I truly enjoyed working with René Dussault over the next five years. We became friends for life.

When Sandra and I headed back to Chelsea, Quebec, in late August, we had a sided, roofed, and shingled two-story cabin with windows, a water-facing deck, and a front door. Margaret continued the work on the inside, painting and so on. She had put up a picture of her dad, whom she'd lived with at Beachy Cove until she was five, when he died of an infected tooth. I would have built this cabin for Margaret years earlier had I known how much she wanted to live at her old family site. I was very pleased with our summer's work. The next time I saw the cabin, she had installed a wood stove, kitchen table and chairs, beds, and other furniture. She also had done a lot of painting.

RCAP appealed to Georges for many reasons. It was an opportunity to do big, potentially transformative work, in every aspect of Indigenous experience. Dickson's sixteen-point mandate was exhaustive. As Georges now says, "No topic was left out, except maybe Aboriginal people on the moon." Also, the topics were huge. Any one of these sixteen points could have been an entire inquiry in itself. Georges would be starting at ground level, with something approaching a blank slate. Like the Aboriginal Healing Foundation seven years later, RCAP would have no staff, or protocols, or policies. The organization would have to be developed from almost nothing, though guided by the terms of reference. This, too, was appealing.

The consensus at the AFN was that Indigenous people should have a say in the commission's work and staffing. An April 24, 1991, *Globe and Mail* front-page headline announced "Aboriginal Affairs Commission Planned," and cited Georges's assertion that Native people would only agree to a royal commission if their leaders had a say in the terms of reference and were allowed to jointly select the members.

Brian Mulroney had already floated the idea of appointing Ed Broadbent as RCAP's chairman. Other names were circulating in the media. Ovide's skepticism about the commission was later affirmed when Jean Fournier, a former Indian Affairs official, was designated RCAP's interim executive director. At this point, critics couldn't be blamed for wondering if RCAP was going to shut out Indigenous people entirely. Still, as early as May 1991, reports were circulating in the media that Georges was going to be appointed. He dismissed the rumours and told reporters that not only had he not been offered the job, he didn't want it. Georges left Ottawa and politics for what he thought would be a nice, long stay in Newfoundland.

I was now free to take a break, which I had promised my wife Sandra, and we were both looking forward to some quiet family time.

Florence Erasmus, 1990s.

We'd planned a June 1991 AFN assembly in Winnipeg, where we were to have an election to replace me. The night before election day, after the reports were done and the previous year's financial report was approved, we had an evening banquet. Folks came to say goodbye, and occasionally they'd roast me in a good way. I remember the CBC reporter, Whit Fraser, gave a funny presentation about how I loved grey suits and how, when I first started in public life, I'd give long speeches in answer to reporters' questions. He added that, now that CBC Newsworld had been created to be able to fully cover in-depth stories, I was giving one-line answers. He had us all laughing. It was a good night of comments and gifts from First Nations across the country.

Over the spring and summer of 1991, former Supreme Court Chief Justice Brian Dickson, chosen by Mulroney to draft the RCAP terms of reference, set to work. Between May 18 and July 5, Dickson held dozens of meetings with Native groups and individuals, experts, federal cabinet ministers, all seven Native parliamentarians, and senior public servants, seeking their guidance. He applied "the most difficult deliberation" to a list of nearly 480 nominations for the positions of RCAP chair and commissioner.

Georges spoke with Chief Justice Dickson a few times, he says, and he gave Dickson a list of items that should be included in the commission's work. "I also told the chief justice that I wouldn't be seeking a role in the commission." As *The Report of the Royal Commission on Aboriginal Peoples* would later put it, Dickson's recommendations for RCAP's mandate "stand out like inuksuit, the Inuit stone landmarks that have guided travellers through the ages. They indicated the direction we were to travel, though perhaps not all the peaks and valleys we would encounter along the way. As we embarked on this voyage of discovery, we were guided by a vision of the renewed relationship that is possible between Aboriginal and non-Aboriginal people in Canada, and this is what we hope will continue to guide Canadians as they read our report, digest our recommendations, and decide on how best to forge our common future together."

By the time Justice Dickson met with Ovide in June of 1991, there had already been some valleys in the journey of a nascent RCAP. Both Georges and Ovide had expressed doubts over yet another government study of Native people. Ovide wanted immediate action on First Nations priorities, not years of waiting for recommendations that would be unenforceable. Georges wondered aloud if the commission was a ploy to garner votes at a time when a recession and failed constitution talks had earned the Conservative government dismal approval ratings. Indigenous leaders across Canada could see the potential of a commission, but only if it was conducted with meaningful Indigenous input and guidance. And at this point there was scant assurance that this would be the case.

The new National Chief expressed his concerns to Justice Dickson. Not only did Ovide insist on a meaningful and substantial role for Indigenous people at RCAP, he had a specific nominee in mind — a certain fellow who just happened to be in a state of semi-retirement, hundreds of miles away, pounding at the roof of a cabin with his hammer.

It has to be said at this point that a royal commission is no trivial affair. An instrument that's been used many times across Canadian history, the royal commission is a tool employed to deal with huge and complex matters not solvable by normal means. The royal commission is invoked to manage complex, big-picture challenges requiring long-term commitments and often social transformation. The royal commission has broad powers, including the ability to issue subpoenas and to compel witness testimony. It is typically well-resourced and staffed by leading figures of society. Royal commissions study critical issues that, if allowed to go unmanaged, could imperil the nation. Royal commissions are serious business.

For someone who'd been National Chief for six years, it would be simple enough to bring in the Indigenous people needed to do the work. There would be a lot of decisions to make, but this was nothing new for a man who at age forty-three had already built and/or led several organizations. Georges took July and August to work on the cabin, and in September 1991, almost exactly one year after the conclusion of the Oka Crisis, he started work on yet another challenge.

The work at RCAP was daunting, to say the least. The sixteen points in our Terms of Reference covered every possible aspect of life for Aboriginal Peoples: self-government, treaties, land and Aboriginal title, the Indian Act, Inuit and Métis issues, Elders, women, youth, urban issues, economics, culture, reconciliation. We started with temporary staff appointed by Canada and offices formerly used by another royal commission. I knew some of the commissioners, like Viola Robinson, but most I knew by reputation or not at all, like René Dussault. We had to get staff so we could begin our work, so it was one of the early areas where commissioners made decisions. One of the people that I wanted desperately to hire was Marlene Brant Castellano, a Mohawk professor and former chair of the Department of Native Studies at Trent University. I'd never met Marlene, but I had heard nothing but good things about her. I wanted her to head our research department.

I remember calling Marlene for the first time. She had just retired and had moved into a house built on land on her reserve. She told me how she had been planning her retirement for some time and how she was just going to begin it in her new home. I tried telling her how seriously she was needed at the Royal Commission and that these opportunities only came up once in a lifetime. It took a couple calls before she agreed to come work with us as research co-director. We hired David Hawkes to be the other research co-director. They ended up being a great team. Canada provided Jean Fournier, an experienced civil servant who knew his way around Ottawa, as our interim executive director until we chose our own. Jean was very helpful in getting us started. Tony Reynolds was eventually hired as our executive director and did a wonderful job in a very challenging role. Jerome Berthelette was our commission secretary, and I was happy to be working closely with him. We knew each other from earlier times, when he was at the Native Friendship Centres of Canada and I was Dene Nation president and then the National Chief of AFN. Together we were looking for allies in the Canadian Constitutional process. These hires were the beginning of our wonderful staff that we had the pleasure of working with over the five years of RCAP.

RCAP's first publication, concerning the inherent right of Indigenous self-government, preceded the public hearings as well as the broader RCAP research agenda. This study concerned the Charlottetown Accord. The constitution discussions had gotten stuck in the business of First Nation self-government and, unable to formulate the right of self-government in a way that didn't affect provincial jurisdiction, Canada turned to RCAP for help. The commissioners acted quickly, enlisting experts such as Brian Slattery to craft a historical overview that could inform and support the work of the constitution process. Traditionally, Canadian constitutional law was developed gradually by the Privy Council, says Slattery. "The provinces are sovereign within their spheres, and the federal government is sovereign within its sphere. And so the logic is that Indigenous Peoples are sovereign in their spheres as well. The question is, how do you figure out what the different spheres are and how they interact?"

The report was a remarkable feat of policy advice as well as an expression of unanimity among the commissioners. The process looked something like the following: First, the commissioners obtained a legal opinion from Slattery. They reviewed the positions held across Aboriginal sectors. Drawing on the expertise and experience of RCAP commissioners and staff, they deliberated until a consensus emerged. In turning out a cogent position on the inherent right question, and within a tight time frame, the RCAP commissioners demonstrated a capacity to tackle enormously complex topics and to reach a unified position. Unfortunately, the impact of this work was, as Research Co-director Marlene Brant Castellano puts it, a little fuzzy, "The clarification of inherent right moved the discussion log-jam, but it didn't appear in the referendum text, resulting in Aboriginal resistance and the failure of the Charlottetown Accord."[1]

I remember I wanted to get the hearings and the research started as soon as possible, so we needed to hire the key people. I wanted a report that was backed up either by what we found out at the hearings or through research, so that we would be on solid ground when we made our recommendations. A parallel process was the launching of the Canada round of the constitution. This round was to come up with the 1992 Charlottetown Accord on the Canadian Constitution. Early in the constitutional process, the parties became bogged down in a question: What would happen to the existing jurisdiction of the provinces and federal government if the Aboriginal Right to self-government was recognized? One of the questions was, did the inherent or original precontact rights of self-government and self-determination still exist after all this time? And if they did, were there any limits to them? Was it still fully sovereign, internally and externally? It became clear that if we didn't intervene with some quick advice, the constitutional process might not be able to proceed.

We very quickly began work on the concept of how the inherent right to self-government had survived the many years since contact with European powers and the construction of Canada and its many laws, including the Indian Act. This was basically a legal document that defended the many years Aboriginal Peoples had taken the position that we had never surrendered our rights to govern ourselves and that we have always had a Nation-to-Nation relationship with the Crown. We were very lucky to have the assistance of people like legal historian Brian Slattery and former Supreme Court Justice Bertha Wilson. It would have made life easier perhaps for many premiers and the federal government if Aboriginal Peoples had taken the approach that the source of the right to self-government didn't matter. But Aboriginal Peoples across Canada were saying the same thing — that the rights to self-government and self-determination are inherent and pre-exist Canada. Indigenous Peoples wanted to exercise their jurisdictions that can be traced back to their Ancestors.

We put forth a document on February 13, 1992, called "The Right of Aboriginal Self Government and the Constitution." In the commentary, we described how the inherent right, in our opinion, still existed and was likely in Section 35 of the Constitution. We argued that there were three jurisdictional spheres in Canada: Aboriginal, federal, and provincial. We presented a way in which three jurisdictions could live side by side, as federal and provincial governments now do, with some jurisdictions exclusive and others shared. We even presented possible constitutional wording or options that could be taken.

We spent some time explaining that the concept of an inherent right to self-government was not "merely technical, shallow symbolism or window dressing." We argued this went to the foundation of how Canada was formed. One view of Canada was that Aboriginal Peoples have no rights of government except what is given to them from Canada. The other view is that Aboriginal Peoples are the heirs to ancient and enduring powers of government that they brought with them to Confederation and still retain today.

This was in the early days of the royal commission, but we were able to speak coherently with one voice to help break the logjam in the constitutional process. The prime minister, the premiers, and the national Aboriginal leaders presented a constitutional package to the country in a referendum on October 26, 1992. This package included wording recognizing the inherent right to self-government. The referendum failed to get enough support to amend the constitution. Many in the Aboriginal community even asked Canadians to vote against the package if they supported Aboriginal Peoples, but that's another story.

Once our research was getting organized and we were settled into our new permanent offices, I wanted us to start the hearings. We decided we'd try to cover as much of the country as possible, no matter how remote or isolated. We travelled in three teams simultaneously, holding hearings in different parts of the country. I remember being told by one of the individuals we'd interviewed to head the public participation position that it would take over a year to organize one set of hearings, never mind three simultaneous sets. I knew we had to hire Aboriginal staff, and that's what we did. Patrick Brascoupé and John Morrisseau were added to the team. Sandra Germain was brought in from the Native Council of Canada, and she was assisted largely by Ava Hill, my assistant at the AFN and now at RCAP. In April 1992, we launched our public hearings in Winnipeg. From there we formed into three groups and started our hearings.

René Dussault was a lawyer, professor, judge, and former deputy minister of justice in the Quebec government. He'd been a legal advisor to a Quebec commission on health and social services, so he knew what it meant to be part of a commission. He was at the Court of Appeal when he received his call from Brian Dickson, and it didn't take him long to render his decision. He'd always been interested in Indigenous issues, and he could see that RCAP was an opportunity to improve the situation of Aboriginal people. It was also an opportunity to see an aspect of Canada he would not otherwise see.

René had confronted many of the issues Georges had, but from a government point of view. Like most civil servants, he was cautious and mild and deliberative. He was pragmatic and logical, and although he would dream about RCAP's potential, he'd been around long enough that he understood how politics work. Now he was co-chair of RCAP, a role he'd share with a firebrand Dene portrayed by the media as a Native radical. A firebrand René was not, but in September 1991 he went to his first meeting with Georges hoping for the best. And the best is what he got, because it turned out that these men of contrasting backgrounds had a lot in common. As RCAP commissioner Mary Sillett observes, "Georges knew what he was talking about, and Aboriginal people felt it. That's why they allowed him to lead, because he captured the essence of the issues. Georges and René were different, but both were intellectuals. When they spoke passionately, and commanded an audience, it was because they understood the issues and were very well read."

Mary makes a good point. If you were looking for a gig that provided lots of reading material, you could do worse than RCAP. Yes, the role of co-chair required vision and leadership, but it also helped if you were at least a bit of a nerd. Georges was an intellectual as much as René was, and they had an instant connection. What the media never knew about the Native radical from Yellowknife was that a good part of him loved nothing more than sitting at home with his nine cats and a book. Georges's love of cats in fact goes back to an early childhood memory.

One of the summers that we rented the Liske home, Dad found someone to chink the log house with a clay compound that might have had some grass in it. It was very interesting to watch being done. The man told my dad and me how to prepare and apply the clay substance, how to make it uniform. This definitely made a difference in heating the house, cutting down any draughts in the walls. A couple years after we moved to the Liske house, we moved again, this time to stay in one of my auntie's former homes. We were still on Latham Island, again on the east side. We had great fun playing in the water just across the street from us, and in the hills just behind the house. This was where I had my first cat, given to me by someone. The little one loved to sleep with me and was our little hunter if any mice made it into the house. I discovered I loved cats and years later had many.

René and Georges wanted to get RCAP going immediately. The first item on their to-do list was a series of informal meetings with provincial premiers, federal and provincial ministers responsible for Aboriginal matters, and regional, provincial, and territorial Indigenous leaders who together represented almost one hundred Indigenous organizations. The point of the meetings was to introduce the commissioners, talk about the issues within the commission's mandate, explain RCAP's approach, and encourage participation in the public consultation processes.

Even as a mere idea, the commission had its critics and detractors. Back in April, Indigenous leaders had debated whether to co-operate with RCAP and speculated that it was an attempt to placate militant Natives or to win votes for the Conservatives. Premiers were wrapped up in other things, top among them the economic woes of the early 1990s. Media obsessed over RCAP's fifty-million-dollar budget, just as they'd done throughout the May contest for National Chief — an $85,000-a-year position, as reporters liked to mention. René and Georges set to bringing leadership on side in a very RCAP-y way, first by listening to the concerns expressed and then by

Georges as co-chair of the Royal Commission on Aboriginal Peoples (RCAP), 1991–96.

offering solutions. "The reception was great," says René, "insofar as we could be helpful for them to solve some of the difficulties."

The biggest challenge was to get the public hearings out on the road. To do this, they'd need staff and a plan, and in the early fall of '91 the commissioners had neither. They knew they'd be travelling across the country, visiting cities and Indigenous communities, and their plan was to begin this work as soon as possible. When the commissioners began interviewing candidates to manage RCAP's public outreach, spring was eight weeks away. Georges recalls one of the leading candidates, who'd just finished doing similar work for another royal commission.

She seemed like a strong candidate until the end of the interview. We asked her about travel, and she told us it would take eighteen months to prepare. A year and a half, just to be ready to start. Well, we didn't have a year and a half. We told her our plan, to be on the road six weeks from that day. "Impossible," she replied. "It can't be done. It will take anywhere from a year to eighteen months just to get ready."

The time frame set by RCAP accommodated several considerations. Commissioners wanted the final report in public hands as soon as possible. The document would be massive, requiring a year and probably more to translate. The writing phase would take at least as long, if not longer. On top of all this, there would be one and a half years of public hearings. Even the most conservative estimate of the time required to reach these milestones provided only weeks to get things moving. Then there was an additional matter, raised by Allan Blakeney. He told his fellow commissioners that a previous royal commission, under the pressure of deadlines, had released its final report before all the research had been finished. Hearing this, the commissioners were insistent that the hearings and the research would be delivered early enough to be included in RCAP's findings and recommendations.

Eventually the commissioners hired the staff who pulled off the impossible task of putting the seven RCAP commissioners on the road in the time allotted. The hearings were organized by a public participation unit lead by Sandra Germain. Patrick Brascoupé would take over in February 1992 and then, beginning in May 1992, John Morrisseau would assume the role of director. Interim public participation director Sandra Germain recalls that

> they started staffing positions that were needed to get the commission on the road. One of them was public participation. I'm not sure how it worked, but I ended up at the time as the director for public participation, knowing that this was a huge, huge responsibility. And I remember thinking to myself, *I'm over my head in this!* We were able

> to sit down and literally map out the areas that the commission could visit, that were in need. And we had a big map up on the wall and, you know, Ava Hill [Georges's executive assistant] is taking charge. We presented a list of communities that could be visited by the commissioners, and with the exception of a couple that were quite isolated, they were accepted.

The seven commissioners broke into three groups, and those three groups held simultaneous hearings across Canada. Three rounds of hearings, five days a week, for eighteen months, with breaks between rounds. The public participation unit got mailing lists from the AFN and the Native Council of Canada, where Sandra Germain had been executive assistant to RCAP commissioner Viola Robinson, then the president of the Native Council of Canada. These were the days before cellphones and internet. Sandra and her colleagues sent flyers in the mail, ran radio and television and newspaper ads, worked the phones and fax machines, and hired community people to knock on doors announcing the arrival of the commission.

RCAP's hearings took just over nineteen months to complete. The first was April 21, 1992, at Fort Garry Place in Winnipeg. A *Globe and Mail* article of that date claims (without attribution) that April 21 was chosen "because it falls between the celebration of Earth Day and the ten-year anniversary of the patriation of the Canadian Constitution, which protects native rights." Both René and Georges are quoted, the former stating that the purpose of the hearings will be "to bring together aboriginal and non aboriginal people to begin setting out the details of a new relationship" and the latter that "the thrust of the hearing process will be to help educate Canadians about natives." April 21 also was one year, almost to the day, after the prime minister had announced his intention to establish RCAP, at an April 23 address to the Native Council of Canada in Victoria: "The government will proceed to appoint a royal commission to examine the economic, social and cultural situation of the Aboriginal Peoples of the country. The Royal Commission should not be seen as a substitute for constitutional reform which is another important part of the answer in resolving the problems of the Aboriginal Peoples."

The commissioners traversed Canada by jet, charter plane, boat, Ski-Doo, dogsled, car, bus, and pickup truck. Over 178 days of public hearings, running to December 1993, the commission visited ninety-six communities, heard from over two thousand people, commissioned over three hundred and fifty research studies, and received written and oral submissions, including via a 1-800 number where callers could make their views known in one of five languages: Inuktitut, Cree, Ojibwa, French, and English.

The first round of RCAP public hearings was a listening phase. The commissioners met wherever the community decided, bringing with them translators and interpreters and support staff. If someone wanted to meet with the commissioners privately, they made it happen. The meetings were largely unstructured, and although the mandate specified areas of focus, RCAP's purview was so broad that participants could talk about pretty much anything. And they did, sometimes well into the night, and even the next morning. One after another after another, community people told the commissioners about their needs, grievances, triumphs, disappointments, miseries, and hopes. Some of the stories went back generations, rehearsing a litany of crimes and abuses and injuries and injustices. After the commissioners left, they produced summaries and discussion documents that were mailed to the communities as a record of what had been said. According to the RCAP final report, "These documents served two purposes: they made sure that we had listened well and grasped the messages presented to us in communities across Canada by parents, teachers, health care workers, counsellors, Elders, school children, and many others. They also enabled us to begin the process of testing the solutions that were starting to emerge, helping to ensure that our final recommendations were firmly grounded in the realities of Aboriginal peoples' lives and reflected their aspirations and visions for the future."

Georges wasn't much surprised by what he heard at the hearings. Treaties, Indian Affairs, self-government, the Indian Act — he expected abundant testimony on these and many other familiar topics. Having been around the Native block a few times, he had a pretty good idea of what the issues were and what people, as a matter of course, thought about them. There was, however, one topic that came up a bit unexpectedly: the residential schools. In 1992 this was still a mostly undiscussed topic, despite having been brought to public attention at the end of October 1990, when Phil Fontaine's residential school experiences were on the front page of the *Globe and Mail*. Fontaine was Grand Chief of the Assembly of Manitoba Chiefs when RCAP held its official launch. RCAP commissioner Viola Robinson remembers his speech on that night. "He made some opening remarks. He had a lot of concerns about residential schools. That's the first thing he talked about. He kept telling us, whatever happens to this commission as you do your work, something has to be done about residential schools. I don't think there was a community I went to that the people weren't raising issues and concerns about residential schools. Later I thought to myself, you know, Phil Fontaine was so vocal and adamant about the work that needed to be done to address the residential schools. And he was so right."

As Georges and his colleagues travelled the country, at each stop someone would inevitably mention the residential schools. Once they did, almost everyone who followed did too. According to residential school Survivor and Aboriginal Healing Foundation board member Garnet Angeconeb (a future colleague of Georges), "Slowly but surely Survivors found a way to start talking about the abuses they suffered at residential school, and that was through the work of the Royal Commission on Aboriginal Peoples." For many Indigenous people, RCAP was the first opportunity to speak to the country about what they'd experienced in residential school, and many took advantage. The scope of residential school effects surprised Georges. "I wasn't blind to it, but I didn't realize the impact."

If Georges could be surprised, imagine what the hearings were like for René. "You couldn't be the same as when you started the work. At the end, you were a different person," he says. The human situation René confronted at the RCAP hearings shocked him, as it did the other non-Indigenous people among the commission's entourage. By his own admission, René "had a lot to learn about the reality and situation in the western part of Canada. It was a real discovery in a country that I had traveled before, but mainly through cities." The hearings helped to populate RCAP's list of issues to be explored more fully, and of course there was also the job of forging solutions. As they toured about, the commissioners listened to each and every speaker, no matter what they said or how long it took them to say it. Georges and René stood firm on the principle that the meetings would be informal and unstructured, and that the people themselves would decide what they wanted to talk about, without prodding or intervention from the commission. The residential school was a good example of why this approach mattered.

Still, Georges didn't want to hear only about the problems. He took to asking speakers for their ideas around possible solutions, sometimes to be told by incredulous participants that solutions "are *your* job." Over time, this problem-solution dichotomy would become a source of division, both among the commissioners and within RCAP as a whole. Of course the problems had to be discussed, and solutions had to be proposed. No one contested that. For some, however, RCAP was spending too much time listening to problems and not enough time pushing toward solutions. Having become frustrated with what he saw as the slow pace of the commission, on April 3, 1993, commissioner Allan Blakeney resigned from RCAP. (He would be replaced by Peter Meekison, former politician, professor, and political scientist from Alberta.) Blakeney's view, according to an April 6 *Globe and Mail* article, was that "the solution [part] was urgent, it would take much longer than we thought, and it was far more important that we start on that than that we continue to have hearings and workshops."

We decided that it would make sense to stop after each two-month period of hearings and do an assessment of what we were hearing. We sat as commissioners and told each other what we saw and heard from those that presented to us. We had a document created to summarize the issues we were hearing. We had an "Overview of the Hearings" for each of the four rounds. We sent this out to a long list of contacts that staff had created from the databases of Aboriginal organizations. This list continued to grow, as people contacted us through mail, telephone, hearings, conferences, and more. We conducted our hearings from April 1992 through to the middle of 1993. We particularly made sure that the overview was sent to communities where we planned hearings next.

Communication was very important for us. We released numerous documents to keep anyone and everyone informed of our plans and activity. A newsletter called "The Circle" was put out regularly. Four overviews of the hearings were sent out. We issued reports on numerous special events: the Urban Roundtable conference; the National Roundtable on Aboriginal Peoples and the Justice System (chaired by Justice Murray Sinclair); *Sharing the Harvest: The Road to Self-Reliance* (the report from the National Roundtable on Aboriginal Economic Development and Resources); *The Path to Healing* (the report on a National Roundtable on Aboriginal Health and Social Issues); and more. Early in the life of the commission we released a Commentary on Aboriginal Self Government, which was followed by *Partners in Confederation: Aboriginal Peoples, Self-Government, and the Constitution* and *Treaty Making in the Spirit of Co-existence: An Alternative to Extinguishment*. It was very satisfying to be involved in efforts like these reports, providing alternatives to extinguishments and explaining how original Aboriginal Title and jurisdiction had survived the passage of time and Canadian law.

We had a film crew follow us into a correctional institute, Stony Mountain, where we conducted a hearing with the inmates. The hearing was open to any of the inmates, but it was primarily Aboriginal inmates that came to the hearing and testified. One interesting fact that came out of these hearings was how many Aboriginal inmates had been in foster care. I have no doubt that if we'd asked how many had parents who were residential school Survivors, most would have raised their hands. After hearing presentation after presentation where the inmate started his story with having spent time in foster care, I asked for a show of hands. How many had been in care? The majority in the room put up their hands.

One very special report was *Choosing Life*, a report on suicide. I remember there was a rash of suicides in Aboriginal communities as we were amidst RCAP's work. It affected us so much that we decided to do a document on suicide that, in addition to giving the latest known information on why and to whom this might happen, we wanted a manual that might be a useful tool for family, friends, or community staff wondering what if anything they might do to help those considering suicide. The report explained that suicide has happened throughout history, and to all sorts of people, rich and poor. One troubling thing that can happen is clusters of suicides, when it seems a sort of pact is made amongst young people to support each other by also committing suicide. We tried to give wide circulation to the little handbook we produced.

One very important report was *The High Arctic Relocation*. This was a report on a very high-handed, arbitrary relocation in the 1950s of Quebec Inuit to Resolute Bay on Cornwallis Island and to Craig Harbour on Ellesmere Island. The purpose of the relocation was to assert Canadian sovereignty in the Arctic at the time of the Cold War. We heard testimony after testimony about how people were just picked up and deposited in the High Arctic, a region they had never travelled to or lived in before. The relocations separated the Inuit from the land, sea, territory, and people that they knew. This was a hard story to listen to, amongst many other tough stories that we heard. We recommended an apology, compensation, and a recognition of the contribution to Canadian sovereignty by the relocated Inuit.

A very important subject for many of us was what kind of justice system did Aboriginal Peoples have prior to contact? What would a revised traditional system look like in the future? Part of the research on this subject was to visit the Navajo justice system. We were able to witness a Peacemaker court in operation. This system was based on the idea of finding peace between the parties involved, including the families of the individuals involved. A young man had assaulted a young woman, he has already gone to jail and served his time, but peace hasn't been arrived at between the parties. The traditionally based Navajo court holds its session to see if peace or harmony can be found between the two families, with the help of a Peacemaker. The Peacemaker sits between the families and gently and quietly talks, first to one party and then to the other, seeking a path to harmony.

We presented a major report with a number of stand-alone, single-issue reports. In the end, we recognized the original deals that had been made. Aboriginal Peoples were Nations with their owns laws and styles of government, many built on the foundations of a matriarchal society that Canada originally treated as equals on a Nation-to-Nation basis, before beginning a colonial relationship. We argued for a twenty-year period of major investment in education, health and social services, healing, economic development, the building of community infrastructure, and the passage of a Recognition Act (an alternative to the Indian Act). We recommended self-government, a fair sharing of land and resources, and a recognition of rights without extinguishment. We predicted that if the major investment we were recommending did not get done, it would cost more in the end, in every way, be it in money or human waste and suffering.

We were very lucky to be able to put money into research that had not been done before in many areas. It was very satisfying to be able to build a foundation that others who came after us could build on. Much of our research was done in time to support the final report. In the end, the hearings, the round tables, and our research all supported our five-volume final report, provided in October of 1996. I was very happy with the massive piece of work that we all did together. I felt that our staff, our researchers, our commissioners, and the people who went out of their way to give us their views all did their jobs and did them well. We got to work and travel with wonderful people for five years.

Within RCAP itself, there was a division between the Indigenous and non-Indigenous staff over where to place their emphasis. Should RCAP be a more aggressive instrument of Native advocacy and grievance, as Georges had been in his AFN years, or an agent of healing and reconciliation? Georges addressed this rift in a September 1994 full staff meeting that was surreptitiously recorded and leaked to media. In an hour-long presentation, he argued for a balanced and realistic approach that accepted the co-existence of Natives and non-Natives and worked toward achievable gains.

This isn't to suggest that the commission was a house divided. Overall, former staff remember their years at RCAP as a time of collaboration and collegiality. So it should have been. The whole point of RCAP was to study the historical relationship between Aboriginal and non-Aboriginal people, the distortion of that relationship over time, the terrible consequences for Aboriginal people of that distortion, and the ways to make it better. The commissioners didn't want to merely outline the character of this better relationship, they wanted to enact it in their own work. Commissioner Mary Sillett recalls that "the people that we hired were really exceptional people, both Aboriginal and non-Aboriginal." RCAP brought together a team that reflected Canada. Roughly 3,500 people applied for the eighty or so staff positions available. Many, many more were contracted to research, write, and edit. The staff was a balance of First Nations, Métis, Inuit, and non-Aboriginal people from across the country.

RCAP research co-director David Hawkes recalls that "the initial plan was to make the institution co-equal, Indigenous and newcomer." Dickson had envisioned this model in his recommendations, which called for a seven-member commission of three non-Indigenous and four Indigenous individuals. This, he surmised, would allow for contributions from the various First Nations communities (Status, on-reserve, urban, and off-reserve) and from Métis and Inuit. It would furthermore provide for geographic, linguistic, and gender balance. As Dickson himself said, at the opening RCAP hearing in Winnipeg, "I was confident the diversity of background and experience of those I recommended would lead to fruitful discussions and broadly supported conclusions."[2]

Departing from Mulroney's off-the-cuff notion to appoint a single chair, Dickson arrived at the idea of two co-chairs, splitting the role between an Indigenous and a non-Indigenous person. The very structure of RCAP reflected its focus of study, a historic partnership that later transmogrified into colonialism. The idea seemed to be that if Aboriginal and non-Aboriginal people could work productively together, as equals, on a four-thousand-page report, maybe they could work together on other stuff too.

Georges had an additional concern about the composition of RCAP. His nightmare was that the commission would be able to hire only non-Indigenous experts and that RCAP would turn in yet another government study of Native people conducted by outsiders. Many others worried about that, too, complaining that Indians had been studied to death. Co-Director of Research Marlene Brant Castellano recalls Georges as particularly passionate about not only involving Indigenous people in the research but providing them with livelihoods and careers as well. "Georges wanted RCAP to reach the young people who had no life ahead, who saw no life ahead. I can't remember the exact words that he used, but he spoke of people with untapped ability and potential, and of unlived lives. He was very emotional about it. Georges's story is a story of spirit, of pouring your life and your passion into opening up a future for those youth that you grieve losing."

To Georges's delight, RCAP was able to recruit an abundance of gifted Indigenous professionals. "We gave people a lot of opportunity that wasn't there before. We helped them with their career." Some of the first people through the door — senior managers like Marlene Brant Castellano, David Hawkes, and Dan Gaspé, who was brought in to lead the communications unit — set upon the work of recruitment. Marlene and David were tasked with setting up the research unit, and as David recalls, "The way we did research was I started by getting in touch with each of the former directors of research for former royal commissions, of which there were quite a few still around. I sought advice on how we ought to organize, and the lessons they'd learned from their experience. There was the Royal Commission on the Status of Women and the Royal Commission on New Reproductive Technologies. The Royal Commission on Transportation. The Royal Commission on Electoral Reform and Party Financing. There was the MacDonald Commission, where Peter Aucoin was the director of research."

Together, David and Marlene identified leading researchers and asked them to draft a short paper of four to five pages identifying the credible research in their respective fields. In some areas (for example, land claims) an abundance of research could be had, while in others (treaties under New France) there was almost nothing. They compiled this information and presented it to the seven RCAP commissioners during a three-day session where areas in need of further research were identified. The result was a research plan including 450 studies, all of which were eventually commissioned and overseen by the research co-directors. Any research commissioned by RCAP had to be relevant for policy-making, forward-looking, a mix of scholarly studies and case studies at the community level, and completed in a timely way. A research advisory committee, composed of Aboriginal and non-Aboriginal scholars and two commissioners, oversaw the work and ensured that the research criteria were met. The research advisory committee drafted a four-page document titled "Ethical Guidelines for Research," endorsed by the research committee and adopted by the commissioners. According to Marlene Brant Castellano, "These guidelines attracted the attention of research agencies in Canada and internationally, and were influential in the subsequent revision of ethical guidance for federally-funded research involving Aboriginal Peoples."

According to Marlene, staffing of the commission required operating "like a telephone tree." First, they found people like Associate Research Director Fred Wien, "good people you could trust." Then these good people went out and found more good people. The commission actively sought out community researchers, who then led them to the people who knew the people who didn't yet have a name but who had potential. "That's the way we started out," Marlene explains. "With concentric circles. A circle of associate directors, unit directors, area directors. We asked everyone to make a list of all the people who they knew were doing good work."

For Commissioner Mary Sillet, "RCAP was like going to university and then having meetings and then many, many briefings and discussions." And then more drafts, more meetings, and many, many more discussions. Here's how Georges remembers it:

> We wanted the hearings to feed into our research, and then the research to feed into our work. Staff identified the research that had been done, that we could build upon. The writers would take a look at all the research coming in, for example on self-government, and they would come to us and tell us what the research was saying. We'd have two or three things on the agenda. In the morning we would start with one subject, and once they'd given us their overview, we would draw from our own experience. We'd look for what was relevant in the research, or what was missing, what the researchers needed to look more closely at. Then we'd send them away to do some more work. And on to the next subject. This time it might be women's issues, and after that, maybe urban issues. We didn't just analyze what was presented to us, we added to it from our own experiences. And as we got closer and closer and closer to the report being completely written, the meetings were less time in between, and that time got shorter and shorter and shorter. After a while it was just like one continuous meeting, and we always had to read for it.

Once the public hearings were over, in late 1993, the commissioners focused on the report. Drafting began in the fall of 1994. As Executive Director Tony Reynolds recalls, "The commissioners came in every two weeks, and staff would organize a report on work done in the previous two weeks. A huge volume of material flowed in to Marlene and David and their team. They had the job of organizing that." Marlene adds that "the final product really flowed through the consciousness, the awareness, the spirit of each of the commissioners working so hard to come together. It was my job to do a lot of editing, so that the length of the product could be brought down to something like a manageable size, because the first drafts were multiple times the 4,000 pages that resulted."

It's hard to exaggerate the amount of work that RCAP did. The staff and commissioners bore a crushing burden. They were able to do so because they were convinced of RCAP's importance and potential. Among the many people who came to RCAP with a powerful sense of mission was a Kanien'kehá:ka (Mohawk) from Kanesatake named Kanatiio, a name meaning "nice village." ("Kanata," or "village," is the word from which the name "Canada" is derived.) Back then, Kanatiio was more widely known by his English name, Al Gabriel. He took over the communications unit when Dan Gaspé left to join TV Ontario. Dan and Al were in Kanesatake during the Oka Crisis and had been working on strategy and land defence with the People of the Pines long before the warrior incursion and the July 11 escalation.

The Oka Crisis was not the only conflict between Canada and Indigenous people in the years leading up to RCAP, but it's unlikely that RCAP would have happened if the violence of the summer of 1990 hadn't occurred. The events at Kanesatake traumatized the community, shocked the country, and exposed an ugliness, a brutality, in the nation's character. So when Al arrived at RCAP, he had a clear sense of purpose. "For us, this wasn't just work. We weren't going in every day to stuff grocery bags or pump gas. We were the subject matter. We were dealing with our own stuff here."

In RCAP, Georges saw an opportunity that would probably never come again. He told Tony Reynolds, the executive director, that the commission would provide Indigenous communities resources they would need for the next twenty years, if not more. RCAP was preparing the ground for the battles of the future, and surrender was unthinkable. Jerome Berthelette (commission secretary and future assistant auditor general of Canada) told staff that, as far as he was concerned, RCAP's responsibility was to align with the weakest of the weak and the poorest of the poor. If RCAP failed, there would be consequences for the families and communities of Indigenous staff. Ottawa's openness to Indigenous-run organizations would be diminished.

By the end, Georges had read the final report, in one form and another, an estimated fifty times. He would get up at four thirty in the morning to read the latest drafts from the various writers. Then, at meetings, the writers would line up outside as the commissioners went chapter to chapter, sending the respective authors away with instructions for revisions. The latest drafts would come in, and Georges would take them home for review, and the process would repeat, roughly from December 1993 to August 1995. David Hawkes says he couldn't believe the amount of stuff Georges read. "I kept thinking, man, he's gonna start hitting me in the head, but no, he would go home and plow through it." Even more astonishing, René did the same with both the English *and* French drafts, ensuring that the content and tone were consistent across the two versions of the report.

In this drafting phase, RCAP faded somewhat into the background of the media landscape. However, there were moments when RCAP made the news. As a result of the special consultations the commission held, several interim reports with recommendations to the government were issued, beginning in the summer of 1994. Two of them — *The High Arctic Relocation: A Report on the 1953–55 Relocation* and *Choosing Life: A Special Report on Suicide Among Aboriginal People* — received particular attention. According to René Dussault, the report on suicide generated "one of the most heated discussions" at RCAP, while the report on the High Arctic relocation not only attracted attention but led to a federal government apology.

The task of going through the many contributions to the report and synthesizing them into a single, coherent unit fell to a small group of staff working with commissioners on final editing. The commissioners were looking for a precise tone: a voice that was calm but not passive, sensitive but not maudlin, alert to injustice but not righteous. Marlene Brant Castellano's skill as an editor in major portions of the final report was evident in her ability to synthesize and balance the academic and Indigenous worlds. It was no small task, as Marlene herself admits.

> There were moments — many, many moments — that were just so dazzlingly important and joyful. Then there were other days. Like the day I stayed up until three in the morning, improving on somebody else's work. I took it to the committee, and as committees do, people started picking holes in it and making the judgment that it needed more work. And I had a meltdown. I said, if it needs more work, somebody else will have to do it. I'm leaving. I left and took the train home, because I had reached that burnout point where I was so tired that I just could not do another thing. This was about a year and a half into the processing of data.

Marlene went home for a time and considered leaving RCAP, but then she remembered why she'd taken on the work in the first place. For her, RCAP was a calling and a role she had been preparing for all her life. On the day she made her decision to join the commission, Marlene saw a double rainbow in the sky above her house. "I don't look for signs, and I don't believe in signs," she says, but for her the double rainbow was a sign that "I could have a new life with family and also take up this responsibility."

Georges experienced a different form of burnout as a result of his time at RCAP. "I'd always loved to read from when I was a very small child. And you know, what the commission did was it burnt me out. I couldn't read nonfiction for years afterward."

As the final report came together, commissioners and staff went beyond analysis of past and present realities and into the realm of future possibilities and solutions. Anyone who has worked with Georges knows that he is the rare person who can engage in big-picture thinking without losing sight of the details. This was invaluable as he went page by page through a report that required blue-sky ideas but also academic rigour. People like Kanatiio valued Georges's ability to manage both the big and small: "If you talk to Georges, he's a small detail guy, and he'll remember the finest detail. If you tell him something now, when you change that twenty years from now, he's gonna call you on it. And he's gonna want you to explain why your opinion has changed. He keeps you on your toes that way, but he never loses sight of the bigger picture. And that's a trait that I've always admired and tried to emulate."

The details mattered to Georges because the facts mattered. David Hawkes's first impression of Georges was that he was tough and straightforward. "He was always willing to listen to all sides of an argument. He was always a great champion of the research. If there was a to-and-fro among the commissioners, Georges would want to know what the research said. He was trying to bring the truth into the decision-making process, not something we see much of these days."

Twenty exhausting months, and the massive full report was drafted. Marlene read through the five volumes to make certain that the positions developed by numerous writers, in the various sections of the report, contained no internal inconsistencies. Next, a team of editors and translators readied the documents for printing. The translation took a year. On Thursday, November 21, 1996, the RCAP final report was released.

Kanatiio recalls the last time that staff (the few who at this point remained) came together. "I think it was on a Saturday. Georges was signing the proofs, the official signatures that were going to be copied into the final report. We had a smudge, and we passed the feather around. Everybody was given an opportunity to speak, and when it came around to Georges, he kind of hesitated for a while. And then he burst into tears. Then it stopped, and he spoke a few words and passed the feather on. It was a bit of a shock for me."

Kanatiio wouldn't have been the only one shocked to see Georges cry. Georges was passionate, as anyone who'd followed his career could see. From a young age he'd had a public life in activism, community organizing, and politics. But if there were one word above all others that best described him, that word was "private." He didn't crave attention and in fact felt uncomfortable getting it, especially if the attention was on him and not on the causes for which he fought. When it came to matters outside of work, Georges didn't just play his cards close to his chest; few knew whether he even had any cards. To people who knew him only through work, Georges could seem a bit aloof, straightforward, unreadable, and tough. All business, all the time. In summation, not a guy who bursts into tears at the office.

On the other hand, RCAP wasn't a typical office job, as Kanatiio reminds us. Together, the staff at RCAP had seen a lot, done a lot, and been through a lot. Together they'd had big discussions and big disagreements, and they'd produced a definitive history of the Indigenous–non-Indigenous relationship in Canada, as well as a twenty-year plan to (as the summary report, *People to People, Nation to Nation*, puts it) "repair the damage to the relationship and enter the next millennium on a new footing of mutual recognition and respect, sharing and responsibility." They'd been across the country and seen the beauty of Indigenous cultures but also the ugly work of colonialism. As René said, by the end, no one who had taken up this work was the same. Fred Wien felt "it was a transforming ethical sort of experience." As Marlene says, the work and mission of RCAP was, at its core, a matter of spirit. RCAP began with Ceremony and ended with Ceremony, and Georges was understandably overwhelmed as he looked back at it all.

> I found the experience of working with all the different people in the Royal Commission an amazing experience. All of these different people putting, you know, their shoulders to the work and pushing it all in one direction. So often, we don't trust each other. But in this case, we all really came together, and it worked really well. The whole thing just all of a sudden hit me, that it was over. *It's over.* We weren't going to come back together as a team to carry on the work. All of a sudden, a dam burst, and I didn't have any control over it.

The final report opens with Kanatiio's rendering of the Thanksgiving Address, "the words that come before all else," introduced as follows: "Those associated with the commission experienced the strength gained when people come together in a supportive manner and for a common purpose. They felt the power that is generated when people use a good mind to come to one mind. It is in this spirit that the commission begins its final report with a thanksgiving address that, in one form or another, was spoken many times at the Commission and from time immemorial among the Haudenosaunee (Iroquois)."

The strength, unity, and common purpose evident at RCAP were doubtless a blessing. Unfortunately, the final report tumbled into a world with a mind all its own. To begin with, there were elements in the federal government that never warmed to the idea of a Royal Commission on Aboriginal Peoples. Tony Reynolds was lectured by a Privy Council deputy secretary who was "very insistent that I understand the limits that the Privy Council felt should be on the commission's report." The Privy Council furthermore objected to RCAP's plan to release the report in stages so that it could be more easily managed. They wanted it out and over with and had little interest in a protracted campaign highlighting the report's details. "I'm afraid that was one change we had to comply with," Tony adds.

The reception wasn't much better when Georges and René visited Prime Minister Chrétien, report in hand. Tony Reynolds remembers the co-chairs returning from his office, a day or two before the report was presented to the House of Commons. "I recall saying to myself, and to my wife, I've never seen two men so deeply disappointed." As far as Chrétien was concerned, RCAP was a creature of the Conservatives, a party now decimated and dismissed by deep unpopularity among the electorate. Georges had never been more discouraged in his professional work, either before or after this meeting with the prime minister.

The prime minister spent our meeting telling us stories of his days as minister of Indian Affairs, the good old days when Indian agents ruled Indian reserves. It was strikingly clear nothing was going to be done under this prime minister. All the dreams of those presenters, researchers, staff, and commissioners were not likely to be addressed unless someone else was in charge.

Georges saw plainly that RCAP was light years away from where Chrétien was. His mindset was still back in the paternalistic days, when the minister of Indian Affairs knew what was best. RCAP was recommending a total departure from that. "Chrétien was in the Dark Age, using terminology that hadn't been used for maybe forty years, and we were in spaceships."

Georges in a spaceship? Maybe RCAP had something to say about Indians on the moon after all. Meanwhile, back on Earth, Chrétien was cutting federal spending in an effort to eliminate a $42 billion deficit. It probably didn't help the RCAP cause calling for annual federal spending increases that would amount to an additional billion dollars by 2003. And then there was the hot issue of Quebec sovereignty, narrowly rejected in a referendum the year before. Chrétien had no desire to entertain Indigenous self-determination, an example that would be certain to electrify the Péquistes. On all the big issues of the day, RCAP was pointing in one direction while the Liberal party was marching in the opposite. Looking back, René Dussault concludes it was a bad time for the report to come out.

The official launch of the Royal Commission on Aboriginal Peoples' final report took place on November 21, 1996, at the Great Hall of the Museum of Civilization in Hull, Quebec. (Today, it is the Canadian Museum of History, in Gatineau.) The federal government turned down the commission's request to have the governor general preside over the submission of the report. Georges and René emphasized the point that Indigenous Peoples have a special relationship with the Crown, and that it was therefore imperative that the Crown's representative be present. The final report concerned nothing less, nor more, than this relationship. The bureaucrats cited scheduling conflicts and busy schedules, and that was the end of that.

On November 22, 1996, Commissioner Paul Chartrand bought five newspapers. The coverage of the RCAP report that day focused on the dollars, with headlines like the November 22, 1996, edition of the *Toronto Star*, which read "Billions Urged for Aboriginals." The Minister of Indian Affairs, Ron Irwin, dismissed the idea that money would make things better, while a member of the official opposition Reform Party, Garry Breitkreuz, complained in the *Star* article that "billions are being wasted on the so-called Indian industry." Bloc Québécois leader Michel Gauthier is quoted in a November 22 *Globe and Mail* article ("Natives Warn Ottawa Not to Ignore Report") saying that "it seems unrealistic in the circumstances that the government could add $1.5-billion to $3-billion to those budgets." The *Toronto*

Star article concludes by noting that "all but lost in the debate about money was the commission's call for modern treaties to confirm self-governing aboriginal 'nations.'" Not to be outdone, Margaret Bridgman, the Reform member of parliament for Surrey North, "equated out" the cost of the RCAP report per page and presented her findings in the House of Commons.

> Mr. Speaker, this morning the Royal Commission on Aboriginal People's report was tabled in the House. This report costs $58 million over five years and consists of approximately 4,200 pages. Equating that out to roughly $13,000 to $14,000 a page I do not think very many Canadians will consider that a bargain. Also the report itself on the aboriginal people notes that more than $10 billion is spent for aboriginal peoples at all levels of government. Yet the royal commission is recommending in the order of a 50 per cent increase in spending. There are three levels of government spending money but only one set of taxpayers. It is time to stop using these billions of dollars to line the pockets of the Indian industry lawyers and consultants. It is time to start putting money where it is needed, with the grassroots aboriginal people.[3]

Yes, the RCAP report recommends investments in existing programs and services, but there's much more in the document than that, as anyone who has bothered to read even a portion of it understands. RCAP's twenty-year agenda for change includes, among other things: a modern-day royal proclamation, stating Canada's commitment to a new relationship; legislation setting out a treaty process and recognition of Aboriginal Nations and governments; creation of an Aboriginal parliament; expansion of the Aboriginal land and resource base; recognition of Métis self-government, provision of a land base, and recognition of Métis rights to hunt and fish on Crown land; and initiatives to address social, education, health, and housing needs, including the training of ten thousand health professionals over a ten-year period.

In just 20 years, the revitalization of many self-reliant Aboriginal nations can be accomplished, and the staggering human and financial cost of supporting communities unable to manage for themselves will end. From that time forward, the return to the country will continue to grow.

Accordingly, we recommend strongly that governments increase their annual spending, so that five years after the start of the strategy, spending is between $1.5 and $2 billion higher than it is today, and that this level be sustained for some 15 years.

In considering the increased outlay we recommend Canadians should keep four things in mind:

- The agenda for change will cost Canada significantly less than a continuation of the status quo, amended piecemeal here and there. The price tag on lost productivity and remedial measures to make up for poverty and other forms of disadvantage is four to five times higher than the cost of the measures we propose.
- Our recommendations constitute an interactive strategy. To work, they must reinforce each other. Implementing self-government and acquiring an increased land base will generate a powerful momentum for economic self-reliance. Economic well-being tends to improve health status. At the same time, progress in healing and education will produce stronger, more confident individuals with the skills and abilities to manage businesses and run governments.
- Changes will have to be negotiated with and implemented by Aboriginal people — in the way they choose. This means that the pace of change will be determined by the capacity of Aboriginal nations and communities to implement their chosen priorities — a capacity that is still developing.

- Governments are reassessing their role in society and cutting back public spending. It would be a travesty of justice, however, if concerted and effective action to rectify the results of a history of dispossession were abandoned on grounds of fiscal restraint. A great debt is owing, and Canadians cannot, in good conscience, default on it.

There are also recommendations that have been taken up by governments or that are underway, such as the establishment of an Aboriginal Peoples' university, recognition of Aboriginal Nations' authority over child welfare, a public inquiry into the origins and effects of residential school policies and practices, and replacement of the federal Department of Indian Affairs with two departments: one to implement the new relationship with Aboriginal Nations (Crown-Indigenous Relations and Northern Affairs Canada) and one to provide services for non-self-governing communities (Indigenous Services Canada).

RCAP's recommendation 1.10.1 specifically calls for a second public inquiry, focused on residential schools:

> The Commission recommends that
> 1.10.1
> Under Part I of the *Public Inquiries Act*, the government of Canada establish a public inquiry instructed to

- (a) investigate and document the origins and effects of residential school policies and practices respecting all Aboriginal peoples, with particular attention to the nature and extent of effects on subsequent generations of individuals and families, and on communities and Aboriginal societies;
- (b) conduct public hearings across the country with sufficient funding to enable the testimony of affected persons to be heard;

- (c) commission research and analysis of the breadth of the effects of these policies and practices;
- (d) investigate the record of residential schools with a view to the identification of abuse and what action, if any, is considered appropriate; and
- (e) recommend remedial action by governments and the responsible churches deemed necessary by the inquiry to relieve conditions created by the residential school experience, including as appropriate,

  - apologies by those responsible;
  - compensation of communities to design and administer programs that help the healing process and rebuild their community life; and
  - funding for treatment of affected individuals and their families.

The "public inquiry into the origins and effects of residential school policies and practices" would be known as the Truth and Reconciliation Commission of Canada, and its work would begin in 2007. Over the next eight years, the TRC would travel the country, hear from around 6,500 witnesses, host seven national events, issue a six-volume final report, and create a detailed historical record of the Indian Residential School System. Its vast collection would eventually be housed at the National Centre for Truth and Reconciliation, at the University of Manitoba, in fulfillment of RCAP recommendation 1.10.3 that

> the government of Canada fund establishment of a national repository of records and video collections related to residential schools, coordinated with planning of the recommended Aboriginal Peoples' International University (see Volume 3, Chapter 5) and its electronic clearinghouse, to
>
> - facilitate access to documentation and electronic exchange of research on residential schools;

- provide financial assistance for the collection of testimony and continuing research;
- work with educators in the design of Aboriginal curriculum that explains the history and effects of residential schools; and
- conduct public education programs on the history and effects of residential schools and remedies applied to relieve their negative effects.

While some of the RCAP recommendations would be enacted, if the RCAP commissioners expected sweeping constitutional and institutional reform, they were destined to be disappointed. Looking back, their judgments today are mixed. For Paul Chartrand, the report has done little more than gather dust. René, despite his profound disappointment back in 1996, is more sanguine: "I find that the atmosphere is so much better. I think that we were instrumental for changes that occurred in the last twenty-six years." Tony Reynolds today considers the report to be a document that has yet to be fully mined. People need to take it out, he says, and reread it every five or ten years. He adds that "since RCAP, there's been a huge shift in the education systems and public understanding and public coverage of Indigenous issues. There's a long way to go, but boy, it's a different country now than it was twenty-five years ago."

Marlene Brant Castellano echoes this sentiment. "In the institutions, particularly the post secondary knowledge brokers, they are now saying that we need to redefine the character and the institutions of Canada. How far they'll go, we don't know. But I see that as a wave of change that is very important. And we did that, too." "I think we all agree as commissioners," says Mary Sillet, "that a lot more of the recommendations could have been implemented. But many of the recommendations required true constitutional change, and that's hard to get." Fred Wien argues that "when First Nations argue that they have the right to do this, or that, or the other thing, they don't need to wait for agreements and so forth. That has its roots in the work of the commission. It had that impact. In many other ways it was impactful as well. The kind of work that was done on residential schools, on the High Arctic relocation, was groundbreaking. Settlements ensued from that, an apology for residential schools, the Aboriginal Healing Foundation. There were all kinds of concrete impacts."

Once the final report had been submitted for translation, Georges was once again asking himself "What am I going to do now?" He and René continued to be involved in running the office and managing media interviews. They participated in editorial boards and continued to meet with political leaders and the minister of Indian Affairs. The commissioners decided to produce a summary version of the report, released under the title *People to People, Nation to Nation: Highlights from the Report of the Royal Commission on Aboriginal Peoples*.

In 2016, Marlene Brant Castellano and Fred Wien collaborated on a twenty-year retrospective of RCAP held in Winnipeg, Manitoba. They sought participants and funding for an event marking the anniversary (they didn't go so far as to call it a celebration) but also making the connection between RCAP and the Truth and Reconciliation Commission of Canada. They invited elected Indigenous leaders, TRC commissioners, academics, and, of course, RCAP commissioners. There is a report on the proceedings of that conference called *Sharing the Land, Sharing a Future: The Legacy of the Royal Commission on Aboriginal Peoples*, edited by Katherine Graham and David Newhouse. The work of RCAP, Marlene says, is like an underground river. It was doing its work over those twenty years, but that work was virtually invisible.

On October 31, 2021, none less than former prime minister Brian Mulroney, who in 1991 called for the creation of RCAP, told *Question Period* host Evan Solomon that the commission "articulated the solution to the challenge Canada faces in dealing for justice with our Aboriginal people, which has to be resolved before anything else can be moved, and the answers are there in the Royal Commission report, and they've been neglected by subsequent governments since 1996, with very little happening, but the solution is there. A government just has to sit down and read that Royal Commission report, and say, hey, I'm going to implement most of this, and I'm going to do it on a priority basis. That's the answer."

5

THE ABORIGINAL HEALING FOUNDATION

Since the release of the Royal Commission on Aboriginal Peoples' final report, in November 1996, the Assembly of First Nations had been pushing the federal government for a tangible response. Indian Affairs Minister Jane Stewart had been approached by National Chief Phil Fontaine, who encouraged her to do something big, and out of their conversations the notion of a government apology and a fund addressing the Indian Residential School System took shape. At some point in 1997, Jane Stewart brought the proposal to cabinet and had several conversations with Paul Martin, the minister of finance. Martin was intrigued, but not persuaded. He recalls, in a 2011 interview, that "there was not a great deal of support for putting up 350 million dollars for anything in the Department of Finance. If you're in the government, you know that the Department of Finance does not spend money easily. Jane came to see me and made the argument very strongly that this healing foundation was an absolute necessity if we were going to begin what was going to be the long road back from residential schools."

Martin didn't say "yes" to the minister of Indian Affairs, but he didn't say "no" either. He told Stewart that he wanted a follow-up meeting with her and

Phil Fontaine. He was sympathetic to the proposal but skeptical of spending a large amount on healing at a time the government was cutting costs across departments to manage its debt. In the space of an afternoon, Paul Martin listened as Phil Fontaine explained why the government should put resources into a healing foundation. According to Martin, the National Chief made the argument "as cogently as I've ever heard it." He challenged the minister to — as Paul Martin puts it — get out of his own skin and put himself in the skin of those who went to the residential schools. "I remember that decision," he says. "It was long." At the end of the day he told Stewart, "I think you're right. The Department of Finance will provide the funding to do it."

Georges was in the midst of a long-overdue holiday when Jane Stewart issued the Statement of Reconciliation and announced the government's $350-million healing fund, as part of *Gathering Strength — Canada's Aboriginal Action Plan*. Delivered on January 7, 1998, the statement began: "Elders, Chiefs, commissioners, my colleagues, leaders, honoured guests, ladies and gentlemen. I have been looking forward to this opportunity to speak to you about the work of the Royal Commission on Aboriginal Peoples and to speak in the broadest terms about the relationships between Aboriginal and non-Aboriginal people in this country. We are here to share what we have learned from the Commission and outline the direction we intend to take, using the insight we now have as a result of its powerful report."

Jane Stewart recalls the day as an "unbelievably emotional time." Her Statement of Reconciliation retraced "our history with respect to the treatment of Aboriginal people" and "the legacies of the past," focusing on the Indian Residential School System. Her audience included Indigenous politicians Harry Daniels (president of the Congress of Aboriginal Peoples) and Marilyn Buffalo (president of Native Women's Association of Canada), the latter immediately dismissing the statement as worthless. The anger in the room was palpable, leading the minister to wonder, "What have I done?" In the years ahead, January 7, 1998, would be a controversial and divisive day among residential school Survivors, some of them embracing the apology and others denying that it had even been one. Stewart herself felt comfortable with the wording of the Statement of Reconciliation and believed it to be an apology "in everything except name."

In early January 1998, when Minister Jane Stewart made public the response of the Canadian government to the RCAP Report, I was immensely disappointed by how little the government was prepared to do. Commissioners, staff, and researchers had all poured their hearts and souls into the RCAP final report and the supporting material. The report had covered every conceivable issue before the country that needed dealing with to achieve reconciliation and justice, most of these issues long-standing, but the government response was completely silent on everything except for a healing fund. There was no way I wanted to lose this fund, as inadequate as it was to do the job.

Georges didn't know it yet, but the next sixteen years of his life would be shaped by *Gathering Strength*, just as the last six years of his life had shaped *Gathering Strength*. In 1996, Georges looked back on the Royal Commission hearings held across Canada and was struck by the prevalence of residential schools in the testimony of witnesses. Between 1991 and 1996, RCAP would spend seventeen million dollars on research, much of it focused on the Indian Residential School System. As he travelled the country, Georges expected to hear about the Indian Act, land claims, poverty, self-government, health, the justice system, and many other topics. The residential schools came as something of a surprise — not because some people were talking about them, but because nearly everyone was. Volume 1 (*Looking Forward, Looking Back*), Chapter 10 of the RCAP final report, authored by Trent University professor Dr. John Milloy, focused on the Indian Residential School System and provided one of the earliest comprehensive academic overviews of what Prime Minister Stephen Harper would later, on June 11, 2008, call "a sad chapter in our history."

The *Gathering Strength* document begins with an evocation of RCAP, whose four-thousand-page final report had been released just over a year earlier: "As the Royal Commission states in its final report, before the renewal of the relationship can begin, 'a great cleansing of the wounds of the past must take place.' It is for this reason that Gathering Strength begins with a Statement of Reconciliation in which the Government of Canada formally acknowledges and expresses regret for the historic injustices experienced by Aboriginal people."

Throughout the months following the completion of the Royal Commission on Aboriginal Peoples' final report (in late 1995 — a year would be spent on the French translation) Georges had been extremely busy giving interviews, travelling, and meeting with Indigenous politicians and community leaders. An interim document, *People to People, Nation to Nation*, had been released in anticipation of the full report and in October 1996, Co-Chairs Georges Erasmus and René Dussault delivered a lengthy address at the official launch in Ottawa. In his portion of the speech, Georges summarized the scope and ambition of RCAP:

> The terms of reference the Government of Canada through the advice of the Right Honourable Brian Dickson set for this Commission were ambitious reflecting the depth of the challenge this country has yet to meet. We were given an unprecedented mandate. And we embarked upon an unprecedented process. We criss-crossed the country, often working in three separate teams. By the end of 1993, we had visited 96 communities, held 178 days of hearings, heard briefs from 2,067 people and accumulated more than 76,000 pages of testimony. The power of the messages unfiltered, forthright, confidently expressed in community surroundings was extraordinary. Moreover, we commissioned over 350 research projects.[1]

Even Georges's partial and cursory description sounds exhausting, and so it was. By 1998 Georges was knackered and, as he had been at the end of his National Chief tenure, ready for a holiday. In early 1998 he had gone into hiding, anxious to escape public view. The Royal Commission on Aboriginal Peoples continued to operate an office and to take calls, but having completed his official duties, Georges had stepped out of the limelight. Jane Stewart's announcement of a healing fund occurred precisely in the middle of the Great Ice Storm of 1998, a massive weather event along the east coast of North America affecting parts of Ontario, Quebec, New Brunswick, Nova Scotia, New York, and Maine. Like many others, Georges was coping with the effects of the storm when he received a desperate call from an official in the Department of Indian Affairs, requesting Georges's involvement in negotiations to establish a healing foundation. "You have to get involved in this," the official said. "I don't have to get involved in anything!" Georges replied.

Only minutes after he had disappointed this official from Indian Affairs, Georges received another call. This time it was the National Chief, who knew Georges but more important, understood how to persuade him. "I'm not looking for a job!" Georges told Phil. "I know, Georges," he replied. "But we're going to lose the money if we don't get an agreement. It's got to be done, or we're going to lose everything." Phil wasn't going to take "no" as an answer. He knew that Georges was the man for this job. He had enormous respect for his AFN predecessor and well understood the important role RCAP had played in securing a healing fund for the Survivors of residential schools. He valued Georges's accomplishments. "People in my position really build on the good work of our predecessors," Phil says. "And we may not have been able to convince the government to do the Statement of Reconciliation and allocate 350 million dollars for the healing fund, if not for Georges and the work his good people did with RCAP."

Phil accepted that in politics it's impossible to please everyone. The Statement of Reconciliation had its detractors, and for some even the $350-million federal commitment to a healing fund was a scandal. There were those who believed that $350 million wasn't nearly enough, and others who felt the money should go directly to Survivors in the form of compensation. In any case, it was now just under two months from the end of the fiscal year. By April 1, 1998, there would either be an entity established to receive this healing fund, or the money would go back into the federal government's Consolidated Revenue Fund and that would be the end of that. It was time for the rubber to hit the road. The Indian Affairs official had called Georges in a panic because time was running out to negotiate a funding agreement with Canada and to do the complicated work of setting up an appropriate entity under the Canada Corporations Act. Georges Erasmus was the logical person to lead this effort, and he wasn't interested.

Phil conveyed the urgency of the situation and appealed to Georges's sense of personal responsibility. Georges made it clear to Phil that he didn't need a job, but Phil in turn made it clear to Georges that a job needed him — and the consequence of saying "no" was that Indian residential school Survivors could lose their healing fund. Georges relented. "It's only going to take six weeks," Phil said. "After that, you can go on your holiday."

In early February 1998, when National Chief Phil Fontaine called me to get involved in negotiating the healing fund agreement and creating an organization to receive and manage the fund, the last thing on my mind was finding a job. I was taking some time off after six very busy years on the Royal Commission on Aboriginal Peoples. I love doing physical work that can give you concrete results, so cleaning up my yard in Chelsea, Quebec, after the Ice Storm of January 1998 was very satisfying.

Phil and I had worked together in the past, and we knew each other well. I let Phil know that I wasn't looking for a job. He was very convincing in letting me know that, as much as he understood my situation, the reality was that the auditor general's office was just not going to let the Canadian government get away with giving the $350 million to a nonexistent entity. An organization had to be formed by the end of the current fiscal year. I realized I was in a unique situation, in between jobs and having just finished a non-political piece of work. I had co-chaired a commission with representatives from different Aboriginal Peoples who were again going to be represented in whatever organization we created to manage the healing fund. I certainly did not want to see the funding return to government coffers without being used to assist in doing some good for Aboriginal people.

The negotiations for the $350-million funding agreement began in February, under great pressure and with everything at stake. No agreement, no money. There was a limited time to work out the details and no way to defer contentious or complex issues to a later date. "There were sixteen meeting days all together," says negotiating team member, Janet Pitsiulaaq Brewster. "We would spend part of our time working on incorporating, in order to receive the funds, and then the Feds would come over and we would negotiate with them." The negotiating team was established with appointees from the Assembly of First Nations, the Native Council of Canada (later renamed the Congress of Aboriginal Peoples), Inuit Tapirisat of Canada (now Inuit Tapiriit Kanatami), and the Métis National Council. Eventually the Native Women's Association of Canada would join, after an initial protest by NWAC president Marilyn Buffalo, who had taken the position that $350 million was insufficient to the point of being offensive. Marilyn had known Georges for years, and their friendship helped to bring her on board. These five national Indigenous organizations would become the appointing Indigenous organizations of the AHF board of directors. Having established a suitable recipient entity, the working group entered negotiations for the funding agreement with the federal government caucus, led by the Intergovernmental Affairs branch of the Privy Council.

"It was an enormous undertaking that generated staggering amounts of debate," recalls AHF lawyer Rick Brooks, "almost like creating Petro-Canada from scratch." The incorporation documents constituted an internal discussion among the five Indigenous organizations, whereas the funding agreement negotiations brought Canada to the table. A political animal, Georges knew the meetings with Canada would unite the Indigenous negotiators against a common foe. More fractious for the negotiating team would be the morning discussions among the Métis, Inuit, and First Nations.

Not long into discussions with Canada, the negotiating team became concerned with the limitations government was imposing on the scope of the organization. At first, research was off the table. RCAP had just spent seventeen million dollars producing a comprehensive report, so the government scoffed at the proposal to give yet more resources to do yet more research. As Georges, however, pointed out, nothing in RCAP had explored healing. The foundation was an unprecedented agency tasked with a unique mandate. Georges took the position that research focusing on the nature and work of healing, and on evaluating the effectiveness of funded programs, made sense. Or was the federal government proposing to spend $350 million on healing and nothing on investigating what it is and how best to do it? Georges dug in, and he prevailed. Research was added to the mandate.

Another point of contention in the negotiations with government was language and cultural revitalization. The government's position was that the healing fund would be used for addressing the legacy of physical and sexual abuse suffered in the residential schools, and not for culture programs. The negotiating team, however, understood that the legacy of the Indian Residential School System extended beyond physical and sexual abuse, as well as beyond the generations of Indigenous people who were institutionalized. The mandate, they argued, should address broader issues and should be open to intergenerational trauma. Since Georges by this time enjoyed a good relationship with Jane Stewart, he approached her to explore the possibility of broadening the proposed terms of reference to include language and culture. He explained to the minister that the legacy of Indian residential schools was much broader than the mandate was contemplating. Georges and his colleagues wanted the authority to address every facet of the Indian Residential School System, not just cases of physical and sexual abuse. Meaningful healing might have to include families and, in some instances, entire communities. The minister explained to Georges that she had done all she could. It would be impossible, she added, to go back to cabinet and reopen these issues. The language in the funding agreement about the intergenerational legacy of the schools was there to address these larger issues, she told Georges, so use it. As for issues such as the investment restrictions, she added, there would be opportunity to revisit them at a later date. Georges took this advice back to the group and they adopted it. The broader legacy of the residential school would be addressed in its intergenerational impacts.

Janet Pitsiulaaq Brewster recalls instances when individual statements had an impact on the federal negotiators.

> I remember very clearly a statement by Paul Chartrand when we were trying to negotiate a more open and impactful foundation, to include especially the Métis, who were mainly at day schools. I remember the numbers being, like, 5 percent of the students were Métis and 5 percent were Ukrainian. I think it was Paul who brought that up. During a particularly difficult conversation, he silenced the room by imploring this federal government representative to take a minute and imagine what his community would be like today in the complete absence of every school-aged

> child. Seeing that sink in with those feds on the other side was, for me … I still get chills, and I still have to catch myself. Through the whole process there was so much passion, and there were so many impactful statements like that.

As promised, Georges gave his six weeks. In that time the negotiating team sent daily drafts of the funding agreement back to the lawyers, who in turn sent back their revisions for the next day's negotiations. It was an intense period of discussion, debate, disagreement, and what felt like endless drafting. Finally, in the early afternoon of March 31, the work was finished. On this day, the government — evidently having grown tired of the back-and-forth exchange of documents — brought the Privy Council and its human and mechanical infrastructure to the meeting. With secretaries, fax machines, computers, and printers assembled, the Privy Council finished the deal on-site, printing and signing the official documents on March 31, 1998, at eleven o'clock. Signing for the Government of Canada was the Honourable Jane Stewart, Minister of Indian Affairs and Northern Development, and for the AHF negotiating team Georges Erasmus, Janet Pitsiulaaq Brewster, Jerome Berthelette, Debbie Reid, Teressa Nahanee, Gene Rhéaume, Paul Chartrand, Wendy Grant-John, and Marjorie "Maggie" Hodgson. The required paperwork was submitted to government, and the government cut a five-million-dollar cheque signed by a federal employee named Terry Goodtrack, who years later would become the AHF's director of finance. The Aboriginal Healing Foundation had come into being.

There was, however, one rub. Late into the negotiations, the negotiating team realized they were not going to be able to establish a founding board by April 1. They decided to turn the matter over to the national Indigenous organizations and to give them three months to appoint their representatives. The negotiators became interim board members and agreed to stay throughout April, May, and June, while the political leaders made their decisions concerning appointments. According to the AHF funding agreement and the bylaw, Canada would have the authority to appoint two board members. These nine appointed board members (three appointed by the AFN, two appointed by Canada, and one appointed, respectively, by

ITC, MNC, CAP, and NWAC) would in turn select the remaining eight directors, for a total of seventeen.

I had told National Chief Phil Fontaine I would do his six-week contract, get a funding agreement, and help create an organization that would receive the funds by the end of March 1998. The national Aboriginal organizations had appointed individuals to represent their interests in the negotiations on the funding agreement and the not-for-profit Aboriginal Healing Foundation. We were so busy getting the funding agreement and the constitution of the yet-to-be-formed organization negotiated that we didn't pay attention to the fact that we would need a board in place at the end of March to sign the incorporating documents and the funding agreement with Canada. The only solution was for the negotiating team, made up of appointed representatives, to become an interim board for a brief period to give the national Aboriginal organizations and the Canadian Government an opportunity to appoint their initial board members for the first two-year term. We gave the national Aboriginal organizations three months, to June 30, 1998, to come up with their appointments.

A very interesting thing happened to me over this period. I began to realize how important healing, properly done, was going to be to achieve the many political goals I'd spent my life working on. Having had sisters, an aunt, and my wife of forty-three years all being social workers — as well as my work in community development for many years — I was well familiar with the economic and social problems plaguing our community as a result of colonization, the Indian Act, residential schools, and so on. We had documented these and many other issues in the RCAP report, and we had proposed solutions.

All that remained was the selection of a founding president and chair. The interim board deliberated the matter and decided Georges was the natural pick. But did he want the job? Once the paperwork was completed, there was a three-month period before the foundation's first board was in place, but the work could not wait, so the interim board began the task of creating an organization from scratch. Georges took this time to think about his next move. Like RCAP, the Aboriginal Healing Foundation would be a departure from his time in politics, where he had addressed big and important issues. The work was going to be different from everything he'd done so far. But as well as being different, it was going to be at least as big and important as anything he'd committed to previously. As an adult he'd been surrounded by social workers, and he was well acquainted with the effects of historical trauma and colonialism on Indigenous people. He hadn't been in an Indian residential school himself, but many of his relatives and friends had. Georges understood that healing was important and that, if done properly, the work of the foundation could make a real difference. "This is exactly what I want to be doing," he decided. Fortunately for his colleagues on the interim board, Georges realized that the work of setting up the Aboriginal Healing Foundation had pulled him in. He was hooked.

What was different from RCAP was that I had an opportunity to play a direct part in the healing process, and it was staring me in the face. I realized that not only did I have the skills to carry this out, but I would love to see successful healing projects that gave concrete results in our communities. The more I thought about it, the more I realized I was ready to do something like this. When it came time to have a meeting with National Chief Phil Fontaine about appointing representatives to the recently incorporated Aboriginal Healing Foundation, in May or early June of 1998, I let him know that he could chose whomever he wished to the three board positions the Assembly of First Nations was entitled to, but that I was open to being one of those individuals. I told him that the more time I was involved with this project, the more I wanted to be involved. Sometime later the AFN sent us a letter with three names, one being me. It made me very happy to be given the opportunity to support healing programs that were created by Aboriginal people for Aboriginal people.

Every year we had a board election. The elections were staggered, with half the board up for election one year and the other half the next. Half the board was nominated by the national Aboriginal organizations, including two members who were nominated by Canada, and the other half was elected by the rest of the board. Over sixteen and a half years, the National Organizations and Canada occasionally replaced the individual they had nominated.

Amazingly, three of us kept being nominated by the Assembly of First Nations: Viola Robinson, Richard Kistabish, and I were reappointed by successive AFN National Chiefs. This created a stability that served us well. Because we were so different and from different parts of the country, we were a good team.

Georges's six-week commitment became a sixteen-year journey. Led by Georges, the board had successes in moving the federal negotiators. While the mandate remained focused on addressing the legacy of physical and sexual abuse in the residential schools, the board argued successfully for a research mandate and convinced the government that the intergenerational impacts of the residential schools had to be addressed. The funding agreement compelled the board to disburse the fund "over a ten year period from the date of approval of the first Eligible Project, or from one year following the signing of this Funding Agreement, whichever comes first."[2] From the interim board's point of view, a longer time frame than ten years made better sense. More time would allow the foundation to invest and grow the fund, like an actual foundation with an endowment, rather than quickly deplete it, thereby squandering an opportunity.

The AHF's financial advisor, Graham Sanders, took pains to invest the healing fund in such a way that all operating expenses would come out of the interest generated by the $350 million. His investment strategy eventually yielded over $107 million in additional revenue. Still, even more could have been done had the AHF been allowed to operate in perpetuity, or even for thirty years, growing its principle like a true foundation. Knowing this, the board made extending the time frame of the AHF mandate a priority as it set about its work.

On June 23, 1998, the AHF announced that a seventeen-member board had been established, as Georges and his colleagues prepared for an upcoming consultation (referred to as the Residential School Healing Strategy Conference) at Squamish Nation, in North Vancouver. From July 14 to 16 board members heard from residential school Survivors, as Georges had during his years at RCAP. The tone of this meeting had been foreshadowed by a community forum hosted by the government four months earlier in Ottawa, as fellow AHF board member Maggie Hodgson recalls: "People were for the first time giving voice to their huge anger. Canada still had the cheque book at that point, because money hadn't been transferred to the foundation. They rented this small room [in Ottawa] that might hold fifty people. Well, I'll tell you, there was a heck of a lot more than fifty people in that room. And they were very angry. A large part of this anger had to do with the fact that they thought that this money for the healing foundation would be coming out of their settlements."

Georges was busy with negotiations when this Ottawa community-forum meeting took place in February. In fact, he wasn't even aware of it. But he was present in North Vancouver on July 14, 1998, when the three day Healing Strategy Conference opened with a welcome from the Squamish Nation hereditary Chief, Bill Williams, who set events in motion with his offer to host a Ceremony seeking the guidance of Survivors. According to Chief Bobby Joseph, the gathering "couldn't have been held at a better place. Here we were in the heart of our spiritual places." Willie Seymour, the conference chairperson and a member of the Chemainus band, spoke of the importance of the event, focusing on Indigenous cultures, rights, and languages. Facilitator Harold Tarbell outlined the conference objectives and presented a brief update on the work of the Aboriginal Healing Foundation, which included the recent creation of the board of directors and the successful negotiation of a funding agreement. Tarbell explained that the conference would provide an opportunity to explore the kinds of projects, programs, and activities that residential school Survivors would like to see the foundation support. Conference attendees were given materials, including an AHF background document and a copy of the funding agreement.

As president and chair, Georges was the first board member to speak. He reviewed the history of the AHF from its inception, and he assured his audience that the foundation would make certain healing services were available wherever they were needed. Georges further emphasized that the conference was being held to listen to the Survivors, in order to receive their guidance. Other board members spoke of their personal backgrounds and of the pain experienced by so many in residential schools. Six of the foundation's board members were not present: Jerome Berthelette, Paul Chartrand (who arrived on day three), Teressa Nahanee, Wendy John (whose husband had just suffered a heart attack), Ann Meekitjuk-Hanson, and Gene Rhéaume, whose attendance was prevented on the first day by a death in the family. After a prayer song by Dennis Charlie, the day began.

A panel made up of AHF board members and government officials (Shawn Tupper of Indian and Northern Affairs, Paul Glover from the Medical Services Branch of Health Canada, Cathy Greene of the Aboriginal Affairs Secretariat in the Privy Council Office) fielded audience questions. A timeline for receiving grant applications was not yet established, they explained, and only projects addressing the legacy of physical and sexual abuse in residential schools would be eligible for funding. The foundation could not duplicate existing services, but it could move into an area if a need was demonstrated.

In Vancouver the anger of residential school Survivors came to the surface, as it had at the February Ottawa consultations. One by one, panel members removed themselves from the stage to sit among the assembly. "One person got up," according to Maggie Hodgson, "and he didn't talk. He yelled for at least three-quarters of an hour." Like many others, this Survivor held within him a burden of pain, and now for the first time an opportunity had arrived to unload it. Eventually, only two board members remained at the table — Georges and Maggie. "I was reluctant even to go and have a pee, because I didn't want to leave Georges by himself. That was an important beginning, showing us the immense volume of pain that existed. It showed how desperately we needed resources like an Aboriginal Healing Foundation."

Survivors representing twenty-one Indian residential schools made fifty-two recommendations grouped into six categories: Recommendations to Board Members, Issues for Board Consideration, Foundation Operations, Program Design and Content, Program Criteria, and Other Recommendations. When the foundation came to Sḵwx̱wú7mesh Úxwumixw Territory, in North Vancouver (referred to, throughout this chapter, as "Squamish"), it was "still a bit of a stranger," according to Chief Joseph. Survivors were in the early days of healing. For this reason, there was mistrust of the board and of the Aboriginal Healing Foundation. The AHF board came to Squamish to show that they meant to listen to Survivors, and to build a foundation that would serve them in a way they themselves had deemed proper and fit and just. Every word was recorded, and with the Survivors' recommendations in hand, the board built the AHF from the ground up. It took time and a lot of work to earn the trust of Survivors and communities. The AHF made mistakes, but the board admitted that — and having learned from their errors, they made changes.

Calls for Georges's resignation at Squamish showed that not everyone believed he was the best candidate for the job of AHF president. His connection to the Assembly of First Nations, where he had been National Chief, led some to suspect he had arrived at the job as a result of his political connections. And of course there is truth in that conclusion. Georges had demonstrated his abilities as National Chief, and his accomplishments in politics and at RCAP had impressed influential colleagues like Phil Fontaine. Perhaps it didn't help either that Georges had been co-chair at RCAP, an institution directly responsible for the establishment of a healing fund. Georges was indeed well-connected, a natural and even inevitable outcome when you've spent decades working among politicians at the highest level. His assets were seen by his critics as liabilities. Some also called for his resignation because he was not a residential school Survivor.

Georges conceded that he had never attended an Indian residential school, but he pointed out that many in his family had. His personal experience had helped him to understand the residential school legacy, and his work at RCAP had only broadened this understanding. As for his political connections and his suitability for the position, Georges explained, at the Squamish Gathering and elsewhere, how he had become involved with the foundation. "If I didn't feel I could do the job with every ounce of me, I wouldn't do it," he said. The Aboriginal Healing Foundation was non-political, he noted, and as president and chair he would speak for no one but the AHF itself. At the conclusion of the conference, a prominent female Elder approached Georges and said, "With your background and all the work you've done, it couldn't be better. You're the guy for it." There were enough Survivors on the board, she added. Not being a Survivor was actually, in her view, an asset.

Georges's colleagues had also decided that he was the perfect person to serve as AHF board chair. He was decisive yet calm, able to think strategically, and also keen to hear the thoughts of others. Quiet and introverted, he was hard to read. Georges struck his fellow board members as competent, objective, and fair. He didn't win others over with charm, as more extroverted politicians often do, but with steadiness and command. In board meetings, Georges would listen far more than he spoke, adding his voice when he could discern the outlines of consensus. He could seem cold and distant, but in the early years of the foundation, when the pain and anger of residential schools was never far from the surface, Georges's disposition helped rather than hindered. Anyone who had followed Georges's career knew well that he had fire within him, and that he felt keenly the indignation shared by Indigenous people. No one mistook Georges's quiet demeanour for weakness or passivity. As the Aboriginal Healing Foundation toured across the country, Georges sat quietly and listened, as he had done in his other public roles. He listened and absorbed the pain and anger at Squamish, and he wondered what the foundation could do.

Richard Kistabish, Georges's vice-chair, had worked out the math. By his estimate, $350 million was $70 per Indigenous person — not exactly life-transforming. Kistabish had joined the AHF board with high but soon-to-be-diminished expectations. One-third of a billion dollars was a handsome sum, but as he would soon realize, the task ahead was enormous: "The first time you've seen the figures, it's a lot, a lot of money. It makes no sense: nine figures before the dot, after which you have the two small zeros. $350,000,000.00. Lordy, lordy. I dreamed all summer about the $350 million. I dreamed I had come upon a magic lantern, and there was that guy straight out of the desert who says, 'You have three wishes, Richard, to achieve what you want to do.' That's how I saw it."[3]

Richard was an Algonquin from the Abitibiwinni First Nation, in Quebec, and a former Chief and Grand Chief. At gatherings of fellow residential school Survivors, he would sometimes say that he had been colonized twice, by the French and then by the English. For years prior he had been active in the health and social services, where among other things he dealt with the legacy of the residential schools. At once worldly and spiritual, Richard was a man led by his heart and known for a wicked sense of humour. You never quite knew what Richard was going to say, only that it would be memorable. In many ways he was the perfect complement to Georges. One serious and private, the other garrulous and playful. Georges brought a keen mind to the work of the foundation, and Richard a big heart. Both would be needed for the work ahead. "I had never approached things on an intellectual basis, to reason things through and to set aside a bit the heart, the emotions," says Kistabish. Together they were a formidable pair.

When the proposals began to arrive, there was no denying that demand far exceeded supply. Copies of every proposal were provided to every board member, a practice that proved costly and that was eventually abandoned. As the deadline for proposals arrived, the office mailroom was filled with the paperwork. For Kistabish it was "an absolutely extraordinary moment," and a huge disappointment too. More than one billion dollars of requests, much of it eligible, arrived in the mail. "I thought it was a lot of money. Heavens, it wasn't very much. It sent me in a hell of a whirl and turned me upside down to be aware of the needs of the communities faced with the amount of money we had." For board member Viola Robinson, "the toughest part was looking at so many applications, so many people and groups across the country, applying for funding support. They were all so good." Given the need for healing across the country, the AHF would have no problem disbursing $350 million.

Squamish provided the board with numerous recommendations, but the reality is that the foundation started with a blank slate. Much had been accomplished by the negotiating team in an intense six weeks and under threat of deadline, but in their first meetings the board confronted a massive list of fundamental questions. "What kind of projects should we fund? How should we fund them? What exactly is healing?" Program design, funding eligibility criteria, youth-focused initiatives, the application review process — dozens of topics required attention. There were no policies of any kind, either for the board or the staff. Georges recalls these early days with the foundation as a steep learning curve. It wasn't as if he, and the other board members, could study other agencies tasked with "addressing the legacy of physical and sexual abuse suffered in the Indian residential schools, including intergenerational impacts." No such agency existed. No such agency ever had existed.

Fortunately, Georges's time in the North had accustomed him to working with Métis and Inuit, as well as with Status and non-Status First Nations people, an approach that was less common in the South but which he adopted both at the AFN and RCAP. As National Chief, Georges had encountered colleagues who "just couldn't see themselves in the same room with non-Status people or Métis." To Georges's disappointment, the AHF board almost immediately settled into camps, the Métis, Inuit, and First Nations representatives each fighting for what they believed to be their fair share of the fund. Georges's career up to this point, in the late 1990s, had made it apparent to him that Indigenous people were being drawn into a despair that made it impossible for them to see, and to seize, opportunities. As the board fought, Georges pondered the self-destructive tendencies of Indigenous people, the multiple ways in which pain and past injustices led them to sabotage their own interests. Now, he believed, the AHF board was doing the same. Furthermore, the Métis and Inuit, who had often been treated as second-class Indigenous people, were right to fear being treated unfairly. Georges knew that the board would either overcome factionalism or it would fail. We have to get to know one another, he concluded. The AHF board Elder, Dorris Peters, intervened, instructing the members to tell one another who they were. "Don't tell me about your job or your title," Elder Peters instructed. "I want to know who you are." Fiercely private, Georges found it awkward in the beginning to talk openly about his personal life. But he understood well the value of the Elder. She calmed things down and played a critical role in managing the conflicts of personalities. Once the board began to open up to one another, they realized they had more in common than they had differences. The result was transformative.

The most important thing that brought us together as a trusting team was the sharing of personal information of each of the board members at each meeting. This came about at the urging of our board Elder, Dorris Peters, who recommended that we do this. After opening our meetings with a prayer from one of our Elders, we went around the table and the room and shared personal information about current experiences and events in our lives. This sharing built a very close-knit group over a period of time. Many former board members still see each other regularly and are close friends.

"All of the issues were avoided or resolved, in my opinion," says the AHF's chief lawyer, Rick Brooks, "because of the strength of the chair of the board. Everyone appeared to, and probably did, respect Georges so much. Sitting in board meetings and watching how he ran meetings — it was abundantly clear that he was incredibly good at getting people to arrive at a solution." For the next sixteen and a half years, up to the dissolution of the AHF in September 2014, every board meeting opened with "Aboriginal Sharing" (as it came to be known). As the board became closer, trust grew. The members could see, as Georges puts it, that the walk and the talk aligned and that the board members were all sincere in what they were trying to do. After a rough beginning, the board came together. "They emerged to become a tight, strong, and trusting group," Georges recalls. "They were still strong personalities, but what's really important is that we evolved to have a common cause and to accept that we had only one employee," the executive director. Georges chaired meetings where discussions could be candid but never rancorous. The drama of the early days yielded to remarkable efficiency. Board members went from being colleagues to friends. The board became, in a word, a model, and it was used as the subject of a case study, *A Legacy of Excellence: Best Practices Board Study Aboriginal Healing Foundation*, written by John Graham and Laura Mitchell and published in 2009 by the Institute on Governance.

With the AHF up and running, Georges and his fellow board directors had turned their attention to approving projects. At the first board meeting to approve proposals, a copy of every proposal was given to every one of the seventeen board members for review. Staff shipped an enormous cache of documents to a board meeting in Yellowknife, at a hefty cost, only to confront the problem of what to do with the paper afterward. (The inelegant solution was to appoint a staff person to burn the documents outside in an oil barrel, a task that took three days.) The board soon realized that the process was a logistical nightmare. A more rational approach was found: the board had a single copy of each proposal made available for their meetings.

Each proposal was reviewed before the board meetings by a body of experts called the "External Merit Review Panel." This panel was made up of people from Indigenous communities across Canada who had experience and expertise in proposal evaluation. The board saw this as an opportunity to promote fairness, since there would be less opportunity for conflicts of interest. The External Merit Review Panel scored each project in relation to criteria set by the board, and the board approved or declined proposals based on the experts' recommendations. The end result was a manageable workload for the board.

One of the many early challenges amongst the newly formed board was creating policy for the organization, since we were starting with a blank page. Because we were going to be a funding agency, we needed criteria on the kind of projects we were going to fund. Office space, furniture, travel policies, investment of the $350 million, the hiring of our executive director — these are just a few of the things we needed to get done, as soon as possible, so we could get the money out to the communities.

At the beginning, we had board meetings several times a month to put in place all the basic policies we needed to run the foundation. But as time passed, the meetings were less frequent. One of the challenges before the board was to create trust among us. Trust would enable us to approve projects fairly. All the board members, whether Inuit, Métis, or First Nation, would be able to tell their organizations that their communities were being treated equally.

This was achieved through a multipronged approach. The board and staff developed criteria for projects we would approve for funding. We decided that we needed independent assessments of the proposals before they came to the board. Only those proposals that were given the green light by independent assessors would be considered for funding. Board members were given material ahead of time so they could brief themselves in advance of meetings. They had access to all project submissions that had come in prior to the cut-off dates of any funding cycle. Giving board members all the time necessary at meetings to ask questions about any funding proposal was critical.

In October 1998, Mike DeGagné was recruited as the executive director, replacing interim EDs (technically interim managers) Paul Kyba and Virginia Toulouse. Paul Kyba had overseen some of the groundwork, including the initial hirings of staff, while Virginia Toulouse had been recruited from the Assembly of First Nations to help organize the June 1998 Squamish gathering and to continue the work of staffing. Virginia was one of the first staff, and she played a number of crucial roles:

> I was contacted by Paul Kyba, who was leading the work with the Aboriginal Healing Foundation. He asked me if I could support him in establishing the board of directors, getting that process in place. I set up the 1-800 number at my home in Cornwall at the time. I ended up establishing, with the interim board, the process for recruiting new board members. Then, shortly after, Paul left, and I was asked if I could take on that role, while the board looked for a new executive director. All of this work took place between about March and November. We worked with a recruitment firm that did the organization structure. The primary consultant for that was Brenda Higgins. She developed the organization charts and identified the staffing requirements. We worked with a subcommittee of the board. We had very little staff. Rod Jeffries was there to set up the "Programs" section and to develop the proposal process. Then I was asked to oversee the proposal review process.

Fleshing out the details of a national Indigenous funding agency was a tremendous challenge. Georges had overseen ambitious work before, but never had he been involved in something of this magnitude.

One of our most important decisions to guarantee a successful organization was hiring the right executive director. Mike DeGagné applied for the job, and on paper he looked perfect, except for one thing. Once we had discussed Mike's experience and the jobs he'd done, I brought up the fact that he'd never stayed very long in any of his positions. I explained that I didn't want to be doing another search for an executive director in eighteen months. I wanted a commitment for at least five years. Mike told me that he could live with that, and he did. Sixteen years later we were shutting down the Aboriginal Healing Foundation together.

Perhaps even more important than hiring the executive director was hiring the executive assistant who would work with both the executive director and the chairman/president. Linda Côté was hired to do this dual job, and we were blessed to have her. She'd worked with Mike before, so he was a known quantity to her. But Linda and I needed to get to know each other. Apparently, I can come across as cool and detached, maybe even scary, LOL. Over time we became friends. Linda kept Mike and I, and our board meetings, organized in such a way that she made us look like we knew what we were doing. We were very blessed to have Linda stay to the end. She helped us close the doors of the AHF for good.

Truth be told, we were very lucky at the foundation to find excellent board members and staff over the course of the sixteen years we were in operation. Many stayed for long periods, and most were sorry to leave, whether they were board members or staff. It was one of the best organizations and groups of people that I had the privilege of working with.

On December 3, 1998, the AHF issued its first call for proposals, under two themes ("Developing & Enhancing Aboriginal Capacity" and "Community Therapeutic Healing") and with a January 15, 1999, deadline. Once the funding began, the pace was hectic. It had to be, with a five-year time frame provided by government to commit the $350 million and ten years to spend it. This highlighted an important aspect of the Aboriginal Healing Foundation — it was not, in fact, a foundation. It was a private, not-for-profit corporation and a national funding agency, mandated to disburse $350 million within ten years of issuing its first grant. The word "foundation" is generally understood to mean an institution possessing an endowment, operating in perpetuity, and issuing grants from the revenue generated by interest. From the very beginning, the working group had pressed for a "foundation" structure rather than a time-limited mandate that would quickly deplete the healing fund. Despite having been unsuccessful at this during the negotiations of the funding agreement, the board took up the cause of a longer-term mandate with revised investment conditions once again.

There were several reasons the board wanted to revisit its investment guidelines and the requirement to "make best efforts to commit the Amount over a period of four years from either the date of the approval of the first Eligible Project or from one year following the signing of this Funding Agreement, which ever comes first" and to "disburse the Amount over a ten year period from the date of approval of the first Eligible Project, or from one year following the signing of this Funding Agreement, whichever comes first." The first was a concern that the funding agreement had the board spending money at what seemed to them an imprudent pace. The funding agreement put considerable pressure on the agency to get money out the door quickly. While this would have been easy to do — there was no shortage of eligible funding requests — the board regarded the ten-year clause as arbitrary and counterproductive. To make matters worse, the foundation's ultraconservative investment restrictions kept the return on investment very low, even as the funding agreement encouraged a swift depletion of the fund. Did the government want to limit the impact of the healing fund as much as possible? To Georges, as to others, it certainly seemed like it.

The board hired KPMG and ScotiaMcLeod to conduct a comprehensive analysis, exploring what it might look like if the investment restrictions were loosened just a bit (while remaining conservative and well within the realm of fiscal prudence) and the pace of expenditures slowed. The object of this exercise was to show that the yield of the $350 million fund could be grown at low risk, providing many millions more dollars to projects over decades rather than years. Again, administrative costs would be covered by the interest generated, and all of the healing fund plus some interest would go to projects. Under the models the KPMG-ScotiaMcLeod analysis provided, there would be a *lot* more money for projects. In fact, one of the models projected over one billion dollars in funding over a period of thirty years, all from the proceeds of the AHF's initial "endowment." The data showed that it was possible to increase the impact of the fund, support more projects, provide resources to more communities, and extend the life of the foundation, all without the need for additional funding.

One of the biggest disappointments of my time at the Aboriginal Healing Foundation was not being able to convince Canada to reprofile the length of time we could take to spend the monies given to us by Canada. Right after the first call for proposals was processed in 1999, we knew that many parts of the country were not ready for our projects. There were large gaps in either the Aboriginal group or part of the country that did not submit proposals, even though we had put out the information across the country. We were fully aware that healing is a very personal journey, and that it can't be forced or rushed. So we would not have been alarmed that some areas would approach us later but for the fact that we were only given a limited window to get the money out. In fact, if we had been able to invest in healing without regard to an early end date, we would have been able to work with communities when they were ready, and for as long as necessary, to get a healthy community with inner strengths that are able to carry on once we moved on to another community.

This call for a longer-term mandate looked to some like a case of securing one's own job security. There were good and practical reasons, however, for extending the foundation's commitment and disbursement phases. At the time the foundation came along, the Inuit were occupied by the pressing work of the Nunavut agreement. They were necessarily focused on negotiating territory and governance arrangements, with all that this entailed. It would be some years before communities in the North were prepared to deal with the legacy of the hostels, tent camps, and boarding homes operated under the auspices of the Indian Residential School System. Likewise, many Indigenous communities across Canada were struggling with basic matters of administrative capacity or other priorities. Assuming they were even aware of the Aboriginal Healing Foundation, Survivors would not necessarily be ready for healing just because the foundation was ready to provide funding. As the board pointed out time and again, the Indian Residential School System operated across several generations, far longer than the decade allowed for healing. Individuals and communities could not be expected to heal on a government timetable. Only when they were ready could the healing begin, and many were not going to be ready within the next few years. And as it would one day turn out, a good many Survivors would be ready only after the foundation, and the projects it supported, had gone away.

The KPMG-ScotiaMcLeod analysis, completed on February 9, 2000, was presented as a PowerPoint to government. The document put several options on the table, from an extension of the disbursement period by a few years to an extension in perpetuity, with the options of fifteen and thirty years falling between. The accountants considered varying mixes of securities in combination with varying disbursement horizons. Government officials received the information and expressed openness to exploring these options. Exploration, however, takes time, especially where the wheels of government are concerned, and time was of the essence. More correspondence followed, as did more meetings. A year had passed when, on March 13, 2001, the KPMG-ScotiaMcLeod document was sent to the minister of Indian Affairs, Robert Nault, and to Denis Desautels, the auditor general of Canada. Georges's covering letter noted that KPMG and ScotiaMcLeod had concluded that prudent modifications of the Aboriginal Healing Foundation's mandate and investment restrictions — "a longer time-frame and a balanced portfolio" — would "allow for a greater return on investment and, as a result, a greater ability to invest in the long-term healing of residential school survivors, their families and descendants." This letter ended with a request "to meet with you to present the Foundation's position on this matter and to seek your support for our objectives."

Georges's letter to the auditor general stated that the foundation's board was "led to believe that your office may originally have had concerns about the length of our mandate" and asked, "Are you aware of any reason we should be restricted to a three- or four-year period to spend or commit the original endowment provided to us by the federal government?" He concluded, optimistically, "I trust that the enclosed study will make apparent the reasons informing our request, and I am seeking your support in this matter, hopeful that we may take this opportunity to maximise the healing fund's long-term effectiveness."

The KPMG analysis had shown that, with a longer mandate and a modification of the investment restrictions that would still qualify as risk-averse, the Aboriginal Healing Foundation could provide communities after thirty years of operation with as much as nearly one billion dollars in funding support ($908.7 million, to be precise) while growing the original $350 million into a $768.4 million endowment. As for operating in perpetuity, the KPMG-ScotiaMcLeod analysis concluded that the capital required to do so at then-current program and expenditure levels ($45.8 million of programs annually, growing at an estimated 3 percent annual inflation) would be $727 million, "assuming that the investment policy was less rigid, to provide for the investment in domestic and foreign bonds, as well as domestic and foreign securities."

The auditor general was not impressed. Even the current ten-year mandate of the foundation (plus one year for start-up activities) had met with his skepticism. Once Desautels was succeeded by Sheila Fraser, the very idea of arm's-length, government-funded foundations would come under intense scrutiny. In early 2001, however, the board's suggestion seemed very defensible. They awaited the minister's response. The reply was, for the board of directors, a matter of both good and bad news. The good news was that the minister had agreed to offer a "Proposal to Amend the Funding Agreement," consisting of a two-year extension of the disbursement deadline, albeit without any loosening of the investment restrictions. The bad news was that the reply came thirty-three months later, on February 19, 2003. In the meanwhile, the AHF had been beholden to the time frame of the 1998 funding agreement. Most of the money had therefore been spent, and the window of opportunity had closed. "I thought it was such a waste," Georges now says. "We knew the AHF needed to be around for fifty years. And it could have been around with that initial money, if we'd been allowed to invest it for the long term." After consulting with his board, Georges replied to the minister of Indian Affairs on April 25 that "it is with regret that I decline your offer of an extension, which was required three years ago to be of benefit to the Aboriginal Healing Foundation."

To this day Georges laments this outcome:

If they had made these changes, the Aboriginal Healing Foundation would still be here. They wouldn't have had to give us the $125 million under the Indian Residential Schools Settlement Agreement, or the $40 million we received in 2005. The foundation would still be doing healing. And healing is still needed. It was a lost opportunity. Unmarked graves have been discovered in many former Indian residential school sites across Canada. The Pope came to Canada to give a version of an apology for the role played by the Roman Catholic Church in the Indian Residential School System. Once again, this has brought forth the pain that is still prevalent in Indigenous communities across Canada. There is still a need for an organization like the Aboriginal Healing Foundation. If anything, it is needed even more than ever, because more former students are ready now for healing than ever before.

The sad reality is that it took over a hundred years of Indian residential schools and colonization to do the damage to Aboriginal communities that we see every day. It will take many years to fully recover. The tragic truth is that Canada would not have needed to invest any more monies beyond the original $350-million grant. The required healing would have continued across the country, long into the future, as required. Canada could have moved on to housing, self-government, community infrastructure, clean drinking water, etc. Had the government moved quickly, when we asked for a reprofile in 1999, the Aboriginal Healing Foundation would have been in business for almost three decades with an extended mandate and better investment criteria. The AHF would likely have been able to put at least a billion and a half dollars into healing, with no end in sight. The immense knowledge that would have been gained by perfecting the programs and projects that do the most in the shortest time frame has all gone by the wayside. The saddest thing is we interrupted so many people and communities in the middle of a healing journey when we had to cut short our healing programs — not to mention all the communities we could have gone into, but never did, with more skills and knowledge than when we started out. What a sad, stupid, and tragic squandering of an opportunity.

Georges had lived a largely public and political life for over twenty years before arriving at the Aboriginal Healing Foundation. Now in his sixth decade (he turned fifty in August 1998, five months after the foundation was established) he was the chair and president of a non-political, not-for-profit organization. Anger, aggression, and agitation had played an important part in Georges's long political career, and one could argue that they had served him well. But Georges had known that what worked at the Assembly of First Nations would not work at RCAP. And it certainly wasn't going to work at the Aboriginal Healing Foundation. A different approach was required, and a different approach was supplied. As chair and president of the AHF, Georges removed himself as far from politics as possible, deferring to his successors at the Assembly of First Nations when journalists called to seek comment on issues of the day, which they often did. Georges was now the face of the AHF and an ambassador of healing and reconciliation, raising awareness of the residential schools and their legacy, wherever he found a receptive audience.

Georges's fiftieth birthday with sons Kristen (left) and Che, August 1998.

Prohibitions against political activity, in particular lobbying, were explicitly cited in the funding agreement with Canada. But even if the foundation had not been constituted as a non-political funding agency, Georges felt that a non-political approach was best. Indigenous political leaders had felt the same. Politics was their domain, and the last thing they wanted was another combatant on an already crowded field. According to AHF executive director Mike DeGagné, Georges took to his new role of public educator and advocate with enthusiasm: "I remember Georges and I flying to these meetings all over the country, to meet with senior politicians and bureaucrats, and someone in short pants would show up to the meeting in their place. So many times I watched Georges patiently explain to these junior folks why healing was important. And I'd say to him, 'Georges, why the hell do you put up with this?' 'Mike,' he said to me, 'this is how it's done, one person at a time. We're going to need them.' And he was right."

Georges's political career had ended in the early 1990s but as the next century arrived, he was still operating in a political environment where diplomacy and persuasion were indispensable. He had taken politics as far as he felt it would go, and now he was continuing the fight for the dignity of Indigenous people by other means. Beginning with RCAP, he would seek change through other approaches. The foundation would not lobby, or participate in demonstrations, or engage in policy. In 2004, Georges stopped giving interviews and offering perspectives on political issues of the day, instead referring journalists to the National Chief. He would only speak about the work of the Aboriginal Healing Foundation and the importance of healing. As for politics, that was now someone else's job.

This decision turned out to have great strategic value. Georges's non-political leadership elevated the cause. Whether with the churches, Survivors, politicians, or bureaucrats, the Aboriginal Healing Foundation cultivated respectful and productive relationships. The AHF was the universal goodwill partner at the table when all others were adversarial. As a non-political agency, the foundation spoke only to the higher purpose of healing and reconciliation. In speeches, Georges would challenge his audiences, but in the manner of a statesman, appealing to the better angels of our nature. Everyone at least professed to want a better future, in which the trauma and pain of the residential schools had been addressed. That, and not the scoring of political points, was the reason the AHF existed.

In 2000, the board took to the road and Georges chaired what the foundation called "regional gatherings." (These gatherings would be held annually over the next seven years.) These events, held in communities across the country, were a blend of conference, shareholder meeting, talking circle, and consultation. As he had done at RCAP, Georges spoke briefly on behalf of the organization before yielding the floor to participants. One after another, Survivors (or in some cases, the family of Survivors) spoke at length of their experiences. To this day the transcripts of these gatherings preserve the wide-ranging expression of dozens of participants: local and community histories, personal narratives, cultural teachings, testimonies of abuse, philippics aimed at the government, criticisms of the Aboriginal Healing Foundation, litanies of injustices committed by Canada, and humour. Through the regional gatherings, the Aboriginal Healing Foundation cultivated relationships with Indigenous people across the country and learned, in an up-close-and-personal manner, what was working and — more to the point — what wasn't. Georges met regularly with community people, politicians, leaders of the national Indigenous organizations, and the churches. He made certain that everyone who wanted to be kept informed was and as a result, trust and support of the AHF grew.

One of the things that I knew was going to be important as a non-political organization was for us to keep everyone informed about the AHF. We took every opportunity to communicate and to listen, and we heeded good advice wherever we found it. Mike and I met several times a year with the National Aboriginal organizations and with members of parliament, senators, and senior bureaucrats. In addition, I would attend AFN assemblies to give reports and answer questions from the Chiefs. I would also attend the assemblies of other National Aboriginal organizations from time to time, but normally we would send the board member nominated by that organization, whether it was the Native Women's Association of Canada, the Métis National Council, the Inuit Tapiriit Kanatami, or the Congress of Aboriginal Peoples. The

Aboriginal Healing Foundation Board of Directors, 2007.

Aboriginal Healing Foundation worked consistently and hard at building good relationships. This served us well over the years, as we knew that no one was in the dark about what we were trying to do or why we were trying to do it.

Once the Aboriginal Healing Foundation Board had (as Garnet Angeconeb puts it) "worked out the wrinkles," Georges's attention turned to the work of public education, awareness raising, and advocacy. By 2003, the AHF had received $1.3 billion in eligible applications from hundreds of Indigenous communities and organizations across Canada but had already committed its funds. (The initial $350 million healing fund was fully committed to projects on October 5, 2003, just ahead of the March 31, 2004, deadline set by the funding agreement.) Georges travelled the country with the message that the healing had begun, but that time and resources beyond what the foundation possessed would be required to complete the work. To anyone who would listen, Georges would patiently explain the history and nature of the Indian Residential School System, its legacy, and the initiatives funded by the AHF to encourage and promote healing and reconciliation. Over the years, the AHF amassed a body of research examining the links between residential schools, historic trauma, addictions, poverty, suicide, and violence. Georges presented many dozens of detailed presentations on these and other topics to community leaders and Survivors and students and politicians and bureaucrats. Once again, Georges fought for a cause, this time healing.

In 1999, you could throw a stone from the AHF's offices at 75 Albert Street and the person it hit would invariably know nothing of the Indian residential schools. Even former students hadn't spoken much, if anything, about them until the 1990s. The learning curve for Canadians was fast and steep. Between 1999 and 2001, Canada's Indian Residential School System transmogrified from obscurity to front-page headlines. Years of lawsuits, advocacy, and Survivor agitation began to yield dividends. Georges's schedule filled with interview and speaking requests, not only in Canada but also abroad. This was nothing new for Georges. Much of the media coverage was ethnocentric, focused on the hazards of residential school lawsuits to the Canadian taxpayer. Georges instead focused on the healing needs of Survivors, whether they took the form of addiction treatment, counselling, or education.

The effort to educate Canadians about an unpleasant aspect of their history met at times with resistance, and even hostility. At the same time that lawsuits were disclosing residential school abuses and abusers, newspapers were publishing defences of the Indian Residential School System. At the *National Post*, David Frum and John Siebert defended the churches and dismissed the legitimacy of calls for healing and compensation. As he wrote in the *North Shore News* on February 20, 2000, editorialist Noel Wright saw in the residential school lawsuits another manifestation of "the native victims industry." The media coverage of residential schools was not all of the same character, but much of it focused on institutional interests and struck the same note as this November 24, 2005, *Montreal Gazette* editorial, "Residential School Payout Goes Too Far": "It's certainly sad that in that process, many of those children lost their language and their cultural identity, but the government and the religious groups who ran the schools acted in good faith and in accordance with the best understanding of the time in preparing their wards for the modern world."

As before, Georges was sounding the themes of justice and fairness. Residential school Survivors had in many cases been denied the fundamentals of childhood: the love of parents, a family, a community, an identity, a sense of belonging. Nor was this denial an aberration of the system. Indeed, it was the purpose of the residential school to sever the bonds of kinship so a generation might be freed from "savagery."

As the public learned about the Indian Residential School System, support for the Aboriginal Healing Foundation grew. Executive Director Mike DeGagné recalls the evening of March 10, 2002, when Georges delivered the Lafontaine–Baldwin lecture in Vancouver.

> The interesting part of that speech, for me, is that it occurred at a time when we didn't know how much support we had out there among the general public. Here we are, having shown up at a hotel in Vancouver. And it's packed — two ballrooms of people. Then a fellow stands up afterward, comes to the microphone. It's the uncle of

The cats birdwatching, Yellowknife, winter 2003.

> Paul Kariya, the Vancouver-born NHL hockey player. "What do we do?" he asks. Georges's response began by saying, "Look at the goodwill of Canadians, as evidenced by the turnout to this speech." It was true. We saw that night the hunger of many Canadians for solutions to these seemingly intractable problems. The political forces, then and later, did not understand how much support there was for the AHF and for this sort of work.

Whether he spoke of the land, poverty, racism, or Native rights, Georges appealed to his audience's inherent decency. The impoverishment of Indigenous Peoples was for Georges a moral outrage, a point he had made abundantly clear in his 1992 speech, "Nothing to Celebrate." Likewise, the residential schools were an offence to basic norms of decency. A system that separated children from parents to deliberately break up the family structures of Indigenous communities was an immoral system. Residential schools devastated Indigenous languages and cultures. Many Survivors attested to the pain, shame, and trauma they suffered in these state-church institutions designed to interrupt the continuity of Indigenous cultures. The AHF spent years studying the effects of residential schools as well as the effects of funded projects. According to *Final Report of the Aboriginal Healing Foundation*, somewhere around 86,000 Survivors were alive in January 2006, the time at which the three-volume report was published, and a further 287,350 descendants of residential school students were intergenerationally impacted, for a total of 373,350.[4] (It may seem odd that a final report would come out in 2006 when the AHF operated until 2014. The timing of the report was determined by the 1998 funding agreement for the initial $350-million grant. Since the AHF received additional funds and operated longer than originally anticipated, the final report came out at what ended up being the midpoint of its existence.)

An estimated 204,564 individuals had participated in AHF-funded healing projects, only one-third of whom had ever engaged in healing prior. Residential schools had disrupted communities for over a century. It was going to take some time to undo the damage.

In the beginning, the foundation funded a broad variety of projects, including gatherings, books, memorials and commemorations, reunions, and plays. It was soon obvious, however, that the board would have to narrow its criteria: the need so far exceeded what the AHF could provide that many projects would have to be declined. In an exercise termed "Applying the Lens: A New Direction," the board decided in September 2001 to focus its resources on a shortened list of activities. The idea was to identify the desired results of AHF-funded programs and the activities that appeared to promise the greatest impact. The AHF would continue to address the intergenerational effects of the Indian residential schools, pursuing a mandate broader than the funding agreement's focus on physical and sexual abuse. But the funding criteria after 2001 would be narrower than previously.

The foundation recognized that healing is a long-term process, and from this it followed that sustaining effective projects should be a priority. Twenty percent of communities were just beginning their healing at the time of the AHF's final report, raising the level of understanding of the residential schools' legacy, chipping away at the stigma and shame of abuse, creating a

Aboriginal Healing Foundation board meeting, 2008.

safe environment to disclose and discuss the legacy of the schools, and building up the capacity of healers. AHF research data suggested that a minimum of thirty-six months was required to begin to see changes in a community, and less than one-third of AHF projects had operated three years or more. Many communities would never receive AHF funding at all. Almost a decade after the Aboriginal Healing Foundation closed, in September 2014, residential schools would continue to be in the news: from the call for a papal apology to the finding of unmarked graves, the legacy of residential schools continues. And so too the need for healing and for a healing foundation.

Even when there was a healing foundation, the needs of communities exceeded the available resources. Over half of the funded projects could not meet the needs expressed by local communities, and over one-third maintained waiting lists for services — everything from counselling to addictions treatment to suicide prevention. Another $140 million would be required just to address the shortfall related to the needs of these funded projects. The data related to residential schools and healing coming in from the communities were both encouraging and stark. Yes, the work of healing was making a measurable difference in real-world human terms, but the work was staggering. The funded projects alone identified over 75,000 individuals requiring services for severe trauma, alcohol abuse, suicidal behaviour, and more. That's enough traumatized Indigenous people to populate a city, and the full number was certainly bigger. Georges and his colleagues could see clearly that the healing had begun, and they could see just as clearly that there was a great deal of work remaining.

The largest category of activities funded by the AHF was healing circles, followed by education, workshops, traditional ceremonies, counselling, traditional medicine, conferences, life skills, land-based activities, residential (in-patient) treatment, parenting skills, family counselling, and alternative Western therapies. The most effective healing approaches (according to participants) were activities involving Elders, ceremonies, one-on-one counselling, healing/talking circles, and traditional medicine. Not surprisingly, participants in AHF-funded projects reported that their healing goals were best supported with services provided by Aboriginal practitioners, and by a "longer involvement in counselling and therapeutic activities."[5]

The board fought hard for this principle of a "longer involvement" in healing. If the government was unwilling to let the AHF invest its initial fund in a long-term strategy, then the other option was more funding. The board pitched this request, and three times the AHF was assured by government that a sizeable endowment was on the way. Three times the endowment did not materialize. The first occasion, in 2004, involved a request for $600 million. The proposal was to put $25 million from this amount into communities each year. Word came that the Aboriginal Healing Foundation would receive the $600 million at some point beyond Christmas. After years of correspondence and PowerPoints and studies and briefings and memoranda to cabinet, it appeared the government was at last acting upon its assertions that the message contained in these exchanges — healing requires a longer-term funding commitment — had gotten through. Everyone went home for the holidays in anticipation of 2005 and a new chapter in the story of the Aboriginal Healing Foundation.

The new year arrived, but the $600 million did not. Over the holidays, on December 26, 2004, a tsunami (the result of a massive earthquake under the Indian Ocean) was headline news around the world. On January 10, 2005, Prime Minister Paul Martin announced the government's decision to increase its relief aid from the $80 million committed in the previous week to $425 million. Rumour on Parliament Hill was that the humanitarian crisis had put political pressure on the government to respond, and that the Aboriginal Healing Foundation had therefore fallen in the list of government priorities. While not confirming that the AHF funds had been redirected to tsunami relief, the government gave assurances that there would be money in the 2005 federal budget — the exact amount was $40 million — and that this would be a bridge fund. The matter of a larger endowment, officials said, would be revisited in the negotiations of a comprehensive residential schools settlement agreement.

Negotiations of the Indian Residential Schools Settlement Agreement (IRSSA) involved lawyers for the government, the Assembly of First Nations, and the churches. Although the AHF was brought into the agreement, as a mechanism for the federal government to provide funding, the foundation was not at any of the negotiating tables. Lawyers negotiating for the feds settled on $125 million as the funding amount, without the input or even knowledge of the AHF. The $40 million bridge led not to an endowment, but instead to a few more years of funding. And while Georges and his colleagues at the foundation publicly expressed appreciation for the $125 million, in private there was frustration with the government's selection of an arbitrary funding amount and the lack of communication and consultation that had preceded it. The government well knew that $125 million fell short of their earlier promises. As before, they gave assurances. The third occasion on which the AHF was assured by government that a sizeable endowment was on the way was when they were told that any money left over from the IRSSA, once the payments had been made, would go into the healing fund. The government claimed that this amount would be as much as hundreds of millions of dollars, easily enough for a long-term endowment. When the Stephen Harper government came into power, in 2006, this arrangement was withdrawn. The AHF would receive the $40 million in the 2005 federal budget and a further $125 million as part of the 2007 Indian Residential Schools Settlement Agreement, rather than the more sizeable endowment required to meet the needs of Survivors.

After 2003, no new projects would be funded by the Aboriginal Healing Foundation. Not only was there not enough AHF money to fund new proposals, by 2003 there wasn't enough to keep all the existing projects going either. The amounts coming in from government were simply too small to keep everything going. Again, all of this was happening against the backdrop of the rejected KPMG proposal, which would have made additional AHF funding requests unnecessary. The board had no option but to cut loose effective community projects. But which ones? Georges and his colleagues struggled with this decision, knowing there were many in urgent need of help. The board felt an obligation to those who had put their trust in an AHF-funded healing project and concluded that it would be potentially harmful to allow those just beginning their healing to suddenly lose the foundation's support. It made no sense to let an effective project lapse in order to start a project elsewhere — especially when the AHF's own research data suggested that thirty-six months at minimum was needed "to move through needs identification, outreach & initiation of therapeutic healing."[6]

Only what the board considered "the best of the best" would receive funding from the 2005 and 2007 commitments, since the additional $165 million received by the AHF was modest in relation to community need. Extensions were offered to a limited number of existing projects identified by the board as having performed, and having managed their resources, effectively. Projects that delivered direct therapeutic services and that served hard-to-reach populations and broad geographical locations were also more likely to receive continued AHF support. One hundred thirty-four funded projects were extended to March 31, 2010, and eleven healing centres to March 31, 2012 (a total of 145 funded projects). The AHF initiated its winding-down strategy, assuming (correctly, as it turned out) that no further funds would be forthcoming,

Georges receiving the Northern Medal from Governor General Michaëlle Jean in 2008.

even though a December 7, 2009, Indian Affairs *Final Evaluation Report on AHF* recommended that "the Government of Canada should consider continued support for the Aboriginal Healing Foundation, at least until the Settlement Agreement compensation process and commemorative initiatives are completed."

Across the country, the closure of AHF-supported healing projects was met by protests, as was the concomitant decision of the Harper government to no longer fund the AHF. An October 1, 2009, CBC article, "First Nations Rally to Save Healing Program," detailed a gathering at the Manitoba legislature to protest the end of an Eyaa-Keen Centre project that provided counselling to former students of Indian residential schools. According to the project's coordinators, Mel and Shirley Chartrand, "Right now, we're helping in a month a couple of hundred people. So that would drop to just a handful. It would be really drastic."

An August 2009 *Northern News Service* article, written by Katie May and titled "It Feels So Good to Help People," looks at the work of an AHF-funded project in Inuvik, NWT, "from grief counselling to breakdancing — aimed at residential school survivors and their families." According to the program's coordinator, Peggy Day, "you just see such a difference in the person [after the workshop] because they're learning how to deal with their past history and learning how to handle it all." An August 19, 2009, article in the *Toronto Star* tells the story of Geronimo Henry, a Survivor of the Mohawk Institute in Brantford, known to former students as the Mush Hole. A Kanien'kehá:ka (Mohawk) and an Elvis impersonator from the Six Nations of the Grand River, Henry for years ran a project funded by the Aboriginal Healing Foundation. He heard stories of the physical and sexual abuse others had suffered at the Brantford residential school. Curious to know if there were more suffering like him, Henry started a group for Survivors called "The Lost Generation" in 1997. He found eight hundred of them.

A Rankin Inlet program, "Somebody's Daughter," was featured in a November 5, 2008, *Northern News Services* article by Darrell Greer titled "Unique Program Provides Skills and Healing." This "on-the-land" program, designed by Inuit women and Elders, focused on women of the

Kivalliq region and combined the teaching of traditional skills (for example, sewing, skin cleaning, and hide tanning) with counselling. The article cites "Somebody's Daughter" participants, like Annie Ollie, who speak positively of the program. "I was one of the first participants in 'Somebody's Daughter' when it started about five years ago," said Ollie. "The program has helped me increase my self-esteem and feel better about myself and my capabilities. I'm a person without a mother, so that often leaves me without anyone to guide me with traditional skills such as sewing, skinning, and tanning. The program has very, very good instructors who, in a lot of ways, replaced my mom in helping me learn important traditional skills."

The North, and in particular the Inuit, came later to healing than other Indigenous groups, but once they had taken up the opportunity offered by the AHF, the Inuit created innovative and effective initiatives. In some remote Inuit communities, AHF-funded projects were the only externally supported programs available. And, thanks to the commitment of the community, they were making a difference. In a February 26, 2006, *Nunatsiaq News* article, "Wellness Centre Gets Credit as Cambay Crime Drops," legal aid lawyer Peter Harte is quoted saying, "We are lucky to have such an excellent community resource here. The work of wellness, combined with the efforts of the RCMP to encourage people to resolve underlying problems, has had a real impact. Cambridge Bay is healing." A Nunavut court judge confirmed Harte's view that wellness is making the difference: "In a makeshift Cambridge Bay courtroom on Jan. 11 Justice Earle Johnson had this to say about wellness in the community: The Wellness Centre here works better than any other community I have seen in Nunavut. I just wish that the Wellness Centre and the programs that they run could be replicated throughout Nunavut. I think it would go a long way in trying to deal with the alcohol problems that I see coming up in court."[7]

In Whitehorse, CBC North reported on a Kwanlin Dun community wellness program that ceased to operate when the Aboriginal Healing Foundation cut its project funding. Kwanlin Dun director of health Stanley Noel is quoted in the December 22, 2004, article saying, "We've had a high volume of people using the services over the years and to me that says success." Media stories from across Canada confirmed AHF data showing that project participants were benefitting from healing, but for the projects the clock was ticking. By 2006, most AHF projects had already been shut down for lack of money.

According to a March 3, 2005, CanWest article, quoting the AHF Executive Director, "What remain are mostly counselling and therapy programs that DeGagné said need $130 million — more than three times what they got — to stay running until 2007."

From the beginning Georges had made the case for longer-term healing support, but in 2010 the federal government, under Stephen Harper, lacked the political will to sustain the Aboriginal Healing Foundation. Over the next few years, the AHF would wind down, overseeing the last of its funded projects (a handful of regional healing centres) while preparing to transfer its research assets to a successor organization, the Legacy of Hope Foundation. On September 29, 2014, the Aboriginal Healing Foundation was dissolved, bringing an end to sixteen years of operation. "As Aboriginal people, we have every reason to be proud of what we've accomplished," Georges said in a statement. "The work of healing and reconciliation is by no means complete. But the past years show us what we can do by working together, and so I urge the public to support Survivors by supporting this work of healing and reconciliation."

6

THE DEHCHO FIRST NATIONS

Several years before the federal government's fateful 2010 budget signalling the end of the Aboriginal Healing Foundation, Georges's professional life had already taken him back home. There was really no need for Georges to remain in Ottawa. The work didn't require it. But where to go? He considered British Columbia and Newfoundland, where his wife Sandra was from. He came close to buying twenty acres just outside St. John's. Eventually, in 2001, Georges sold his Chelsea, Quebec, house and moved back to Yellowknife, where he had first been called upon as a leader. From that time forward, he split his time between Ottawa and Yellowknife. Georges's career had begun in the Northwest Territories over forty years earlier, and now life had brought him full circle.

In the late 1990s, Sandra and I started discussing where we might want to live next. She had always wanted to live in Newfoundland again. We looked around St. John's and came close to buying a beautiful piece of land that was a number of acres with shorefront, minutes from the city. The only thing that stopped us was the land didn't have direct access to the nearest community road. I regret to this day not buying the land, even as an investment. It would have been a wonderful place to live.

We considered other Atlantic provinces and looked at land as we drove to Newfoundland. We had purchased a motorhome, which we used to transport our cats on our travels, mainly to eastern Canada and the United States. Later, we started travelling across Canada and into the western half of the country, including the north. We wanted to live by water, and Sandra wanted to return to salt water. I was open to anything, as long as it was near water. We spent a number of years considering eastern Canada and visiting a number of shorelines, without settling on a piece that we both wanted. We would usually end up in Newfoundland, and we agreed that if we were going to live in the Atlantic, it may as well be Newfoundland. We then thought we would give British Columbia a try, but we couldn't bring ourselves to considering the amount of money that was involved. Remote properties were less expensive, but we had no interest in isolating ourselves. We decided to return to Yellowknife and renovate our house.

By the time we returned to Yellowknife, in the summer of 2000, we'd been renting our Yellowknife home for fifteen years. We told our family and friends that we were coming back and that we would renovate and move in. We removed the carpet and replaced it with tiles and other flooring. While we got a lot done, there was just too much to do in one summer, so we returned to Chelsea to spend another winter there. In the spring of 2001, we once again drove our motorhome across the country to Yellowknife and continued the renovations. In the fall of 2001, we transferred our motorhome registration to the NWT and drove back to Chelsea to sell the house we'd been living in for sixteen years. Many of our neighbours had taken years to sell their properties. It took us three days.

We sent the contents of our Chelsea house to Yellowknife and we drove to Newfoundland in our motorhome. Before we had left Yellowknife, we'd arranged to purchase a PT Cruiser and return a rental car that we had been using. Sandra wanted to spend the winter with her mother in Moreton's Harbour while I spent the winter working with the Aboriginal Healing Foundation, travelling back and forth. My instructions from Sandra were to open as few boxes as possible so that we could properly unpack and settle in when we were back in Yellowknife in 2002. That is exactly what I did. I packed the extra boxes in the bedroom and in part of the living room, and I opened only the boxes containing what I needed to get through the winter.

I was able to spend time away from the Aboriginal Healing Foundation because, unless we had a board meeting or other event that needed my attention, I was now only working a few days a month. I set up a home office in Yellowknife and started working by phone, text, and email. I made it a practice to be at the Ottawa office at least three to five days a month.

In the spring of 2002 we drove across Canada in our motorhome, opened the rest of our boxes, and properly settled into our Yellowknife home. We had been gone for seventeen years, and we both loved being back to the land of the midnight sun. I remember our first night back, Sandra was outside at midnight pruning a willow bush in front of our bay window. We were living by water again. While we had both enjoyed our Chelsea home in Quebec, in the middle of beautiful, tall pine and oak trees, it was nowhere near water. Nevertheless, we loved our little acre of land, and we told the new owners we wanted a chance to buy it back if they were ever to sell it. About three years later, it was for sale again. We were offered the chance to buy it. There was a significant increase of the selling price, and by this time we were very into being in Yellowknife. We declined the opportunity.

We continued renovating the Yellowknife house, doing most of the work ourselves. One of the things I remember was staining the cedar siding using just ladders, with no scaffolding to reach the very high spots. This required reaching across more than twenty feet. I'm not sure how I did it. We also went back to planting a garden in our front yard and once again tried getting different kinds of roses to grow. We decided to plant a hedge using local spruce trees, something we'd seen in another part of town. We had a lot of rock on our property, and to plant the hedge we had to bring in dirt. Over time we were able to plant a row of trees in front of and up both sides of our property. We also got the roses and the gardens going.

When Georges left Dene politics in 1983 he had no intention to return, and he certainly didn't expect to be negotiating with the federal government on behalf of the Dehcho more than twenty years later. In 1977 the Berger Inquiry recommended a ten-year moratorium on the Mackenzie Valley gas pipeline, with the expectation that land claims could be settled within a decade. At the end of that decade, Georges was beginning his second term as

National Chief of the Assembly of First Nations. The Dene and the federal government had crafted a final agreement dealing with the land. As the 1990 Oka confrontation was occurring at Kanesatake, the proposed agreement was being presented at joint assemblies, one held by the Dene Nation and the other by the Métis Association.

The final agreement was the result of seven years of negotiation. It offered the five Dene regions $500 million, surface title to 181,230 square kilometres of land, and subsurface rights to 10,000 square kilometres. But there was a catch. The federal government made extinguishment of existing Aboriginal land rights and titles (such as the constitutionally entrenched Section 35 rights of hunting, fishing, trapping, and occupying lands) a condition of the agreement. Georges had gone home to oppose the agreement, not as the leader of the Assembly of First Nations but as an individual Dene who saw deep flaws in the agreement.

It was an agreement that dealt only with land. It had extinguishment of our rights, and there was no self-government discussion whatsoever. The only self-government was being achieved by the GNWT, which was getting all kinds of recognition and power.

The term "extinguishment" refers to the long-standing government policy that Indigenous people must "cede, release, and surrender" all their rights and titles to land as a precondition of entering into treaty, whether the numbered historical treaties or the modern-day treaty and land claims processes. With no assurances of Indigenous powers of the sort that the territorial government was receiving, the Dene and Métis voted to reject the agreement presented to them at the assemblies. "We all expected to go back to the negotiating table," says Georges. But it was not to be. Enraged, the Associate Deputy Minister of Indian and Northern Affairs, Rick Van Loon, thundered out of the meeting, declaring that there would be no more negotiation with the Dene as a whole. From now on, the federal government would deal only with the individual regions. Indian Affairs then cut funding to the Dene and called for repayment of the forty million dollars borrowed to finance the negotiations. The prospect of a Pan-Dene land and governance settlement was dead. On November 24, 1990, Georges told the *Edmonton Journal*, "They're back to square one, but obviously you never really go back to square one."

In July 1990, Georges was at the Dene Nation Dettah assembly for the vote on the Dene Métis Final Agreement. (The morning of the vote, thirty-one-year-old SQ Corporal Marcel Lemay was shot and killed at Oka.) "I was not in favour of it at all," Georges says. "Even though I wasn't a community delegate, I asked permission to speak, as was the right of any Dene in our constitution." Georges voiced the grounds of his disapproval: first, that self-government was not included in the agreement-in-principle and, second, that it was based on extinguishment (which the Dene had been campaigning against for many years). The amount of land offered was insufficient, but Georges told his audience that the land issue could wait for another day, once self-government was added and extinguishment taken out. "Thankfully," Georges says, "both the Dene Assembly and the Métis Association Assemblies rejected the agreement."

The vote to reject the final agreement was unanimous across the various Dene Peoples, but disagreements soon arose over how to proceed. The assembly's Mackenzie Delta delegates rejected a resolution to affirm Aboriginal and Treaty Rights in the land claims agreement, while the Sahtu delegates abstained. Gwich'in negotiator Robert Alexie walked out of the meeting, followed by the members of his team. (Patrick Scott, one of the CBC reporters at the assembly, says that in a conversation years later, Alexie told him that "we were shocked that they let us walk out. We were bluffing, but they didn't stop us.") In the years ahead these northern regions of the Mackenzie River delta would form the Aboriginal Pipeline Group and Inuvialuit leader Nellie Cournoyea would advise Georges and Dehcho Grand Chief Herb Norwegian not to get in the way of "their pipeline." (As premier, Nellie Cournoyea would also sign the 1993 Sahtu Dene and Metis Comprehensive Land Claim Agreement on behalf of the NWT government.) From July 1990 forward, the various communities and regions of the Dene Nation would go their own ways, pursuing their own agreements with Canada. The events of 1990 had exposed the emerging cracks in the Dene coalition. Eventually, the Gwich'in, Sahtu, and Tłı̨chǫ regions would withdraw from the Dene Nation. In 1993, a Dene Nation Review Committee visited the communities of Denendeh (Dene territory) to discuss the future and to consider possible amendments to the Dene Nation Constitution.

For decades, Canadian politicians had dreamed of an NWT resource economy that would rival, if not exceed, the Alberta oil and gas industry. As a September 5, 2016, *Globe and Mail* article puts it, "Residents of the Mackenzie Valley thought a boom was coming in 1958, with Diefenbaker's 'Northern Vision.' It never arrived." But at the end of the century, the conditions once again were propitious. Technological advances and global events made development of the oil sands economically feasible. A spike in the price of crude oil beginning in 1999 and peaking in June 2008, the September 11 attacks in 2001, and the American invasion of Iraq in 2003 all made development of the region more attractive. Gas shipped south from the delta could also be used in the capital-intensive extraction of oil from Alberta bitumen, home to 70 percent of the world's proven reserves. As the economic picture brightened for the oil and gas industry, investors once again revisited the prospect of a Mackenzie Valley pipeline.

In 1999 the Dehcho were finally about to go ahead with negotiations in a regional process. The Dehcho Grand Chief, Mike Nadli, hired a Toronto lawyer named Chris Reid, who played a double role as chief negotiator and legal counsel. The Dehcho saw this as an efficient and cost-prudent arrangement, never mind that their new land claims negotiator had never negotiated a land claim. For the Dehcho this was a bonus. They weren't pursuing a land claim and didn't want someone working for them who'd been in the land claim business.

The Dene had been pushing back against the term "land claims" since at least the 1960s. The concept of a claim implied a contestable assertion. You don't claim that two plus two equals four; you merely acknowledge it. Because there is no disputing the long-standing Dene occupation, stewardship, and use of lands, there's no need for a land claim. Needless to say, neither the federal nor territorial government shared the Dene view that there was no room for dispute of these basic facts. The Dene mapped their land back in the 1970s and determined that over 450,000 square miles of land was theirs. When the Dene entered into land negotiations, the mapping project provided them a framework and a vision.

The reality is that no government in Canada is going to enter into a negotiation process where the endpoint is Indigenous control over 100 percent of traditional territories. Just as the Dene had a process and a goal in mind, so too did the federal government. Here is how Chris Reid describes it:

> The typical land claim formula in Canada for this kind of land claim is based on something called land selection, where the Indigenous party ends up, at the end of the process, agreeing on the Indigenous government owning a certain amount of land, usually somewhere between 15 percent and 20 percent of the total Traditional Territory. And usually they select the parcels of land that they're going to own, based on the quantum that's been agreed to. And then the Crown owns the rest of the land. [This amount, 15–20 percent, is specific to North of 60, but wouldn't apply to BC, for example, where 5 percent is a more likely number.]

The Dehcho have continued to reject a formula that would chop the land into blocks, some owned by the Dehcho and most others by the Crown. This fundamental dispute had been the principal reason that there is no agreement to this day concerning who owns the land and who has jurisdiction over it.

It was Georges's wife Sandra who first heard that the Dehcho were looking for a new chief negotiator.

After we had been in Yellowknife for about a year, Sandra noticed that the Dehcho First Nations and the Akaitcho were looking for negotiators. She told me I should apply. This surprised me to no end. Before coming back north, she'd said that she didn't want me travelling as much anymore. "I thought part of what we were doing was having more time together," I said. "Yes," she answered, "but if you don't apply for the job, some southern lawyer who knows nothing about the Dene will get it. You have all this experience and skill, plus these are your people and you know them. You must apply!"

Soon Dehcho Grand Chief Herb Norwegian was petitioning Georges as well. Grand Chief Norwegian strongly encouraged Georges to apply, and although Georges responded that "I'm not really looking for a job" he promised to give the opportunity serious thought. "I had a meeting with the Akaitcho, but once I heard the negotiating position and their general approach, I decided I wasn't interested. On the other hand, when I reviewed the general approach of the Dehcho First Nations, I got excited." Georges became very interested in negotiating their approach. He applied for the position of chief negotiator with the Dehcho First Nations in the fall of 2003 and was interviewed in Hay River. Once again, he was working for the Dene. Although he continued as chair of the AHF board until the agency's closing in September 2014, he also took on a role with the Dene. A January 12, 2004, Dehcho First Nations' press release announced the hiring of "legendary Dene leader and activist Georges Erasmus" as the chief negotiator of the Dehcho negotiating team, tasked with the enormous work of resolving long-standing jurisdictional disputes with Canada and the Northwest Territories over lands and resources. (As mentioned earlier, Georges had actually taken on the negotiator role the previous fall.)

The Dehcho First Nations position was laid out in a document called "The Dehcho Proposal." Dehcho Grand Chief Mike Nadli had given this to Minister of Indian Affairs Jane Stewart on January 21, 1998. It had originally been given to Minister Ron Irwin in March 1994. The Dehcho didn't want to be part of the federal government's Comprehensive Claims Process and had convinced Canada to call their process the Dehcho Process. A framework agreement was signed in May of 2001, providing the roles of the three parties — Canada, the Dehcho First Nations, and the government of the NWT. The GNWT was to be involved in some but not all items, especially land, which continued to be a federal jurisdiction for bilateral discussion with the Dehcho. The framework included subject matters for negotiations, the approval process, timing of negotiations, the stipulation that all negotiations would be open to the public, and funding. The Dehcho insisted that they wouldn't borrow money for the Dehcho Process, and, during the time Georges was chief negotiator, they never did.

In the fall of 2003 Georges joined the two new assistant negotiators on the Dehcho team, Sam Gargan (a former Chief of the Deh Gáh Got'ı̨ę First Nation, former mayor of Fort Providence, and former MLA and Speaker of the Territorial Legislature) and entrepreneur Ria Letcher, of Łíídlı̨ı̨ Kų́ę́, a.k.a. Fort Simpson. In 2006, Sam and Ria would leave, and Richard Lafferty would replace them as assistant negotiator. The former chief negotiator, Chris Reid, stayed on the team to focus exclusively on the legal issues facing the Dehcho. The negotiating process was coupled with a Dehcho strategy of ensuring protection of vulnerable areas. They negotiated an expansion of the Nahanni National Park Reserve with Canada and designated certain hunting areas as unavailable for development. This initial move to protect sensitive lands took roughly half of the Dehcho's 215,000 square kilometres of territory off the negotiating table.

The whole process between Canada and the Dehcho First Nations was based on what they called the 21 Common Ground Principles. It was clear that Canada and the Dehcho disagreed on ownership of the land, sovereignty, and jurisdiction, but both wanted to reach clarity in their relationship. The 21 Common Ground Principles laid out the process that would reach agreement on land, governance, and rights, amongst other things. With the twenty-one principles agreed to, the Dehcho and Canada began the Dehcho Process.

Interim Land Withdrawals had already happened before I became chief negotiator. Land withdrawals had put aside major areas of land that were important to the Dehcho, taking a large amount of land from any economic activity while negotiations were underway. Normally, the lands set aside might be later selected by the Aboriginal party as a part of their land selection but in this case much of the land was traditionally important to the Dehcho for activity on the land for harvesters.

An Interim Measures Agreement had been reached and signed by Grand Chief Mike Nadli and federal minister Robert Nault on May 23, 2001. The Interim Measures Agreement deals with numerous issues including land use planning and the Nahanni Park; forest management; the Environmental Impact and Review Board; the NWT Protected Areas Strategy; agreement to negotiate an interim management arrangement for the Nahanni Park; tourism; Great Slave Lake Fishery; sales and leases of federal and territorial lands; land and water regulations; and land withdrawals and funding for the Dehcho involvement in these processes, including land use planning.

Finally, an Interim Resource Development Agreement had been negotiated and signed on December 2, 2002, by Grand Chief Mike Nadli and federal minister Robert Nault. The agreement provided revenue for the Dehcho from a percentage of the federal resource royalties collected from the Mackenzie Valley in the previous year, based on a formula. A process was set up for new issuance cycles for oil and gas exploration and consultation, plus a process for consultation and the reaching of impact and benefit agreements on new mines in the Dehcho territory. A map of the territory was agreed to by the parties.

An important boundary agreement with the neighbouring Tłįchǫ had been reached and signed on October 31, 2002, by Grand Chief Mike Nadli and Grand Chief Joe Rabesca. This boundary settlement was needed for the Tłįchǫ First Nation to conclude their agreement.

The framework agreement made it clear that the negotiation of a Dehcho government would be a negotiation for a public government, open to all citizens that met the residency requirements, based on Dehcho laws and customs and other Canadian laws and customs. This was the centrepiece of the Dehcho Process. The Dehcho government was to be the primary government in the region, delivering programs and services to residents in the Dehcho territory within the NWT.

The final agreement was to clarify and build on the existing treaties between the Dehcho and the Crown, providing certainty and clarity of rights respecting land, resources, and governance for both the Dehcho Dene and Métis. It would also provide for the use, management, and conservation of land and water, plus wildlife and fish and their habitat.

I found that the road map for my role was very clear. I felt totally confident in bringing the Dehcho position to the negotiating table. We began the slow process of building the agreement-in-principle. We began to outline the way we would do the mechanics of bringing position papers to the table. At one point, the federal team offered to let us use a common storage place in the electronic cloud where we could, with a password, retrieve any document brought to the table by one of the parties.

The Dehcho First Nations are a Tribal Council representing eight Dene and two Métis communities, with a population nearing 4,500. Georges describes the Dehcho First Nations as "kind of like a federation," with communities and leaders coming together to work on something, occasionally dropping out, and then coming back again. With 44 percent of the 1,220-kilometre pipeline route going through Dehcho territory, it would be difficult to complete the project without their involvement and consent. The Dehcho debated among themselves. Should they get involved in the project and reap the economic benefits as other Indigenous groups in the region, like the Inuvialuit, had done? The decision was no involvement until the issues of land title and restrictions were resolved.

When I took the position of Dehcho chief negotiator, I thought that we could reach an agreement very quickly, perhaps in two to three years. I was seriously disabused of that once the negotiations got underway. Part of the delay was waiting for the governments to come back with the reaction of their superiors or bosses. It might take months just to get a reaction to a particular idea or position. Both governments were amazingly slow in coming back with replies to important issues or subjects from the table. In the spring of 2004, we had a very interesting meeting in the Nahanni Park, at the lake above the Victoria Falls. The federal negotiator when I began negotiating for the Dehcho was Robin Atkin. He had negotiated the Interim Agreements, with Chris Reid representing the Dehcho. We were beginning to make progress when a court case centred on the MVRMA, or Mackenzie Valley Resource Management Act, and a proposed Mackenzie Valley pipeline interrupted the negotiations for a year.

The Dehcho did not have a representative on the MVRMA like others who had settled their claims and had final agreements. This was one of the issues put forth in the suit. Another was the desire of the Dehcho First Nations to create a Dehcho Resource Management Authority (DCRMA) for the Dehcho territory. The authority would have the participation of both governments and the Dehcho government. Whatever communities were impacted by a proposed development would be consulted. Both governments, as part of the Crown, and the Dehcho First Nations would have veto powers. When there was consensus on a development, it would be approved. The Dehcho had not been able to get this on the table to negotiate. The Dehcho took the position that they had never agreed to the MVRMA having any authority on their lands, and that the MVRMA could not decide on a project that would be 40 percent or more in their territory.

The fundamental underlining disagreement with Canada (or the Crown in Right of Canada) was over title to the land and the original sovereignty of the Dene of the NWT, of which the Dehcho First Nations were a part. The Dene had two numbered treaties with the Crown that Canada said extinguished title and sovereignty. The Dehcho, like other Dene, take the position that these were Peace and Friendship Treaties. This was the argument made in the Paulette case in the early '70s, which ended with Judge Morrow coming down on the side of the Dene and the Supreme Court ruling only on the caveat request by the Chiefs. The court took the position that a caveat was not possible on Crown land. It did not challenge Judge Morrow's decision that Treaties 8 and 11 did not extinguish Dene title or jurisdiction. This looked like one of those situations where the Dehcho could get clarity from the courts, once and for all, on whether title and jurisdiction was still alive and well for the Dehcho Dene.

Nine months after Georges assumed the position of Dehcho chief negotiator, negotiations with the feds shifted focus to an out-of-court settlement of a lawsuit challenging the application of the Mackenzie Valley Resource Management Act and the pipeline Environmental Assessment Process. A September 3, 2004, *Globe and Mail* article quotes the Dehcho Grand Chief, Herb Norwegian, as saying, "This is the only recourse that we have." The Dehcho stuck to the positions that the MVRMA didn't apply to the Dehcho and that they would not be part of this federally imposed resource development process, but also that no pipeline would traverse their territory. The lawsuit suspended the pipeline project, and it caused the suspension of the Dehcho land negotiations with government.

Georges recalls an assembly at Kakisa, in the summer of 2004.

Once the Dehcho filed their suit, Canada shut down the negotiations in the Dehcho Process and brought in Tim Christian to negotiate an out-of-court settlement. Part of the deal was to get the feds to agree to discuss the DCRMA, because that's what the whole lawsuit was about.

It took most of a year but finally, in July 2005, a settlement was reached. In keeping with the settlement's terms, the Dehcho agreed not to challenge the MVRMA again for seven years and to negotiate the DCRMA in the Dehcho Process, and the government paid out $31.5 million, spread over several years. In the end, the Dehcho decided it wasn't worth the risk or the time for a court case to wind its way all the way to the Supreme Court, as cases have been known to take up to ten years. Once again the pipeline was not built, but this time because the project had become too costly. There were cheaper places to get gas by fracking, in the U.S. and elsewhere in Canada.

"We settled, and we put half the $31.5 million in a trust," says Richard Lafferty, "and we used the other half for negotiations and running the main office."

Federal negotiator Robin Atkin had moved on to other assignments with the government. Tim Christian became the federal negotiator and negotiations resumed. Over time, we negotiated what a Dehcho public government, based on Dehcho First Nations laws and customs and other Canadian laws and customs, would look like. We negotiated a regional government with provincial-like powers, and we negotiated community governments that allowed anyone who met a residence requirement to run for office and to vote in both community and Dehcho government elections. We also negotiated guaranteed seats for Dehcho Dene, both at the regional and community government levels. In addition, the Grand Chief and the Community Chief had to be a Dehcho Dene.

The current municipal community governments, the Dene Band Councils, and the Métis locals would all be merged into one government structure. We came to the table seeking a ten-year residency requirement, then reduced it to five years. Canada and the government of the NWT are seeking two years. It became apparent that, with guaranteed seats, there was not as much need for an extra-long residency requirement.

A lot of work went into what a world with the Dehcho government replacing the current government of the Northwest Territories would look like. We negotiated fifty chapters in the draft agreement-in-principle. The AIP chapters included Preamble, Definitions, General Provisions, Dehcho Government, Dehcho Community Governments, Eligibility & Enrolment, Dehcho Community Lands, Early Childhood Education, Kindergarten to Grade 12, Post Secondary Education, Out of School Care, Adult Education and Training, Child and Family Services, Social Housing, Income Assistance, Adoption (including Custom Adoption), Marriage, Wills and Estates, Language and Culture, Traditional Healing and Health, Heritage Resources, the Administration of Justice, Taxation, Dispute Resolution, Approval of the AIP, Ratification of the Dehcho Agreement, and Implementation.

The approach adopted by both Canada and the government of the Northwest Territories was that every head of power enjoyed by the Dehcho Government had to also be exercised by one of the other governments. This meant that the government that had paramount authority in any jurisdiction would override if there was a conflict in laws. Usually, any jurisdiction to be exercised by the Dehcho government that was provincial-like would mean the Dehcho jurisdiction would override any conflicting jurisdiction from another government. The sticking point in the jurisdiction area was and is the position from both governments that exclusive jurisdiction is something they have denied the Dehcho so far.

The Royal Commission on Aboriginal Peoples had recommended that Aboriginal Peoples be able to exercise exclusive jurisdiction in important internal matters that were central to the health and survival of Aboriginal Peoples. Legal experts like Brian Slattery and former Supreme Court judge Bertha Wilson thought the idea of exclusive jurisdiction was very reasonable and no threat to Canada. Neither government has been open to recognizing even minor heads of jurisdiction so far. There were a small number of heads of power we continued to push for exclusive power. We included sections in the agreement titled "Structure of Dehcho Government" and "Internal Matters," and the "Management and Exercise of Rights and Benefits" provided under the Dehcho Agreement, including those "Related to the Harvesting of Wildlife, Fish, Migratory Birds, Plants and Trees." Very modest demands, but both governments are steadfast in their opposition to the jurisdiction.

Like most modern treaties, the Dehcho Agreement was a way out of the Indian Act. Dehcho Lands, called Dehcho Ndehe, would not be reserve lands. Everyone would pay taxes, and Canada would collect GST and the personal taxes of those in the Dehcho communities or on Dehcho Lands/Dehcho Ndehe. Canada would give the federal portion of taxes collected back to the Dehcho Government for its programs and services to Dehcho citizens and residents. The government of the Northwest Territories took the position that they would hand over the taxes they collected in the heads of power that the Dehcho Government started exercising. This meant that if the Dehcho would take over the schools or develop a Dehcho Education Act for kindergarten to grade twelve, the government of the NWT would turn over their education dollars.

A Dehcho constitution, which will be the supreme law of the Dehcho and which all laws must be consistent with or be void, must be completed before the final agreement. Work has begun on this. It will outline all those who can participate, including Dehcho citizens, resident Canadians, and permanent residents in Canada. It will outline the structure of Dehcho Government and Dehcho Community Governments and will list a Dehcho Charter of Values, Rights, and Freedoms important to the Dehcho Dene and Métis. The rights included are the right to speak their traditional languages, the right and duty to exercise and pass on their languages and culture, and the right to practice their spiritual, cultural, and religious beliefs without fear of discrimination. The Dehcho Government will enact laws and implement measures to ensure that all persons shall enjoy reasonable protection against all forms of violence, coercion, and discrimination. The Dehcho Government will enact an Official Languages Act, setting out measures to protect Dehcho Dene and Michif languages. The Dehcho Charter makes it clear that the Canadian Charter of Rights and Freedoms applies to the Dehcho Government.

Additionally, the Dehcho Charter outlines some unique areas. The constitution expresses the fundamental values of the Dehcho Dene and Métis, reflecting their unique spirit and values, including respect and support for each individual living in a community of shared resources and responsibilities. The Dehcho government must pass worker safety laws and has the responsibility to protect the lands and waters of the Dehcho Territory. It will enact laws that balance the duty to protect lands and waters with the need for economic activity in the Dehcho.

In February 2006, Prime Minister Stephen Harper assumed office and identified the Mackenzie Valley pipeline as a top priority for Jim Prentice, the minister of Indian Affairs. A February 25, 2006, Don Martin article for the *National Post* (headlined "Prentice Already Walking the Walk on Native Issues") quotes Prentice saying that "it's not just a pipeline, but a spine of northern development. It will change the east-west axis of oil and gas development northward from the Alberta border to the Arctic Ocean. When it's finished, the Northwest Territories will be a driving engine of our economy." The Harper government offered $104 million and 39,000 square kilometres of land with subsurface rights, roughly 17 percent of the Dehcho Traditional Territory. At one point, Stephen Harper was offering the Dehcho terms that were better than the terms of the GNWT, which was led by an Aboriginal premier.

Land, a fundamental and sacred issue for the Dehcho, became the major sticking point. Tim Christian presented the federal government's position. What Canada was prepared to agree to fell far short of what the Dehcho thought was fair. We presented a simple formula: offer the Dehcho the same as you'd offered the Tłı̨chǫ, surface and subsurface rights multiplied by the population. Unfortunately, we were unable to get agreement.

The government was offering the Dene 39,000 kilometres. The Tłı̨chǫ had title to 39,000 square kilometres under *their* agreement, despite the Dehcho having a much larger population. Applying the population formula used to calculate the Tłı̨chǫ land quantum, the Dehcho arrived at 70,000 square kilometres as an equivalent offer. In response, the federal government increased the land quantum offer to 45,810 square kilometres. Neither the feds nor the territorial government were offering anything near the Dehcho number. The GNWT insisted that the Dehcho accept the "standard model" for a land claim agreement, called "land selection," severely constricting the eventual Dehcho territory. As Chris Reid explains, "The territorial government came out with a new policy, claiming that it had always been their policy even though it's never been mentioned anywhere, anytime before. And according to their policy, after you complete a Dehcho land claim, at least 45 percent of the land in the Dehcho territory must be open Crown land. Well, half of the territory is protected, and another huge chunk of it is not economically accessible. We said, 'but that's all that there is. I mean, you get it all. The Dehcho will never have economic development.'"

The GNWT demand was a massive affront to Dehcho interests and aspirations, leaving only 15,000 square kilometres of open land to the Dehcho Dene communities. The GNWT "intend to give these open Dehcho lands away to oil companies and mining companies in exchange for tiny royalty payments," the October 2013 *Report on the Dehcho Process* bitterly concluded.[1]

To make matters worse, the Government of Northwest Territories knew that devolution was coming. On June 25, 2013, the territory signed an agreement with Ottawa that would take effect on April 1, 2014. Soon the NWT would have provincial-like powers over lands and resources. The GNWT took to slowing down the process, contesting every detail of the negotiations. Devolution undercut the Dehcho negotiations by formalizing key matters like resource sharing and jurisdiction. As Chief Edward Sangris noted, in a February 28, 2014, *Globe and Mail* article, "The very thing the feds are transferring to the [NWT government] is included in our discussion." Georges saw the effects of devolution too.

All of a sudden, the GNWT role at the negotiating table completely changed. They now were the ones that were speaking on land and resources, and they became very, very covetous of the new powers and responsibilities that they thought they had. And so, they were very reluctant to come up with a fair agreement. We tried but couldn't budge the NWT. Land is still the outstanding question before the Dehcho Process today. Canada and the government of the NWT eventually made a joint offer that increased the amount of land, but it's still shy of what the Dehcho feel is fair.

Over many years, the negotiations between representatives of the Dehcho and the federal and territorial governments had taken place in various locations. They met often in Yellowknife, but also in Fort Simpson, Ottawa, Edmonton, the Nahanni National Park Reserve, and elsewhere. Conveniently, the southern sessions took place in early December and were attended by northern Chiefs who came as observers — and as shoppers. The Dehcho negotiations were open to the public, and the point of meeting in different locations was to allow for broader public attendance. "Not that very many people came, or were enamoured by the sessions," Patrick Scott says, "because they were pretty dry and pretty slow going."

"Not because of us!" adds Georges.

We'd have these items and Canada wouldn't accept our position. Canada would think something else, and the GNWT would have yet another opinion. So we'd put the disagreements into a footnote. So many of these things were absolutely minor details, here and there, that oh my god. We'd try and push them on these details but, no, we couldn't get anywhere. Okay, let's move on then, and find something else. Page such-and-such, chapter such-and-such, footnote such-and-such.

Patrick Scott describes the negotiations as endless, incredibly tedious, and very obtuse at times when dealing with Canada, and particularly with the GNWT. "I mean, the level of patience and self-control that's required when government is being totally, totally unresponsive to any reasonable discussion … it drives you nuts. I don't know how Georges sustained his calmness in those situations, but certainly he did."

In the early days, the federal and territorial teams were made up of negotiators, lawyers, assistants, and bureaucrats, but over time the rosters shrank to a negotiator, a lawyer, and one or two support staff. Georges assumed the role of chair and, since no one objected, he continued on in that function to the end of his tenure. "I thought it was better that the Dehcho lead, since it was the Dehcho's negotiations for land and governance. I started acting as chair, and no one challenged, so I just kept chairing." Negotiating with the folks across the table was only a small aspect of Georges's role. There isn't simply the business of negotiating, there's also managing staff and budgets and the egos of lawyers and politicians and bureaucrats.

And then there are the people on your side of the ledger, who have to be managed as well. As the GNWT became increasingly intransigent, some Dehcho leaders refused to compromise. Georges persuaded the Dehcho leadership that even though they didn't like what was on the table, it was in their interest to keep negotiating. "I'm not sure a lot of people have that particular ability," says Chris Reid. "The stature of Georges as a former National Chief enabled him to talk to Dehcho leaders in a way that I wouldn't have dreamed of." The majority of Georges's work was ensuring that leadership were informed and on board.

> Some would say, "Well, you just convince the government that we signed a treaty and, you know, we never gave up anything. All you got to do is just tell them, you know, just tell them, and all the land will be ours."

There were many times Georges would have to say, "That's not the way it's gonna work." Successful negotiation would have to mean that both sides think they're coming out as winners. There would have to be mutual benefit and compromise, and compromise did not necessarily mean selling out. Something would have to be given up for something to be gained. This wasn't a message that everyone wanted to hear, but it was definitely a message Georges would have to deliver. And that's what he did, community by community and assembly by assembly.

Sam Gargan, Georges's co-negotiator and later on, Grand Chief of the Dehcho First Nations, also notes the communications challenges faced by the Dehcho throughout the negotiations. "Unlike the Dene Nation, we still don't have a team of fieldworkers in the region. So there's still some hurdles that we're faced with every time that we want to inform the community." Georges agrees. "That is really a hindrance. When the Dehcho were reduced in funding, it really hindered the work. It's stupid that government did that. And it was simply because the Dehcho didn't want to borrow money. So the government started reducing how much money they were providing. First, it was $2.1 million, and then it went down to a million. When I left, it was down to half a million a year. It really diminished what the Dehcho could do, because there really was a need for community staff to inform people."

On Georges's effectiveness as a leader, Patrick Scott is clear. "I think it must be because he is so tuned into Elders. They believe in what they value, and he's good at translating their worldview into contemporary realities. His deep sense of awareness of where Dene society has come from, what it has been, and what is important to it, enables him to put the puzzle pieces together. It's not just knowing. You've got to go past knowing. You have to care to take the path that Georges has taken, to take the journey he's travelled."

Although he'd resisted taking on work, negotiating for the Dehcho was "like coming home." Georges found the work interesting and even fun.

Living and working amongst the Dene again was a delightful thing that felt so comfortable and enjoyable, even during the tough periods. I felt so at home and self-assured in the work and in the rightness of what we were seeking. It was a perfect fit for me. It was especially enjoyable to work with the Elders and Herb Norwegian, who had become a good friend during our days at the Dene Nation. It took me a little while to get completely caught up to events that had happened during the sixteen years I'd been away. But eventually I reached the point where it felt like I had never left.

Unfortunately, work meant that once again Georges was doing an enormous amount of travel. "One good thing was the ability to video conference our negotiation sessions." Over the twelve years that he was chief negotiator for the Dehcho First Nations, Georges saw the negotiators for the other parties change a number of times. When Georges resigned, the negotiators for all three parties lived in Yellowknife.

Ka'a'gee Tu First Nation Chief Lloyd Chicot says that Georges had "a better perspective as to what we were negotiating about, so that's one of the reasons that my community chose him as the chief negotiator." And he thought the Dehcho were making "pretty good progress. A lot of the things the Elders talked about in the past, we pretty well hit that nail on the head there when we were negotiating with Canada. I think Georges pushed the Dene perspective a little bit more, on the whole. We wanted a little bit more than what Canada was willing to offer. But we went as far as we could, and we really, really pushed the envelope to get our views on file."

Georges also felt he'd gone as far as he could. By 2015, he'd concluded that an agreement wasn't in the foreseeable future. He signed on for what he thought would be, at most, a four-year job, and now he was twelve years in with nothing to show for his effort.

> We were totally stalled on land, and that was the principal thing left. I thought, this is going to go on for a long time, and you know what, I've already been at this for twelve years and I don't see an end in sight. I couldn't tell myself that, in a year or two, we're gonna get into it more. It was obvious we were in a quagmire, and we were going to be there for a while.

Negotiations were scheduled to resume in November. In the summer of 2015, Georges was alone, his wife Sandra visiting family in Newfoundland. He'd stayed behind to work on the deck of his Yellowknife house, an activity that gave him ample time to think about the negotiations and about his future. "It's not a great comparison, I'm sure, but it was like Pierre Trudeau having a walk in the snow. I concluded that this work was not going to go anywhere quick."

The Dehcho First Nations announced on September 8, 2015, that Georges was stepping down as their chief negotiator. Their press release began

"Georges Erasmus has led the region's land claim and self government negotiations for the last 12 years. The 67-year-old says he's retiring for personal and family reasons." The personal reasons concerned the impasse at which Georges had arrived in the Dehcho negotiations. The family reasons, kept from public view, referred to Georges's wife, who in 2015 was in remission from cancer. Georges wanted to be at home, spending precious time with his wife.

I'd become the Dehcho First Nations chief negotiator in late 2003. Eight years later, in 2011, we discovered that Sandra had cancer. After about a year of surgery, radiation, and chemotherapy, the cancer went into remission. I was torn about my job, because I don't like to leave something clearly unfinished, and spending more time with Sandra. We discussed what we should do. She

Georges and Sandra, 2016.

was strongly in favour of staying the course with the Dehcho First Nations if the end was not far around the corner. Interestingly, both governments were using final draft legal language, borrowing from other final agreements where appropriate. Normally, everyday common language is used to negotiate an agreement in principle. We reasoned this would mean a quick turnaround between the AIP stage and the final agreement, so we also took to using legal terminology on the Dehcho side of the table. Sandra and I decided we would begin taking more time for holidays, which we spent mainly in Newfoundland.

We bought a new motorhome, our old one now being twenty years old, and we drove across the country, visiting friends and family. We began renovating the Knight family home that Sandra had acquired when she and her brothers divvied up the properties their parents had left without wills. The home was built in the 1950s and needed some work. We spent three months over a summer, with more work remaining to be done. The new deck made a wonderful place from which Sandra could oversee where she grew up. She had also watched the family business from this spot.

We both loved being in Newfoundland in winter, having spent many Christmases there. We would come for a month for our yearly holiday. Unfortunately, the work I was doing never allowed us an extended time in Newfoundland. During the summer of 2014, I bought cedar in Yellowknife to replace the deck, which sat for a winter in our yard. In the spring of 2015, I noticed that weather damage was starting, so I began to tear up the deck. I replaced the supports that needed replacing, and I put a double coating of clear stain on both sides of the cedar. It was slow and labour-intensive work. Sandra made a trip to Newfoundland on her own while I finished the deck.

During the quiet time that I had repairing and replacing the deck top, I thought about my work. We had tried to get an agreement on the land quantum over the past few years, with no movement at all from the government of the NWT. We had been stuck for years, and I didn't see any quick agreement on the issue — I decided I had better things to do with my time. I notified the Dehcho First Nations that I was resigning. Grand Chief Herb Norwegian tried to talk me out of resigning, but my mind was made up. Six years later, I was asked to assist in a workshop for the negotiating team. There had been no movement, except that Canada and the government of the NWT had come together and made a joint offer of land. The offer fell short of the fair deal that the Dehcho First Nations wanted.

In 2016, Sandra's cancer returned. This meant chemotherapy again, along with naturopathic treatments. Together these took up a lot of time. By late fall we started to keep away from crowds, as Sandra became very susceptible to catching anything and everything. I became her main caregiver, but thankfully our doctor was prepared to make house visits, and home care provided nurses from time to time. I really didn't believe that she would die, even at the very end. I kept thinking that something would happen to heal her, and that we would have the retirement we had always been planning, spending more time in Newfoundland with her family and friends. Eventually we had a wheelchair. Then a hospital bed. Her two brothers came to Yellowknife, and we took turns staying up with her.

In late 2016 or early 2017, we were told there was no need for any more chemo. The cancer was not responding to the treatments. All the medical professionals could do now was assist with the pain and keep Sandra comfortable.

Sandra was a remarkable individual. I was very lucky to have her in my life for the nearly forty-three years that we were together. She was very spiritual and intuitive and would read material that was always helping her grow spiritually. I read them the Zen way by looking at the covers and occasionally reading a page or two. She also was amazingly brave. She would say and do things that others would think are way out there. If she thought it was helpful, she would speak her mind.

She did one of those things not long before she passed. She started telling people, including me, that I would have another person in my life after she died. When she told me that privately, I said there will be no need for that, you'll make it through this. She would quietly and patiently say, "Georges, you know I am very sick." She didn't push, she just let me process the things we talked about. I think probably the hardest for her was telling her two brothers that I would have someone in my life after she died. I couldn't put my mind there and asked her to quit saying these things. I realized afterward that she was doing what she could to assist me after she passed on. I found emails that she sent to friends and family where she was asking people to look out for me, because I was going to take her passing very hard. I felt so close to her, and it felt like we were going down a rabbit hole together as she got sicker and sicker. I was kind of surprised when I didn't die when she did.

Her brothers, Ted and Ken, and I would stay up with her, since she would only doze from time to time. We thought we should always have someone up with her. At one point, when it was my turn to be awake with her, she asked if I would still drive across the country in our motorhome as we had planned on doing together. I said, I still don't believe you will die but yes, if you die, I will still drive to Newfoundland this summer. She asked what I would think if she asked her brothers to join me, each going one way. I said that would be okay with me. On a Friday morning, we took her to the hospital in an ambulance. She fell asleep, for the first time in a while. Early the next morning, around 5:00 a.m. on April 15, 2017, Sandra quietly passed on. I was in shock. I expected her to wake, and that we would spend more time together.

That summer I drove across Canada with Sandra's brothers. Ken went east with me and Ted returned. It was a great time. I learned new things about both brothers. We visited friends and camped in the campgrounds that Sandra and I used to use when we crossed the country. It was bittersweet. When I was in Newfoundland, we replaced the shingles on the cabin that Sandra and I had built for her mom. I discovered notes that Sandra had left for me throughout the family home, as if she knew she was never coming back. It broke my heart, and I had moments of grief when alone, thinking about our many years together and all the support I had received from Sandra while I pursued my work in the Aboriginal struggle. I still found it hard to believe, but I knew I eventually had to accept that Sandra was gone.

When Patrick Scott was working with Georges, he was diagnosed with cancer. Needless to say, it was a very difficult time. "Georges stood with me," he says. "He supported me in profound, simple ways that he probably doesn't even understand how important they were to me at the time." Patrick becomes quiet and serious. "I think it's important for you to hear this," he says. His voice breaks as he holds back the tears. "I know from having worked with him for eleven years, directly, you will never find a more kind person than Georges Erasmus. He can be the most intimidating political bully in the room, but on a humanity level, he is one of the kindest people I know.

I say that with a lot of emotion, because it's that public persona that people see, and they miss the soul, and he has an incredible soul."

For years, Georges didn't want to write this book, or at least he didn't want to write it enough to commit. "I'm too busy with other things," he decided. After Sandra died Georges grieved, afflicted by the raw calamity of loss. It must have seemed to him as if life was over. But of course, life goes on for the living.

7

CONCLUSION

Not long after Sandra had passed, I started walking every day, began lifting weights again, and making sure I didn't isolate myself from people. In May I bought a small cabin from my brother Guy, and I went there from time to time.

In the summer of 2017, I made a trip across Canada in my motorhome and planned my return so I could be back in Yellowknife for the Labour Day long weekend. It had been forty-three years earlier that Sandra and I had started our relationship on this weekend, and I wanted to be back in Yellowknife for it. I spent it alone, lost in memories and thoughts about the forty-three years we had spent together. I went to places we used to enjoy, walking the paths and trails around Yellowknife. September 15 was five months since Sandra had passed away. I remember it being a hard day for me, but I knew I had to move on.

A few days after the five-month anniversary of Sandra's death, something interesting started to happen to me. I started to get a prompt to contact Evelyn Lyons, better known as "Eve." I had met her in June of 1972, while she was working at the Indian Brotherhood as assistant to the president, James Wah-Shee. I was still with the CYC in 1972. She'd left town in the fall of that year to eventually return to Ottawa. Somehow, we had hooked up for a while in late 1973 and 1974, which ended when I began my relationship with Sandra.

I hadn't had contact with Eve for forty-three years and I wasn't really sure if she was alive. I ignored the prompts the first day, but they only got stronger the next day. Finally, I started looking for an address in some old address books. I found an old Hotmail email address that I sent an email to, which bounced back. I thought, well, I tried, so that should be it. The next day the prompts were even stronger. I went back to that old address book, and I found what looked like a cellphone number. I thought, no way is this still relevant. But I sent a text message anyway, and I waited. Nothing happened for about an hour, then I received a text: "Georges?" Then a second text: "From the NWT?" I couldn't believe it. Somehow I had reached her. Of course, I had no idea what her situation was. Married, perhaps. Children, grandchildren. I had no idea what to expect. I replied that, yes, it was me, one and the same.

We had a few texts that evening and arranged a call for the next evening, after dinner. I had an anxious day, but the prompts immediately stopped once we connected. Finally, she called me, and we talked. She was alone, unmarried, and had not had anyone in her life for twelve years. She was taking care of her ninety-eight-year-old mother, soon to be ninety-nine, in her Toronto condo. She was still working, with a five-year plan to retire. I told her that I was semi-retired, and that Sandra had died in April after five years from the first cancer. Eve tried to quickly tell me all the things that she had experienced since we had last seen each other. I could tell from her voice that she still had feelings for me. I was amazed.

We started calling each other regularly over the next number of weeks. I had a conference in Vancouver that I was attending in October just before the Thanksgiving long weekend. I suggested she come and meet me in Edmonton for the weekend. She said she would need to find someone to care for her mom. In the end, I decided to go to Toronto to see her because she was unable to find a caregiver on short notice and then travel to Edmonton. Eve picked me up at the airport and took me to my hotel so I could check in. Later, after she had arranged supper for her mom, we went out to a local restaurant and had a wonderful meal together. After the initial awkwardness on the drive into the city, everything started to feel like it was yesterday that we had been together. Eve was the other person who I had told Sandra I loved and had given a piece of my heart. Sandra would tease me about Eve over the years, even though she didn't have a name and never asked for one. "Do you think your other love could do it better? Ha, ha," or "You could always ask your other love." The years melted away. Eve and I were together, and we wanted to be with each other.

Sometime after Eve and I reconnected, I had an interesting discussion with an Aboriginal Elder in Yellowknife. She started telling me about a prompt to get into her car and drive out on the highway, so she did. She was told when to stop and to look at the sky. In the sky, she watched as the clouds changed to spell out the initials of the young person in her family that had died not long before, who she was concerned about. She said that it made her very happy to know that the young person was all right. I then told her about the prompts that I had received to call Eve, and how we had finally connected. She said, that is your wife Sandra; she wants you to be happy. You must always listen to your prompts.

I started going to Toronto regularly and rented a furnished condo for seven months just ten minutes' walk from Eve's condo. During this time, Eve had

Georges and Eve by Great Slave Lake, January 2019.

decided to retire at the end of June 2018 and move to Yellowknife for good to be with me.

Two years after we reconnected, Eve and I were married in front of family and friends in Yellowknife. Several of Sandra's family came to the wedding from the East Coast and continue to keep in contact with us. We try to spend time with family and friends on a regular basis and get in some fun travel. So far, we have been to Ireland, Scotland, London, and New Zealand, plus an extended trip with our motorhome across Canada and to the Yukon twice. Eve traded in her car as a down payment on a truck, which I barely let her drive. It has become very useful in renovating the cabin I bought from my brother.

Eventually Eve sold her condo in Toronto, and we started planning a major renovation to our Yellowknife home. First, we did the kitchen and two existing bathrooms, along with replacing the hot water boiler and many other things. Sandra and I had wanted to update the kitchen and somehow add an ensuite to the master bedroom. Interestingly, Sandra had suggested going over the existing living room or dining room and taking up some of the high ceiling space for a new bedroom suite, but I didn't want to lose even part of the high ceilings we had. In the end it was exactly what we did. We took up part of the dining area ceiling, still leaving a nine-foot ceiling, and going out both south and east over our deck, to also create a covered deck area that we had always wanted. It took a few years, and Covid doubled the costs, but we love what we did with the house. I didn't think I would find happiness again, but I could not be happier.

I've been spending more time with my two sons and their families. My eldest son, Kristen, lives in Yellowknife, so I get to see him more frequently. We also arrange one or two trips a year to BC for visits with my younger son, Che, and his family. My son Kristen and I are renovating the cabin, so we are regularly involved in doing work and spending time together. Over the last couple of years my son Che and I have been going fishing at Frontier Lodge, near Łutsel K'e, or Snowdrift. Last year it was part of his fiftieth-birthday-year bucket list, and this year his wife joined us along with Kristen. Che has two boys, six and nine. Eve offered to take care of them while the rest of us went fishing. Some of us had fun.

Mike Mitchell and Georges in Whitehorse, November 2019.

It was never my intention to spend my whole life in the First Nations rights struggle to regain control of our lives and to be self-determining, with control of our lands. One situation led to another, and it seemed the next opportunity would simply open up in front of me. I always had an inner sense that I was doing the right thing, like I had agreed on the other side before being born that I would take on this struggle. Most of my jobs fit me like a glove. I truly enjoyed all my jobs, even the ones with challenges. I knew that I was carrying on the work in our struggle that had been started a long time before me and that it would carry on after I was finished with my input in advancing our rights. As the saying goes, I knew I was standing on the shoulders of giants, without any doubts.

There came a time that I realized this was going to take longer than I originally thought. At some point, it became clear to me that I would not be part of the implementation of our self-government. I had started my work with our people thinking I could make better laws, or our people could make better laws or policies than what I was seeing forced on our people. I came to the realization that I was setting up the conditions and institutions for others to implement, legislate, and govern. That's when I came to fully appreciate the amazing work of those who came before me and who set the conditions for me to carry on their struggle, which I was very happy to do.

Two of the organizations I was instrumental in helping create in the north, the Tree of Peace and the Denendeh Development Corporation, are still in operation today. One runs a friendship centre with social programs and the other is the economic arm of the Dene of the Northwest Territories.

Two organizations that I worked with and led are the Assembly of First Nations in Ottawa and the Dene Nation in Yellowknife. Both are being challenged as to their relevance today. In the case of the AFN, the organization is amid an internal discussion as to its relevance at the grassroots level and at the national level. An AFN charter renewal has been underway for some time now, and hopefully it will assist in bringing the organization to a point where it is once again relevant to the majority of First Nations. The Dene Nation is also looking at its constitution and wondering about its future, because the role of the organization has changed since many regions are settling land and governance agreements. In both cases the future role may be more like the UN, where governments come together to decide common action together. In the same way that the United Nations is not a government, neither will be the Assembly of First Nations or the Dene Nation.

A big part of the message that I grew up with from the Dene was we never gave up our land, or our ability to manage and control it. In other words, we did not extinguish our title or our right to be self-governing and self-determining. This was central to much of the work that I did throughout many of the different roles I assumed in my career. One of my jobs with the Indian Brotherhood in 1973 was lobbying Ottawa to create a way in which we Dene, and other First Nations, could negotiate a land and governance regime. It took many years to get to the point where Canada finally agreed to negotiate so-called land claims. It took two court cases that went all the way to the Supreme Court — the 1973 Nisga'a Calder case from British Columbia, on Aboriginal

Eve and Georges in New Zealand, March 2020.

Title, and the Paulette case from the Northwest Territories on Treaties 8 and 11, which did not extinguish Dene title. This, along with continued lobbying, forced the Trudeau government to reverse its direction of removing Aboriginal and Treaty Rights and to begin a negotiation process based only on land and extinguishment.

We continued to lobby for an alternative to extinguishment, and for the addition of self-government, in what became known as the "Comprehensive Claims Process." There was a brief period (in 1976, when Warren Allmand was the minister of Indian Affairs) that the government was open to negotiating both land and self-government. Trudeau quickly closed that door and shut our negotiations down. He started negotiations with the Inuvialuit and others on extinguishment and just land, not self-government. This was still the model being used when the Dene Nation and Métis Association process to negotiate an agreement-in-principle took place in the late '80s. This model was discussed and rejected at two general assemblies in Yellowknife in 1990.

After the Dene-Métis process came to an end in July 1990, over time the regions started their own negotiations in the Comprehensive Claims Process with Canada. The Mackenzie Delta Gwich'in 1992 agreement and the Sahtu Dene and Métis agreement of 1993 continued to use the same model as the Inuvialuit Final Agreement of 1984, with extinguishment or cede, release, and surrender of rights rather than recognition of them, and no self-government. The Tłı̨chǫ entered the Comprehensive Claims Process but kept pushing for an alternative to extinguishment and for an opportunity to negotiate self-government, rather than the creation of corporations to manage their rights. During the RCAP process, the Tłı̨chǫ would contact us for any models that we were working on that were actual ways in which rights of Aboriginal Peoples could be recognized and not extinguished. We provided the Tłı̨chǫ with a recognition model that they used at their negotiating table. Following the failure of the referendum on the 1992 Charlottetown Accord, which included a self-government clause, the federal government in 1995 took the position that Section 35 of the Canadian Constitution did include the right to self-government, as Aboriginal Peoples had been saying all along. The RCAP report of November 1996 recommended that Canada negotiate self-government at the land claim tables, and it recommended alternatives to extinguishment.

It took the Tłı̨chǫ longer than the other regions, but their insistence that self-government be part of their agreement was accepted. The fight for an alternative to extinguishment paid off in the end. On August 25, 2003, exactly eighty-two years after Treaty 11 was signed by Tłı̨chǫ Chief Monfwi, in 1921, the Tłı̨chǫ Land Claims and Self-Government Agreement was signed, with a recognition clause, not extinguishment.

Thankfully, Canada has now taken the position that Aboriginal groups that were forced to accept extinguishment in the modern treaty process can now have that removed and can now also negotiate self-government just as Délı̨nę in the Sahtu has over the past few years. This clearly is the result of the ongoing lobbying being done by those still at the negotiating tables, dealing with land and governance, and those that have the agreements based on extinguishment and that included self-government. It was wonderful to see the James Bay Cree be able to go back to the negotiating table and negotiate a self-government agreement. My old colleague René Dussault was on the government side of the table, and no doubt he had a feeling of satisfaction to see a completed governance agreement arrived at for the Cree. The Gwich'in

Tribal Council of the Mackenzie Delta in the Northwest Territories are now at the table negotiating a regional government.

With the Tłı̨chǫ model in place, I thought that negotiating an agreement for the Dehcho First Nations was going to be quick. We now had the ability to negotiate land and governance, without extinguishment. Unfortunately, it was not quick. In fact, the process continues today with former Grand Chief Mike Nadli as chief negotiator. There are high hopes that it can be successfully concluded in the next number of years.

A lot has changed for First Nation Peoples in Canada during my life. For the first eleven years of my life, until 1959, Status Indians were regarded as so-called wards of the state. We could not vote, own property, hire lawyers to defend ourselves, and much more, because we were not recognized as human beings with citizenship rights to act in our own right. That changed when Prime Minister Diefenbaker amended the Indian Act. The Indian Residential School System finally ended in the late '60s, after over one hundred years of trying to destroy Aboriginal languages and cultures and world views. (The schools continued to operate in many of our communities up until the late 1990s.) While the Indian Act is still in place, we have over two hundred negotiation tables across Canada to move away from the act and have self-government for First Nation communities. Unfortunately, negotiation takes so long, but the fact that these processes exist is a positive development. Much has changed, but much still needs to be done.

One of the ongoing areas for continued lobbying is in the governance arena, the need for Canada and provincial and territorial governments to accept that Indigenous governments must be able to exercise exclusive jurisdiction in certain areas. Governments must get over whatever foolish fears they have in this area and come to the negotiating tables to negotiate exclusive jurisdiction.

Healing and Reconciliation with the Indigenous population of Canada will not be complete until we have a full implementation of the Royal Commission on Aboriginal Peoples' report. It is not too late at all to implement that report, as it looked like Prime Minister Justin Trudeau was going to do a few years ago.

There is no doubt in my mind that the Indian Act must go, but it cannot be done in a way that the White Paper of 1969 attempted. The RCAP recommended a Recognition Act that would put in place Regional First Nation Governments, with a long list of powers or jurisdictions, which mostly were provincial-like. Once a particular group of First Nation communities came together, outlined their existing land base, developed a constitution, and developed a membership process open to all their descendants, they would be recognized. No one would be forced to leave the Indian Act until they were ready and wanted to. The Recognition Act was a quick way to start with some areas of jurisdiction when leaving the Indian Act. Negotiation on more land, funding, and additional issues or jurisdiction were all on the table. The two hundred or so tables that are now negotiating self-government is what we now have instead. With the Recognition Act, First Nations would be able to have jurisdiction immediately and go back to the table for what was missing.

One of the things I learned along with everyone that was involved in the Aboriginal Healing Foundation is how much personal damage was done by the Indian residential schools. More and more unmarked graves are being found and known about across Canada. Last summer I was again shown where the unmarked graves are in Fort Providence, NWT, next to where an Indian residential school was run for a very long time. The pain and trauma of the residential school Survivors and their families needs to be healed. It is great that Canada currently is sending counsellors into Indigenous communities for personal counselling, but it doesn't replace the work that the Aboriginal Healing Foundation was funding. There is still a need for an organization like the AHF to fund healing in the future. It took over one hundred years to create the pain and suffering caused by the Indian residential schools and it will take at least that to remove the damage done.

When I began my work for my people, I was very determined that being right always meant fighting for the complete acceptance of everything that we were fighting for, without compromise. I remember one of the premiers in the constitutional process saying, "Georges, you need to be able to accept a little water in your wine." I have learned that, indeed, there are times to accept a little water in your wine and that the other side must do the same. It doesn't have to mean that what you accept must be in place forever, but it may be the way forward for a time. For instance, we are now seeing areas in Canada that originally negotiated land agreements come back decades later and now negotiate self-government.

Don't let perfection stand in the way of a fair compromise that would greatly improve your situation today. Let the coming generation take the next step to complete the battle or the work you started.

A comment on the inherent right to self-government is worth being made, to understand what Aboriginal Peoples mean when we use those words. We seek recognition for as much jurisdiction from our original authorities that our Peoples exercised before contact as possible. Most Aboriginal Peoples are satisfied with the usual powers that provincial governments exercise in Canada, over land, education, health, justice, language and culture, etc. Some seek more. The main point that needs to be understood is that we were not defeated in war; our treaties are peace and friendship, so we maintain that we have not extinguished our original sovereignty. Legal experts don't seem to make a difference between a jurisdiction being created by federal or provincial legislation or a right created by a treaty. Most Aboriginal Peoples that have been in the struggle for the recognition of the inherent right to self-government would make it clear that what we are after is the *recognition* of the original jurisdiction our people exercised precontact, regardless of the means of recognition, be it legislation, constitutional amendment, or treaty. It must be clear that recognition is happening, not the creation of new jurisdictions.

A comment on the right to self-determination is also worth making, as this also is something that Aboriginal Peoples have been seeking to have recognized. As Peoples that have territory, language, culture, history, world view, institutions, and a clear idea of our collective selves, we clearly have the right to self-determination. It is only right that the United Nations have recognized the rights of Indigenous Peoples to self-determination. The discussion on the rights of Indigenous Peoples that began in Geneva in the fall of 1977 took some forty years to reach agreement in the UN, but this has been the norm for the recognition of Indigenous rights. Those in the struggle, and those that are allies in the struggle, must plan for the long term when pursuing the recognition or the implementation of Aboriginal Rights.

Because it takes so long to achieve the proper recognition of Aboriginal Rights or Treaty Rights, it might mean sometimes that the generations that fought for certain rights being recognized are not necessarily alive when the

Georges at his cabin on Ingraham Trail, NWT, March 2024.

recognition happens. In other cases, the struggle for recognition might be over only for the struggle for implementation to begin. For the young people taking up the struggle of your forefathers and foremothers, don't despair. It will take time to get what you want, but history is on your side. Move forward with a confident stride, and like the generations before, you will prevail — if you stay the course.

POSTSCRIPT

Readers of this book well know that Georges has planned respites and retirements many times, only to be drawn back into the fray. They may not be surprised that, in May 2024, Georges agreed to return to his role of Dehcho chief negotiator. "I'm so early to the job that I have no way to gauge how long it will take to settle the Dehcho Process," Georges says. Perhaps a future edition of this book will have more to say.

ACKNOWLEDGEMENTS

Many people gave their time to interviews and thereby enriched this book. We thank each and every one who spoke to us. In alphabetical order, they are: Aunt Cecilia, Paul Andrew, Garnet Angeconeb, George Barnabe, John Bekale, Jerome Berthelette, Marlene Brant Castellano, Janet Pitsiulaaq Brewster, Gerry Cheezie, Lloyd Chicot, Lawrence Courteoreille, Mike DeGagné, René Dussault, Bill Erasmus, Jeannette Erasmus, Joanne Erasmus, Sean Erasmus, Cousin Kathy, Rick Fader, Phil Fontaine, Sam Gargan, Dan Gaspé, Sandra Germain, Freddie Greenland, Nancy Hall, David Hawkes, Steven Iveson, Marilyn John, Manny Jules, Kanatiio (Allen Gabriel), Richard Lafferty, Pat Madahbee, Rose-Alma "Dolly" McDonald, Ovide Mercredi, Joe Miskokomon, Mike Kanentakeron Mitchell, Dave Monture, Antoine Mountain, Herb Norwegian, Gord Peters, Chris Reid, Tony Reynolds, Miles Richardson, Viola Robinson, Lyle Sayers, Patrick Scott, Mary Sillett, Konrad Sioui, Brian Slattery, Virginia Toulouse, Frank Tseleie, John Tseleie, Fred Wien, and Norm Yakelaya. A few of the quotations in this book are sourced from interview notebooks from other projects, such as *Full Circle*, a 2014 book on the Aboriginal Healing Foundation. An interview with former prime minister Paul Martin is one example. We especially thank Marlene Brant Castellano and Patrick Scott, who reviewed the RCAP (Marlene) and Dehcho (Patrick) chapters and provided corrections and improvements. Thank you to Jody Wilson-Raybould for kindly agreeing to write a foreword, and to Antoine Mountain, Bob Rae, Shelagh Rogers, Konrad Sioui, and Norman Yakeleya for their provision of promotional blurbs. Thank you to Antoine Mountain as well for his many phone calls and advice at different points in writing the book. Thank you to the team at Dundurn Press, who worked closely and patiently with us: Kathryn Lane, Susan Fitzgerald, Elena Radic, and Laura Boyle. Thank you to Eve Erasmus for her valuable contributions at many stages along the way.

NOTES

1: Young Georges

1 See "About Us," Dene Nation, accessed March 22, 2024, denenation.com/history/.

2: The Indian Brotherhood

1 As quoted in Antoine Mountain and Susan Quirk, *Dene Nation: An Analysis*, a report prepared for Dene Nation under a contract for the Royal Commission on Aboriginal Peoples (Sòmbak'è, Denendeh: Dene Nation, 1993), publications .gc.ca/collections/collection_2017/bcp-pco/Z1-1991-1-41-158-eng.pdf.

2 *House of Commons Debates*, 29th Parliament, 2nd session, Vol. 1 (1974), parl .canadiana.ca/view/oop.debates_HOC2902_01/1.

3 Mark Rendell, "Inquiring After Berger," *Edge YK*, March 2, 2015, edgenorth .ca/article/inquiring-after-berger.

4 Interview, May 27, 2022.

5 Northwest Territories Archives, "Some One Interviewing Geo. Erasmust [Erasmus]" (Item N-2001-016: CN-131A-1; sound recording), gnwttest .accesstomemory.org/n-2001-016-cn-131a.

3: The Assembly of First Nations

1 Ian Waddell, "How Pierre Trudeau Relented on Indigenous Rights," The Tyee, April 23, 2021, thetyee.ca/Culture/2021/04/23/Pierre-Trudeau-Relented -Indigenous-Rights.

2 Interview, December 2014.
3 "Indigenous Leaders Meet to Amend the Canadian Constitution in 1982," *The National*, aired March 16, 1982, on CBC, archived video clip, cbc.ca/player/play/1.3334702.
4 "Jody Wilson-Raybould's Father Tells Pierre Trudeau His Daughter Wants to Be PM," CBC News, posted November 5, 2015, YouTube video, youtube.com/watch?v=vhPnnLK6Znc.
5 "Indigenous Leaders Meet."
6 Paul Watson, "70 Indians Held in Ottawa Sit-In Protest," *Toronto Star*, April 15, 1989, A3.
7 "Georges Erasmus: Deal with Us Now!," *The National*, accessed March 22, 2024, archived video clip, cbc.ca/player/play/1.3594850.
8 "Georges Erasmus: Deal with Us Now!"
9 "Native Fight a 'Time Bomb,' MP Says," *Toronto Star*, June 4, 1988, A3.
10 *Globe and Mail*, September 27, 1990, A4.

4: The Royal Commission on Aboriginal Peoples

1 Brian Slattery sees the importance of this work differently: "With respect to the impact of RCAP's first publication, *Partners in Confederation*, I think that the suggestion that it was 'a little fuzzy' in the context of the Charlottetown Accord underestimates the long-term significance of the publication, which lies primarily in the Canadian courts, whose decisions hold sway in the political realm as well. The publication has already been cited a number of times in Supreme Court judgments (see below) and it is likely to be cited once again when the Supreme Court decides to fully endorse the concept of the inherent right of Indigenous self-government, as it surely will in the next couple of years."
2 Royal Commission on Aboriginal Peoples Hearing Transcript, Fort Garry Place, Winnipeg, Manitoba, April 21, 1992, central.bac-lac.gc.ca/.item/?id=rcap-220&app=Rcap&op=pdf.
3 Margaret Bridgman, "The Constitution," *Statements in the House*, November 22, 1996, openparliament.ca/politicians/6897/?page=2.

5: The Aboriginal Healing Foundation

1 "Address for the Launch of the Report of the Royal Commission on Aboriginal Peoples," Government of Canada, rcaanc-cirnac.gc.ca/eng/1100100014639/1572549038231.

2 Funding Agreement between Aboriginal Healing Foundation and Her Majesty the Queen in Right of Canada, as represented by the Minister of Indian Affairs and Northern Development, March 31, 1998, ahf.ca/files/98-funding-agreement.pdf.
3 Interview, 2011.
4 Aboriginal Healing Foundation, *Final Report of the Aboriginal Healing Foundation*, vol. 1, *A Healing Journey: Reclaiming Wellness* (Ottawa: Aboriginal Healing Foundation, 2006), ahf.ca/files/final-report-vol-1.pdf.
5 Aboriginal Healing Foundation, *Final Report*, vol. 1.
6 Aboriginal Healing Foundation, *Final Report*, vol. 1.
7 Sara Minogue, "Wellness Centre Gets Credit as Cambay Crime Drops," *Nunatsiaq News*, February 24, 2006, nunatsiaq.com/stories/article/wellness_centre_gets_credit_as_cambay_crime_drops/.

6: The Dehcho First Nations

1 Dehcho First Nations, *Report on the Dehcho Process* (Fort Simpson, NT: Dehcho First Nations, 2013), dehcho.org/wp-content/uploads/2022/03/DFN_Negotiations_Process_Report_2013_10-5.pdf.

IMAGE CREDITS

British Museum: 106
Busse, Henry: 11
Chambers, Cynthia: 29
Chretien, Tapwe/Native Press: 172
Christoff, Anita: 239
Election Campaign: 73
Erasmus, Georges: 65, 87, 96 (*bottom*), 131, 169 (*top & bottom*), 237
Erasmus, Jean: 268
Erasmus, Kristen: 275
Erasmus, Reanna: 232
First Air: 138
Fisher, Joanne C.: 124, 125 (*top & bottom*)
Fumoleau, Rene: 71, 74, 78, 81 (*top & bottom*), 82 (*top & bottom*), 83, 88, 89, 91, 92, 99, 134
Gabriel, Allen Kanatiio: 235
Goddard, John: 123
Governor General's office: 243
Knight, Sandra: 167
Lyons Morse, Deirdre: 279, 284
NDP Campaign: 86
Official RCAP Photo: 180
Sigurdson, Carole: 95 (*top & bottom*), 96 (*top*)
Unknown: 8, 19, 21, 75, 77, 79, 85, 112, 119, 120, 170, 277

INDEX

ABOUT THE AUTHORS

GEORGES ERASMUS, First Nation's Dene leader, is an outspoken proponent of self-determination for the Native Peoples of Canada. Born August 8, 1948, at Fort Rae, NWT, he was raised and educated in Yellowknife. Georges has been described as "the personification of his people's demands for self-determination." As a charismatic leader with a talent for clear, impassioned oratory, Georges rose quickly to prominence. His political involvement began in the late 1960s with the Company of Young Canadians, where he developed organization skills as well as a radical political stance that made his transition to the larger political scene a controversial one. Active in the IBNWT, first as director of community development and later as president of its successor organization, the Dene Nation. In 1983, Georges stepped down as president of the Dene Nation and shortly after he became the Northern Regional Chief of the Assembly of First Nations. He was elected National Chief of the AFN on July 30, 1985. He easily won a second term in 1988, a position he held until he decided not to seek re-election in 1991. In the aftermath of the Oka Crisis in 1990 Erasmus was asked by Prime Minister Brian Mulroney to co-chair the Royal Commission on Aboriginal Peoples to assess both the historical and contemporary relationship between Indigenous and non-Indigenous Canadians. After a short hiatus he was again called on to be chair and president of the Aboriginal Healing Foundation, an organization focused on helping those affected by the legacy of residential schools through community-based healing. Land and governance negotiations were in progress in the Dehcho region of the NWT, and Georges was hired as the chief negotiator. He held this position until 2015 when he stepped down for family reasons. Georges lives in Yellowknife with his wife Eve.

WAYNE K. SPEAR is a Kanien'kehá:ka (Mohawk) citizen of the Haudenosaunee with thirty-five years' experience working in, and with, Indigenous organizations and communities. His work has appeared in the *National Post*, *Huffington Post*, CBC, *Ottawa Citizen*, and elsewhere. Wayne was a weekly CTV News panelist and host of *The Roundtable Podcast*, featuring interviews with prominent Indigenous leaders and professionals. His book *Residential Schools, With the Words and Images of Survivors* was a 2015 TD Canadian Children's Literature Award finalist and winner of the 2016 Forest of Reading Golden Oak Award. *Full Circle: The Aboriginal Healing Foundation & the Unfinished Work of Hope, Healing & Reconciliation* was published in 2014 and tells the story of the Aboriginal Healing Foundation, where he was director of communications.